Learning to Request in a Second Language

Second Language Acquisition
Series Editor: Professor David Singleton, *Trinity College, Dublin, Ireland*

This new series will bring together titles dealing with a variety of aspects of language acquisition and processing in situations where a language or languages other than the native language is involved. Second language will thus be interpreted in its broadest possible sense. The volumes included in the series will all in their different ways offer, on the one hand, exposition and discussion of empirical findings and, on the other, some degree of theoretical reflection. In this latter connection, no particular theoretical stance will be privileged in the series; nor will any relevant perspective – sociolinguistic, psycholinguistic, neurolinguistic, etc. – be deemed out of place. The intended readership of the series will be final-year undergraduates working on second language acquisition projects, postgraduate students involved in second language acquisition research, and researchers and teachers in general whose interests include a second language acquisition component.

Other Books in the Series
Portraits of the L2 User
  Vivian Cook (ed.)

Other Books of Interest
Cross-linguistic Influence in Third Language Acquisition
  J. Cenoz, B. Hufeisen and U. Jessner (eds)
English in Europe: The Acquisition of a Third Language
  Jasone Cenoz and Ulrike Jessner (eds)
Foreign Language and Culture Learning from a Dialogic Perspective
  Carol Morgan and Albane Cain
An Introductory Reader to the Writings of Jim Cummins
  Colin Baker and Nancy Hornberger (eds)
Languages in America: A Pluralist View
  Susan J. Dicker
Language Learners as Ethnographers
  Celia Roberts, Michael Byram, Ana Barro, Shirley Jordan and Brian Street
Language Revitalization Processes and Prospects
  Kendall A. King
Language Use in Interlingual Families: A Japanese-English Sociolinguistic Study
  Masayo Yamamoto
Motivating Language Learners
  Gary N. Chambers
The Other Languages of Europe
  Guus Extra and Durk Gorter (eds)
Reflections on Multiliterate Lives
  Diane Belcher and Ulla Connor (eds)
The Sociopolitics of English Language Teaching
  Joan Kelly Hall and William G. Eggington (eds)
World English: A Study of Its Development
  Janina Brutt-Griffler

Please contact us for the latest book information:
Multilingual Matters, Frankfurt Lodge, Clevedon Hall,
Victoria Road, Clevedon, BS21 7HH, England
http://www.multilingual-matters.com

6. 2007

SECOND LANGUAGE ACQUISITION 2
Series Editor: David Singleton, *Trinity College, Dublin, Ireland*

Learning to Request in a Second Language
A Study of Child Interlanguage Pragmatics

Machiko Achiba

MULTILINGUAL MATTERS LTD
Clevedon • Buffalo • Toronto • Sydney

For Yohji and Yao

UNIVERSITY OF CHICHESTER

Library of Congress Cataloging in Publication Data
A catalog record for this book is available from the Library of Congress.

British Library Cataloguing in Publication Data
A catalogue entry for this book is available from the British Library.

ISBN 1-85359-612-4 (hbk)

Multilingual Matters Ltd
UK: Frankfurt Lodge, Clevedon Hall, Victoria Road, Clevedon BS21 7HH.
USA: UTP, 2250 Military Road, Tonawanda, NY 14150, USA.
Canada: UTP, 5201 Dufferin Street, North York, Ontario M3H 5T8, Canada.
Australia: Footprint Books, PO Box 418, Church Point, NSW 2103, Australia.

Typeset by Wayside Books, Clevedon.
Printed and bound in Great Britain by the Cromwell Press Ltd.

Contents

Tables, Figures and Appendices

Tables

Figures

Appendices

Summary

This volume examines the acquisition of requests in English by a seven-year-old Japanese girl, over a period of 17 months from the beginning of her second language learning experience, during her residence in Australia.

The principal purpose of the study has been to determine what strategies and linguistic devices a child second-language learner uses in order to make requests in English and what developmental path the learning process follows.

The data were collected in the child's home in Australia during her natural interaction with three different types of interlocutor: a peer, a teenager, an adult neighbour; and with the child's mother, who conducted the research. The child's interaction with each addressee was both audio- and video-recorded. These recordings were supplemented by diary data.

The study focuses on the development of the child's requestive repertoire, as well as how this aspect of her language use varied in relation to goal and addressee.

A developmental profile resulting from this study demonstrates that strategies, linguistic exponents and modifications show a steady developmental pattern. The results also indicate that the developmental patterns of request realisation varied substantially according to goal. This strongly suggests that requests for goods, for the initiation of action, for the cessation of action, and for joint activity emerge as distinct areas of learning and behaviour. Differences in relation to addressee were remarkably subtle. The child's request behaviour seemed to be shaped significantly by the play situation. While not distinguishing greatly between her peers, the teenager and the adult, she did make readily observable distinctions between her play partners and her mother, who was outside the context of her play. The child showed a sensitivity to the social context that over-rode the age-related influences imposed by the addressees.

This study has attempted to clarify our understanding the pragmatic development of a learner's interlanguage, about which we yet know very little.

Acknowledgements

Many people helped me at various stages of this project. I am particularly grateful to Howard Nicholas, Lloyd Holliday, Susan Ervin-Tripp, Gabriele Kasper and Kenneth Rose for their critical readings of an earlier version of this book. Their invaluable comments helped clarify a number of the issues I wanted to address. I am also indebted to Professor Kasper for suggesting the book title. Of course, however, I alone am responsible for any shortcomings in the book.

In addition, I would like to thank all those who served as interlocutors for the subject, Yao: Hannah Glynn, Emily Berry, Janice Brommer and many of Yao's friends. Janice also helped me with the tedious task of transcribing the tape recordings. My gratitude also goes to Diane Worrell for her expertise as a computer specialist and statistician.

I am also indebted to my colleagues for their support, particularly to Yuko Kobayashi, Professor Emeritus of Tokyo Woman's Christian University, who kindly undertook additional responsibilities during my absence from the university while starting this project in Australia. I would also like to thank Richard Spear, a former colleague, for casting a native speaker's eye over the final manuscript.

Special thanks go to the series editor, David Singleton, for including this book in the series. My sincere gratitude is also due to an anonymous reviewer for his or her cogent remarks on the preliminary manuscript. I would also like to extend my deep appreciation to the team at Multilingual Matters for their highly efficient work as well as for their very friendly, supportive manner and great patience.

I must also thank Yao Achiba, a most cooperative subject, for helping me maintain my sanity during this lengthy project. My final gratitude goes to Yohji Achiba, who ensured that I had the time free at home to write this book.

Chapter 1
Introduction

1.0 The Background of the Study

This study was occasioned by my coming to Australia with my daughter, Yao, in May 1992. During our stay, I observed her pragmatic development in a variety of contexts over a period of 17 months, as she gained command of English. For the purpose of this study, which was begun when Yao had had no prior learning of English, I gathered data in the particular context of play situations so that I was able to control the data gathering using both audio- and video-tape recording. The quantified data of the study comes from these recordings. In order to document her process of learning, I also kept a diary with notes on her utterances in English and the comments she made with regard to her language learning.

1.1 Interlanguage Pragmatics in Second Language Acquisition Research

Interlanguage pragmatics has been defined as 'the study of nonnative speakers' use and acquisition of linguistic action patterns in a second language' (Kasper & Blum-Kulka, 1993: 3). A growing interest in interlanguage pragmatics over the last two decades is reflected in the substantial body of research that has been undertaken (see Ellis, 1994; Kasper & Dahl, 1991; Kasper & Rose, 1999; and Thomas (in manuscript) for review). However, the bulk of the studies have focused on second language use rather than pragmatic development. That is, the great majority of research has been on the ways in which and the extent to which learners of a second language use pragmatic knowledge differently from native speakers of the target language. Consequently, the greater majority of the research has been cross-sectional and focused on adults. (Not surprisingly, the bulk of the studies with children have concentrated not on second language but first language acquisition.) There are only a few longitudinal studies that have investigated L2 pragmatic development (e.g. Bardovi-Harlig & Hartford, 1993, on 10 adult learners of English; Ellis, 1992, on two child learners of English; Sawyer, 1992, on 11 adult learners of Japanese; Schmidt, 1983, on one adult learner of English). In

1

contrast, among the mainstream second language acquisition studies, which are primarily concerned with the formal linguistic properties of the learner's interlanguage, there have been a great number of longitudinal studies on developmental patterns and sequences of specific syntactic features. This rich literature commences with Cazden *et al.* (1975), Hakuta (1976), Wong-Fillmore (1976), Itoh and Hatch (1978) and Pienemann (1980), and is continued by more recent studies such as those by Nicholas (1987), Liu (1991), Tarone and Liu (1995) and P. Clark (1996). Thus, we know a great deal about the development of a learner's linguistic features. But as pointed out by Ellis (1994), Kasper (1996), Kasper and Rose (1999), Kasper and Schmidt (1996) and Schmidt (1993), we know very little about how a learner's pragmatic aspects develop. What we need now are longitudinal studies that unravel pragmatic development by observing learners from the onset of their language acquisition process. It is the purpose of this study to contribute to the fulfilment of that need.

1.2 Speech Acts

As a means to investigate pragmatics, the speech act approach has been used effectively for both in first and second language acquisition research. This approach finds its origin in linguistic philosophy (Austin, 1962; Searle, 1969; 1975; 1976). According to speech act theory, speakers perform *illocutionary acts* by producing utterances. An illocutionary act is a particular language function performed by an utterance. That is, through their utterances speakers convey communicative intentions, such as requests, apologies, promises, advice, compliments, offers, refusals, complaints and thanking. The study of speech acts provides a useful means of relating linguistic form and communicative intent. An utterance, here, is treated as the realisation of a speaker's intention and goal in a particular context.

Because there is no easy way to map the literal meaning of an utterance into its function, both the performance and the comprehension of an illocutionary act is a highly complex matter. One utterance can have a multitude of functions, and the speaker's intent is not always clearly perceived. For instance, an utterance like 'Can you reach that book?' can count as a request to pass the book when addressed to a person sitting close to it. However, when Yao broke her collarbone and was visiting the doctor for the second time, he used this utterance as an information question to determine the extent of her recuperation. The literal meaning of 'can you …?' in both contexts is 'are you able to …?' but only in the utterance in the latter context is this literal meaning central. Another example of this complexity is an utterance such as 'I'm hungry'. This can be a simple statement of fact but only rarely is. It can, on occasion, even be an attempt to be excused from piano practice when produced by a child who has been told by her mother to practise. As Fraser (1975: 189) suggests, a single utterance can and often does serve a number of illocutionary acts. An addressee has to draw pragmatic inferences to know why the speaker said what she or he said. This calls for considerable pragmatic as well as linguistic ability on the part of the addressee, especially when he or she is a learner.

1.3 The Choice of Speech Act for Research

The illocutionary act of requests has been chosen for the present study for several reasons. First, and most obviously, requests are useful and occur frequently, especially among learners of a new language. Learners may get along without performing other illocutionary acts, but without requests it would be difficult to function effectively. Secondly, among the different types of speech acts that have been studied in second language research, the illocutionary act of requests has been studied most. Therefore, there is a firm framework upon which to base further study. Thirdly, requests occur in particularly useful contexts for the investigation of the development of a learner's pragmatic competence. Because requests are realised by a variety of linguistic forms (e.g. imperatives, declaratives or interrogatives), express a variety of functions or intentions, and encode the relative status of the speaker and the addressee, they create an environment in which there is substantial opportunity to examine how linguistic forms are related to intentions. Fourthly, they make use of various direct and indirect forms in accomplishing successful communication. Fifthly, a request constitutes *a face-threatening act*, a term introduced by Brown and Levinson (1978; 1987), and so a speaker, in order to reduce the threat and to minimise the potential face damage, will need to make use of strategies and modification. Finally, it has been said that 'requesting is close to being the prototype case of a social transaction' (Bruner *et al.*, 1982: 93). Requests thus provide insights into many different aspects of a learner's acquisition of pragmatic skills.

1.4 The Purpose of the Study

The present longitudinal case study investigates the developmental process of one illocutionary act – requests – in a child second language learner. It does so by observing systematically a Japanese child's use of English in natural settings in Australia over a period of 17 months from the onset of her second language learning.

The purpose of this study is to examine how and to what extent the child learns to realise requests in her second language over time. In so doing, it is hoped to contribute to our understanding of the pragmatic development of the learner's interlanguage, about which we know very little, as stated in Section 1.1.

1.5 The Organisation of the Book

After these introductory remarks, Chapter 2 will review the pertinent literature on pragmatic development, specifically as it is seen in requests. Much of the literature reviewed will be on L1 children's acquisition of requests, since there is a rich literature in this area. The chapter concludes with the research questions for this study. The following chapter describes the subject, the data collection procedures, and the coding scheme of the study.

In Chapters 4 through 8, the results are reported and discussed, with each chapter addressing a specific question. Chapter 4 traces the emergence of strategies and the various linguistic exponents used in the performance of requests. A detailed examination is made of direct and conventionally indirect strategies. Chapter 5 focuses on another strategic resource that forms a special category – the use of hints. In Chapters 6 and 7, we will look at variations in the use of requests, examining the extent to which Yao's requests vary with situational contexts, in particular with request goals and addressees. Chapter 6 attempts to identify the relationships between the goals of requests and their realisation, while Chapter 7 examines the relationships between addressees and request realisation. In Chapter 8, the focus shifts from strategies and linguistic forms to another dimension of request realisation – modification.

The final chapter synthesises the results detailed in Chapters 4 through 8 and presents the conclusions.

Chapter 2
A Review of the Literature

2.0 Introduction

As noted in Chapter 1, most of the studies of interlanguage pragmatics have focused on second language use rather than pragmatic development. Consequently, much of the research on requests deals with the extent to which and the ways in which the pragmatic knowledge of L2 learners differs from that of native speakers of the target language; or it makes comparisons between learners with different languages and cultural backgrounds with respect to their pragmatic knowledge of requests. Much of the research has been cross-sectional and has not focused on the interlanguage development of requests. There have only been a few longitudinal studies and thus we know little about how L2 learners realise requests and what kind of developmental path their acquisition follows. In contrast, in first child language research, there is a comprehensive literature on the development of such pragmatic knowledge. It is on this literature, concerning L1 children, that we will concentrate in this chapter in order to provide a framework for investigating the L2 child's development of requests. The literature from cross-sectional studies on L2 adult learners will, however, be reviewed briefly, in order to document findings relevant to the present study. The longitudinal studies of children and of one adult acquiring an L2 will be looked at closely.

In this chapter, after defining requests and their direct and indirect strategies, we will review the relevant cross-sectional and longitudinal L2 studies. Then we will examine the development of L1 children's request realisations, including the variation in their request behaviour as they are influenced by social factors. Finally, two studies on the relationship between request behaviour and its goals will be looked at, one ethnographic, the other of a bilingual classroom.

2.1 Defining Requests

Since the terms 'request' and 'directive' have been used inconsistently in the literature, the term 'request', as it will be used in the present study, requires a careful definition.

Searle (1976), in his theoretical study, distinguishes five basic speech acts: representatives, directives, commissives, expressives, and declarations. He defines 'directives', the most studied major category, as 'attempts by the speakers to get the hearer to do something' (1976: 11). The verbs that evoke this category, according to him, are 'ask', 'order', 'command', 'request', 'beg', 'plead', 'pray', 'entreat', as well as 'invite', 'permit', and 'advise'. These illocutionary verbs differ in the degree to which they mark the intensity of the act (e.g. 'I ask that you clean up the room.' vs. 'I order that you clean up the room.'). However, in Searle's taxonomy (1969), 'order' and 'command' are categorised under 'request'. There are others who have also treated these illocutionary verbs under the category of 'request' (e.g. Fraser (1975); House and Kasper (1987)).

The terms 'request' and 'directive' also have been inconsistently employed in empirical studies, some researchers equating requests with directives and using the terms interchangeably. For example, Ervin-Tripp (1976; 1977) employs a label 'directives' and divides directives into six types: need statements, imperatives, embedded imperatives, permission directives, question directives, and hints. Her classification scheme has been widely used in studies of L1 children's requests. Gordon and Ervin-Tripp (1984) adopt the same classification system but use the term 'request' instead of 'directive'. Wolfson (1989), citing Ervin-Tripp's classification, also equates directives with requests. However, many researchers see 'requests' as a subtype of 'directives' (e.g. Andersen, 1978; James, 1978; Schmidt, 1983), while yet others see 'directives' as a subtype of 'requests' and define directives as requests for action (e.g. Read & Cherry, 1978; McTear, 1980). A broader definition of requests is provided by Becker (1982):

> ... 'request' refers inclusively to an utterance that is intended to indicate the speaker's desire to regulate the behaviour of the listener – that is, to get the listener to do something. (Becker, 1982: 1)

According to this definition, what Searle (1976) has labelled a 'directive' is called a 'request'. Becker (1982), on the other hand, suggests, a 'request' is more common and less manipulative when compared with the term 'directive'. For this reason we will use the term 'request' instead of 'directive' for such a speech act and define 'requests' as 'attempts by the speakers to get the hearer to do something' (following Searle (1976: 11) and his definition of directives). They may range in illocutionary force from 'ordering' to 'begging'.

2.2 Direct Strategies, Conventionally Indirect Strategies and Nonconventionally Indirect Strategies

Requests, as defined above, can be made at different levels of directness.

2.2.1 Direct vs. indirect strategies

According to speech act theory the same act can be performed either directly or indirectly. Direct strategies are defined as utterances in which the propositional content (sentence meaning) of the utterance is consistent with the speaker's intent (speaker meaning) (Holtgraves, 1986), while indirect strategies are defined as utterances in which the speaker's meaning and the propositional content are not identical. Thus direct strategies convey only one meaning or illocutionary force, while indirect strategies convey more than one (H. Clark, 1979). For direct strategies a speaker's intention is explicit. In contrast, with indirect strategies his or her intention is conveyed implicitly. According to Holtgraves, intentions in direct strategies are conveyed more efficiently and unambiguously.[1] However efficient and unambiguous such strategies might be, they can be awkward when used in ordinary conversation. For example, when you want to borrow money from a friend, you may seek an indirect way to pursue your illocutionary goal, saying, 'Could you lend me some money?' or 'Do you have any spare cash?' rather than using an imperative such as, 'Lend me some money'. It is generally agreed that indirect strategies are used for the sake of politeness (Brown & Levinson, 1978; 1987; H. Clark, 1979; H. Clark & Schunk, 1980; R. Lakoff, 1973; Leech, 1983; Searle, 1975), with Searle (1975: 64) suggesting that 'politeness is the chief motivation for indirectness'. Leech (1983: 108) argues that 'indirect illocutions tend to be more polite' because of their optionality. However, Blum-Kulka (1987) and Gibbs (1983) have demonstrated that the indirect strategies that are conventional or formulaic have politeness values associated with them and are perceived as polite, noting that all the indirect strategies are not always so perceived.

2.2.2 The two types of indirect strategies

In the speech act literature we find two types of indirectness: one uses conventionally indirect strategies and the other makes use of nonconventionally indirect strategies. The latter are known as hints.

2.2.2.1 Conventionally indirect strategies

Searle (1975) states in relation to conventional indirectness:

... there can be conventions of usage ... I am suggesting that *can you, could you, I want you to*, and numerous other forms are conventional ways of making requests, ... but at the same time they do not have an imperative meaning. (Searle, 1975: 76)

H. Clark (1979) distinguishes between two types of convention in indirectness: *conventions of means* and *conventions of form*, which comprise what Searle (1975) calls conventions of usage.[2] Conventions of means determine the semantic device by which an indirect request can be made. For example, a convention of means is used when a speaker makes a request indirectly by questioning the hearer's ability, such as in 'Can you close the door?'. The conventions of form specify the exact wording used for a particular indirect request: e.g. 'Can you close the door?' or 'Could you close the door?'. Note here that 'Are you able to close the door?' is not conventional. For conventional indirectness, both types of convention shape what the speaker can do to signal requestive force.

In addition, there is another typical feature of conventional indirectness. Blum-Kulka (1989) labels it *pragmatic duality*. Conventionally indirect strategies can always be interpreted on at least two levels, the literal or the requestive. By using conventionally indirect strategies the speaker can convey either an information-seeking question or a request, or both, as in 'Can you help me with my homework?' The speaker's inquiry about the hearer's ability is an initial step toward an ulterior goal and is, therefore, part of the request (Blum-Kulka, 1989; Leech, 1983). Another example of this is seen in a teacher's being unable to hear a student and saying, 'Can you speak more loudly?' The student may answer, 'Sorry, I can't. I have a cold.' While the teacher was most likely making a request, the student responded to it as a question. Thus, a hearer can interpret an utterance on either one of the two levels or on both, and vary the response according to his or her interpretation.

2.2.2.2 Nonconventionally indirect strategies (Hints)

Blum-Kulka (1989) defines nonconventional indirectness as follows:

> For conventional indirectness, conventions of propositional content (means) and linguistic form combine to signal requestive force. Non-conventional indirectness, on the other hand, is in principle open ended, both in terms of propositional content and linguistic form as well as pragmatic force. Thus, there are no formal limitations.
> (Blum-Kulka, 1989: 42)

One of the benefits of this strategy is that a speaker can avoid the responsibility for making a request (Brown & Levinson, 1978; 1987). A hint has more than one possible interpretation and the addressee is obliged to make an inference to recover what the speaker actually intended. The speaker can thus avoid responsibility for having committed him- or herself to a particular act. The other benefit is associated with face-management. According to Brown and Levinson (1987: 73), a speaker 'can satisfy negative face to a degree greater than that afforded by the negative-politeness strategy'.[3] Hints, called an 'off-record' strategy by Brown and Levinson (1987: 71–5), are regarded as more polite than 'on-record' strategies. This view is shared by Sifianou (1993) and Thomas (1995).

Contrary to the current theories of politeness, however, empirical studies have demonstrated that hints are not always perceived as the most polite strategy. Blum-Kulka (1987) has shown that native speakers of Hebrew and American English judged conventionally indirect strategies, rather than hints, to be the most polite. Her argument is that politeness requires both pragmatic clarity and avoidance of coerciveness and that a certain balance between the two is essential. This balance is achieved by conventionally indirect strategies, while it is not by nonconventionally indirect strategies, hints. The latter lack pragmatic clarity. Walters (1979a; b) has also found in his experiments with native speakers of American-English and Puerto Rican speakers of Spanish that nonconventionally indirect strategies (e.g. 'Where …?' in English, 'Donde …?' in Spanish) were perceived as less polite than their conventionally indirect counterparts. Ervin-Tripp (1976) claims that hints are frequently used among families and communal groups. If this is so, it is difficult to regard hints as the most polite form of requests.

Since nonconventionally indirect strategies, hints, carry multiple pragmatic force (Blum-Kulka, 1989; H. Clark, 1979; Gordon & G. Lakoff, 1975; Leech, 1983; Thomas, 1983; Weizman, 1989; 1993), an utterance such as, 'It's freezing in here' conveys more than one meaning. Alternately, you may utter this without any specific goal other than the maintaining of a friendly relationship, as Leech (1983) suggests. Because nonconventionally indirect requests tend to be less transparent than conventionally indirect ones (H. Clark, 1979), understanding them requires more inference by the addressee, who must make use of his or her knowledge of the speaker and the context (Gibbs, 1981).

If the use of hints is not motivated by politeness and if it also means the speaker has to take a chance on having the addressee misinterpret his or her intentions, then there may be other reasons for using hints. This issue will be explored in Chapter 5.

2.3 Studies in L2 Request Realisation

In this section we will review both cross-sectional and longitudinal studies on the realisation of second language requests from the point of view of both development and variation.

2.3.1 Cross-sectional studies

We will begin the review of cross-sectional studies with what is known about the adult learner and then in the following section examine the child learner.

2.3.1.1 The adult learner

A number of studies have examined how learners produce requests in an L2. Much of the research has been cross-sectional in nature and has investigated adult learners. The Cross-Cultural Speech Act Realisation Project (CCSARP) (Blum-Kulka *et al.*, 1989a; Blum-Kulka & Olshtain, 1984) has been the most extensive study of this kind. This project investigated speech act realisation patterns cross-culturally, and by means of the Discourse Completion Test/Task (DCT)[4] collected its data from both native and non-native speakers of several languages. CCSARP has provided a great deal of information concerning cross-cultural comparisons of the request behaviour of L2 learners from differing backgrounds.

Blum-Kulka's cross-cultural comparisons (1989) in CCSARP have shown conventional indirectness to be the preferred request strategy in all the languages examined (Australian English, Canadian-French, Hebrew and Argentinian Spanish). This is consistent with the findings obtained by Trosborg (1995) from her study of role-playing subjects (Danish learners of English aged 16–30, Danish native speakers aged 20–35, and English native speakers aged 20–35). The findings of the House & Kasper study (1987), using data obtained from native speaker subjects (Danish native speakers, German native speakers, and British English native speakers) and learners (German learners of English and Danish learners of English), are consistent with these two studies, although the learners underused the conventionally indirect strategies.

Using CCSARP data, Weizman (1993) compared learners and native speakers in their use of nonconventionally indirect strategies (i.e. hints). She found that learners' use of hints was not much different in frequency from that of native speakers. A low frequency of hints was observed for both native speakers and learners. According to Weizman (1993), unlike direct and conventionally indirect strategies, learners do not need to acquire hints anew, and in fact, hint selection by Hebrew learners matched Hebrew native speaker norms from the very beginning. Fraser *et al.* (1980) note that what the learner learns about the concept of requesting in his or her first language will carry over into the second. Hints, therefore, can be said to be one of the pragmatic concepts that learners bring to their second language.

Faerch and Kasper (1989) in CCSARP, as well as House and Kasper (1987), have compared the use of modification of L2 learners with that of native speakers. Their study reports that 'grounders'[5] (reasons, explanations, or justifications) were the most frequently selected means of all the supportive moves,[6] but that they were used more frequently by learners than by native speakers. They suggest that learners give priority to clarity over brevity.

The tendency of L2 learners to be verbose (Faerch & Kasper, 1989) is also found in the research of Blum-Kulka and Olshtain (1986), who investigated the utterance length of requests produced by native speakers of Hebrew and English learners of Hebrew at three proficiency levels. They report an under-use of supportive moves at the low proficiency level, an over-use for the high-intermediate group, and finally a use approximating target norms for the highest group. As a reason for the verbosity in the high-intermediate group, Blum-Kulka and Olshtain suggest that learners with a high but still nontarget-like proficiency want to ensure that they are understood.

Blum-Kulka and Olshtain, as seen above, found a developmental aspect in L2 learners' acquisition of requests by examining learners at various proficiency levels. There are other studies that focus on the developmental aspects of the learner's request performance. Scarcella and Brunak (1981) examined such performance in beginning and advanced Arabic learners of English and in native speakers of English. In role-playing situations, subjects were asked to speak to superiors, familiar equals, and subordinates. The advanced learners used imperatives mainly with familiar equals and subordinates and declarative statements to superiors, while beginning learners used imperatives to all the addressees regardless of social distance and power differences. A positive politeness[7] feature, the inclusive 'we', frequently occurred in the L1 speakers' speech. In contrast, in the speech of both beginning and advanced learners it was absent. Scarcella and Brunak (1981: 64) suggest that the 'inclusive 'we' may be acquired quite late (or not at all, except by the most adept L2 learners) in adult L2 acquisition'.

S. Takahashi and DuFon (1989), using role-play situations, investigated the request strategies used by Japanese learners of English at the beginning, intermediate, and advanced levels. They report that as proficiency increases learners proceed from less direct to more direct levels in their choice of strategies. S. Takahashi and DuFon attribute the early learners' less direct strategies to L1 transfer.

Hill (1997), employing a DCT, investigated the use of requests by Japanese EFL learners of English also at three levels of English proficiency. He found that Japanese learners used more direct strategies and fewer hints than did native speakers. With greater proficiency, direct strategies decreased, but there was little development in the use of hints.

There is another study concerning Japanese learners of English, but one not directly related to proficiency levels. Tanaka (1988) compared the request performance of Japanese students at an Australian university and that of Australian students as native speaker informants. In role-play situations, the subjects were instructed to ask to borrow a book from a friend and a lecturer who were native speakers of English, in ways that differentiated addressees with respect to social distance and degree of power. She found that the requests of learners were less indirect and less tentative than those of native speakers. In addition, learners did not use positive politeness (e.g. the mention of a first name), nor did they give reasons for their requests. Furthermore, learners did not vary their requests to suit the social context.

Along the same lines as Tanaka, Fukushima (1990) compared the request performance of Japanese students at a Japanese university with that of native speakers of English. Using DCT in situations where the status was the same but the degree of familiarity was different, Fukushima reports that the learners' request performance was direct and that it did not vary to suit the social context. Tanaka's study, as well as Fukushima's, suggests that 'although highly context-sensitive in selecting pragmatic strategies in their own language, learners may under-differentiate such context variables as social distance and social power in L2' (Kasper, 1997: 2).

The studies of L2 learners we have reviewed here indicate that direct strategies, conventionally indirect strategies, and nonconventionally indirect strategies (i.e. hints) are all available to L2 learners. Their distribution, however, may differ between L2 learners and native speakers as well as among learners at varying proficiency levels. These studies also indicate that learners are unable to perform requests in effective ways, as a consequence of the verbosity of their supportive moves and their lack of the inclusive 'we'. Learners also seem to have difficulty in varying in appropriate ways their requests according to social factors such as their addressee. The studies make varying claims with respect to the extent to which low-proficiency learners make use of direct strategies.

2.3.1.2 The child learner

Only a few studies have investigated cross-linguistically the L2 children's production of requesting behaviour. In Walters (1980; 1981), role-plays were performed with the help of puppets. This methodology is often used in the studies of L1 pragmatic development (e.g. Andersen, 1978; 1990a). In 1980, he examined the relationship between children's grammatical ability to produce request forms (e.g. imperatives, can, could, will, would, etc.) and their sociocultural ability (i.e. their degree of politeness). His study involved four experiments with groups of bilingual and monolingual children ranged in age from six years and nine months (6;9) to 15;6. In each experiment, the child was asked to assist a puppet in making requests to other puppets differing in age, sex, and race. The settings and topics were also varied. Walters' study demonstrates that grammatical skill and sociocultural knowledge are relatively independent abilities. Some of the utterances produced by the L2 children exhibited appropriate sociocultural knowledge in terms of politeness, but the forms they used were ungrammatical (e.g. 'We borrow your basketball please?', 'Do you know where is the can opener?'), while some grammatically well-formed utterances were inappropriate when they were addressed to adults (e.g. 'Hey, buy a ticket') (1980: 341–2).

Walters' 1981 study investigated the ability of bilingual children to vary their requests in accord with various contextual factors. There were 32 children studied, ranging in age from 7;7 to 11;4. Here too, each child was asked to assist a puppet in making requests to other puppets of varying age, sex, and race. To elicit requests, four settings were used, each having two topics. For example, the topics in the 'supermarket' setting were 'a request to be shown rice' and 'a request to be allowed to get ahead of someone in the checkout line'. The contextual factors investigated were: the sex of the subjects, the setting, and the age, sex, and race of the addressee. The results for both English and Spanish show that setting had the strongest effect of all the contextual factors on requests. The only other factor to have a significant effect was the sex of the addressee. In both languages requests addressed by children to female puppets were more deferential than those addressed to male puppets. The age of the addressee had no significant effect on the requests. The children treated their peers and adults in the same way. Walters speculates that the age of the addressee had no significant effect on the requests because the addressees were adults and peers. He further notes that if the peer puppets in his study had been younger than the children, they may have produced significantly less deferential requests with younger puppets than they did with adult ones. There are, thus, several issues that remain open with respect to how addressee and setting interact in shaping the behaviour of the speaker, suggesting that this is a particularly complex social phenomenon for the learner to analyse.

A final cross-linguistic study of L2 children's request behaviour that deserves attention is Rose (2000). This study, using a cartoon-based oral-production tasks, charts developmental patterns of EFL and Cantonese requests, apologies, and compliment responses at grades two, four and six in Hong Kong. For request strategies, there was a movement from direct to conventionally indirect strategies and an increasingly greater frequency of supportive moves. However, these children showed little sensitivity to situational variation.

2.3.2 Longitudinal studies

As stated in Chapter 1, there are at present few published longitudinal studies that have investigated L2 pragmatic development: Bardovi-Harlig and Hartford (1993); Ellis (1992); Sawyer (1992); Schmidt (1983). Of these Bardovi-Harlig's study is on suggestions and rejections made by advanced adult learners of English in advising sessions. Sawyer's study is on the acquisition of the Japanese sentence-final particle *ne* by adult learners of Japanese. Only Ellis (1992) and Schmidt (1983) have investigated L2 learners' performance of requests, and therefore these two studies will be reviewed.

Ellis (1992) examined how two L2 learners, J (aged 10) and R (aged 11) produced requests in a classroom setting. The study showed that J and R used imperatives and the 'can I ...?' formula frequently throughout the observation period (16 months for J and 21 for R). But they hardly ever used hints. They modified their requests (for J only 10% and for R 27%) by using the politeness marker 'please', or by repeating or paraphrasing their requests. There were few grounders. The study also found that they did not vary request forms according to addressee except for negative request forms, which were used mainly with peers. In general, neither of the learners developed beyond a basic ability to make requests. Ellis gives two possible explanations: one that the developmental process of the two learners was incomplete, the other that a classroom environment with its familiar people did not create the need for the face-work and its resultant use of indirect requests and extensive modification. The second reinforces the findings of Walters (1981), described in the previous section, concerning the complexity of the social phenomena that the learner must analyse and the overall significance of the setting as a part of that phenomenon.

Schmidt (1983), over a three-year period, examined the acquisition of English by Wes, a Japanese artist living in Hawaii. He analysed the acquisition of Wes' communicative ability in four components: grammatical, sociolinguistic, discourse, and strategic competence. This case study, while not focusing directly on request realisation, does provide developmental evidence with regard to Wes' ability to perform requests.

Wes' early requests consisted of a limited number of formulas, such as 'shall we …?', 'can I …?' and 'let's …?'. In addition, instead of the imperative form, he used the -ing form (e.g. 'Please, never thinking' meaning 'Don't think about it' (1983: 152)). From the beginning, Wes relied heavily on the use of hints (e.g. 'Uh, you like this chair?' meaning 'Please move over' (1983: 153)), which were not always understood by native speakers of English. But by the end of three years his ability to perform requests had become much improved, with 'shall we …?' and 'let's …' now used productively. Schmidt notes, however, that his request behaviour was still far from perfect, sometimes inappropriately using the form 'can I …?' where 'can you …?' should have been used.

The studies by Schmidt (1983) and Ellis (1992) suggest that beginning learners rely on a limited number of formulas that only later become available for productive use. However, while the subjects of both studies had acquired a limited range of request strategies and forms by the end of observation period, their use was often socially inappropriate. Further, the two studies come to different conclusions with respect to whether learners begin with more complete and perhaps formulaic version of request, or whether they make use of non-standard expressions, which are used as hints. The differences in age among the subjects may also be a significant factor. These matters will only be resolved by further study.

2.4 The Development of Request Realisation in L1 English-speaking Children

To help provide a framework for this study, we will review the literature on children who acquire English as their first language. Section 2.4.1 traces the pragmatic aspects of their development from pre-school years through elementary school, while Section 2.4.2 looks at the variations in the request behaviour in relation to social contexts. The final section, 2.4.3, compares the requests of children with those of adults.

2.4.1 The production of requests by L1 English-speaking children

Ervin-Tripp (1977: 175), in agreement with the findings of other studies (e.g. Dore, 1977a), suggests that at the age of three a child starts using a variety of forms to convey requests, including embedded imperatives[8] (e.g. 'Can you give me one car, please?'), permission forms (e.g. 'Can I have my big boy shoes?'), or modal embeddings (e.g. 'You can make a crown'), as well as simple imperatives.

Gordon and Ervin-Tripp (1984), in their case study of a four-year-old boy, T, report his making requests in his interactions with others over a period of seven months. They examined his requests in terms of 'self-oriented requests', 'rule/norm oriented requests', and 'activity- or external goal-oriented requests' (1984: 312–4). For self-oriented requests, which were used when T wanted an object or to do something for himself, he used the forms, 'I want …', 'I want to …', or 'can I …?'. T's self-oriented requests were rarely accompanied by adjuncts of reason. On the other hand, his 'rule/norm oriented requests', which were used in situations where he wished to change what was going on, were accompanied by adjuncts of reasons, such as 'it goes there' in 'That doesn't go there, it goes there' (1984: 312). T's final type of request, 'external action requests', was used to get co-operative actions from others. These requests were basically in the imperative form and occurred usually during shared activities such as imaginative game play. Imperatives were also used when co-operation was assumed. T used imperatives more often than any other request form. Polite requests such as, 'can I' or 'could you', though the least successful, were used only when he was afraid of noncompliance. Gordon and Ervin-Tripp (1984) conclude that the primary determinant of T's choice of request forms depended on whether his requests were self-oriented, rule/norm oriented, or external action oriented, while subordinate to this was the degree of his expectation of compliance. This suggests a strong role for goal in shaping request behaviour, one perhaps of even greater significance than setting or addressee.

Ervin-Tripp *et al.* (1990), in the videotaped data of peer and family interaction in a natural setting with children aged from two to eleven, report results quite similar to Gordon and Ervin-Tripp (1984), for polite request forms and their compliance.

According to Ervin-Tripp *et al.* (1984) and Ervin-Tripp *et al.* (1990), children, in spite of their failure to get their way, continue to produce as they grow older more varied types of polite request forms as well as justifications (i.e. supporting statements). They give two possible explanations for children's use of polite forms. One is that regardless of their compliance, polite forms to adults are not usually ignored and do get attention, while other forms are often ignored. The other is that the use of polite forms is motivated by children's desire to sound competent.

Ervin-Tripp *et al.* (1990: 328) proposes that 'politeness from the start is a social index, not a persuasive device'. By age four or five, they note, children reveal their knowledge of socio-linguistic skills in role-playing by knowing who to be polite to and when it is most appropriate to use polite forms.

Andersen (1990a) makes similar claims concerning modifications in children's language use, including politeness markers such as 'please', suggesting that they reflect the acquisition of socio-linguistic skills based on the development of their social cognition, rather than on their concern for efficacy.

These studies (Gordon & Ervin-Tripp, 1984; Ervin-Tripp *et al.*, 1984; Ervin-Tripp *et al.*, 1990; Andersen 1990a) show that polite forms are not effective in obtaining compliance from adults. On the other hand, Ervin-Tripp *et al.* (1990) and Wood and Gardner (1980) found that for high cost requests (e.g. a request for goods that belong to and are being used by the addressee) polite forms were effective with peers or older children. Acquisition of native-speaker-like request behaviour, therefore, requires a sensitive assessment of the nature of the request, the likelihood of compliance, the social status of the addressee, and the setting in which the request is made. The speaker must then, having made these evaluations, marshal the appropriate linguistic resources to make the appropriate linguistic differentiations.

Perhaps one of the most comprehensive and systematic works on the production of requests by children is the study done by Garvey (1975). She examined requests in 36 dyads of nursery school children ranging in age from 3;6 to 5;7 years, observing their spontaneous speech during peer interaction. Her results showed that in both the younger dyads (3;6–4;4) and the older (4;7–5;7) direct requests predominated. There were no examples of hints.

In a study of nursery school children, O'Connell (1974, cited in Ervin-Tripp, 1977: 176) reports that four-year-olds often hinted to adults for help when they were unable to do something (e.g. 'Daddy, I can't get this out') or when they were in difficult circumstances (e.g. 'Jason's trying to take my stuff'). Ervin-Tripp (1977) notes that by the age of four, and possibly earlier, children begin to use hints. She also notes that hints are used more often with adults than with other children. This may be one of the reasons why Garvey's children did not hint, her data being based on peer interaction.

Garvey reports that out of a total of 565, only seven want/need statements functioning as requests. This finding seems to contradict the results reported by Ervin-Tripp (1977) and Gordon and Ervin-Tripp

(1984), who report that want/need statements are used early by children when addressing adults. One of the major request forms produced by a four-year-old boy in the Gordon and Ervin-Tripp case study was a want/need statement such as 'Mommy, I need some cold medicine' (1984: 313). As to the paucity of want/need statements among peers in Garvey's study, Read and Cherry (1978: 235) note that this is not unexpected since children are not accustomed to having their desires or needs satisfied by peers. These findings suggest that the addressee plays a significant role in shaping requests, with age a key factor.

Levin and Rubin (1983), in a study of 60 children at levels pre-school (4;5 years), first grade (6;5 years) and third (8;9 years), investigated the development of their requests. Children of the same grade and same sex were placed in dyads and asked to play with toys. The proportion of indirect requests did not change between the ages 4;5 and 8;9 years, accounting for 20% of the total number of requests.

The studies discussed above have shown that children, even before their elementary school years, have acquired a basic grasp of the diverse syntactic forms used for conveying their requestive intentions. However, some development seems to occur only during the elementary school years. Liebling (1988), in her cross-sectional research, investigated elementary school children (in grades one, three, and five) with respect to comprehension and production of, and reasoning about requests varying in degrees of politeness. She found that although the children did equally well on the comprehension task, they performed unequally on the production and the reasoning tasks. In the production tasks, the children in grade one did not use polite forms with the conditional (e.g. 'would' and 'could'), while children in grades three and five demonstrated control of embedded request forms with the conditional often softened by the addition of 'please'. However, when asked to say 'Mommy, mommy, I need the hammer' in a nicer way, only fifth graders used indirect, nonexplicit questions, such as 'Do you know where the hammer is?' (1988: 92). Liebling notes that even fifth graders rarely used inexplicit forms such as hints and nonexplicit questions spontaneously. Her findings suggest that with respect to production of request forms there is a great improvement in pragmatic skill during the elementary school years, and that by grade five, children are able to use a variety of request forms. Inexplicit types, however, continue to require improvement.

Liebling found that pragmatic reasoning too develops during the elementary school years and continues to improve beyond grade five. In her research, first graders were usually not able to grasp the pragmatic relationship of form, function, and context. Children in grade three were more able to do so, but often failed to deal accurately with their relationship. Only fifth graders were able to explain their relationship with accuracy and consistency.

According to Ervin-Tripp and Gordon (1986), marked changes in children's language use take place around age eight (the third grade). At around this age 'children's speech begins to address the viewpoint of the hearer, [and] recognises problems of intrusiveness as a social issue' (1986: 87).

Gordon *et al.* (1980) also report the sensitivity of children to their intrusions into the activities of an addressee. In their study, 81 children in kindergarten through the fifth grade had to go to two unfamiliar adults who were busy talking and make requests. They found a significant difference in the forms used by children below the third grade and those older. For children below the third grade, approximately 50% of the requests were 'need statements' (e.g. 'I need a blue marker.' (1980: 8)). They also made a large number of 'location questions' (e.g. 'Where's the marker?' (1980: 8)). 'Need statements' produced by children below the third grade reflected the assumption that the addressee had what they wanted and would comply with the request. 'Location questions' did not assume compliance but assumed that the addressee had the desired object and would respond. In contrast, children in the third grade and above recognised that they may have been intruding and might be confronted by noncompliance. These children were more likely to use interrogative forms to make requests than were the younger children. Of those interrogative request forms, 50% were 'possession/existence' questions (e.g. 'Do you have a green marker?'; 'Are there any more markers?' (1980: 8)). These examples show that the older children did not assume that the addressee had the object and would give it to them. In addition, the older children often added a tag (e.g. 'I can use') to the interrogative requests, such as 'Do you have a blue marker I can use?' (1980: 5). Tags were not used by the children below the third grade. Gordon *et al.* (1980) note that the presence of this qualification among older children may reflect their wish to make clear that the questions were not meant as requests for information.

Data from both Ervin-Tripp and Gordon (1986) and Gordon *et al.* (1980) above show that children become aware of the perspective of others around age eight. This corresponds to the cognitive changes claimed by Piaget (1959), who argued that children before age seven or eight are egocentric and fail to understand other people's points of view, and it is not until seven or eight that the habits of social thought begin to form.

Although considerable pragmatic knowledge is acquired during pre-school years, some development occurs during elementary school (e.g. indirect requests with the conditional 'would' and 'could'). Nino and Snow (1996: 140) state:

> Ultimately, during the school years, continued development in control over polite request forms is driven in good part by the maturation of social abilities, in particular the capacity to take the perspective of the request recipient.

Clearly, therefore, the task of acquiring the pragmatics of requests involves a substantial element of social growth and, at least in one's first language, considerable cognitive development as well. This means that a child learner is confronted not only with the task of analysing his or her situation, but also that his or her ability to perceive the dimensions of that situation is maturing. For the second language learning child such complexity is compounded by the fact that the factors distinguishing situations and the way those distinctions are signalled are unfamiliar.

2.4.2 Variations in the request behaviour of L1 children in relation to addressee

As seen in the previous section, children are able to produce a variety of request forms. In English, requests can be realised in a variety of syntactic forms, and the range of request strategies may vary from the most direct to the most indirect. The actual choice of request strategies and forms, however, depends on a variety of social factors. Research on requests performed by adult native speakers of various languages have shown that adults, when making requests, are sensitive to social factors such as age and role of addressee, social distance between interlocutors, and their status relative to each other: for American English (Ervin-Tripp, 1976; 1977); Israeli Hebrew (Blum-Kulka *et al.*, 1985); and Hebrew, Canadian French, Argentinian Spanish, Australian English and German (Blum-Kulka & House, 1989). Blum-Kulka *et al.* (1985) found the age of addressee relative to the speaker was significantly related to choice of request strategy. When adults addressed children, they predominantly used direct strategies. In contrast, when children addressed adults, they more frequently used conventionally indirect strategies.

Much of the research has shown that children too are sensitive to addressee factors. This section deals with variations in language use by L1 English speaking children within a developmental perspective, focusing on the studies that concern the choice of request strategies and forms according to addressee. A number of studies have reported that children vary their choices according to the status relationship between themselves and the addressee. The age and the role of the addressee appear to be important indicators of status and thus major influences on such choices.

Ervin-Tripp *et al.* (1984) report that at ages two and three children use polite forms to researchers 60% of the time and to parents only 10%. When addressing other children, the ratio is between 14% and 24%. At age four they show no consistent pattern of differentiation. By ages five to eight, however, they become more deferent to adults than to children, and to peers and older children more than to younger ones. Significantly more imperatives are used to mothers than to fathers, and requests to fathers are frequently mitigated.

In a doll-playing experiment with 21 children aged from 4;6 to 5;2, James (1978) investigated the influence of the addressee's age on a child's requests. In her study, children were asked to talk to dolls representing addressees from three age groups (adult, peer, and younger child). In the situations where the children were telling the doll to stop doing something such as taking their ball away, they issued direct imperatives (e.g. 'don't ...') most frequently to the doll representing younger children and least to adults. Indirect requests such as interrogative forms (e.g. 'can you ...?') were used most frequently to adults, while modified imperatives (e.g. 'don't ... please') were addressed to peers. In situations where the children were asking a favour, request forms became more indirect than those produced in the other situations. Requests addressed to adults were significantly more indirect than those to younger children. However, there was no significant difference in the request forms used to peers as opposed to adults and younger children.

McTear (1980) investigated the requests of two girls over the period of two years from ages 3;8 and 4;0 to 5;9 and 6;1 and provided evidence showing that children vary their request forms according to addressee. The children in his study used personal need or desire statements and hints to adults and imperatives to each other.

Based on a series of student projects involving nursery school observations of a large number of children, Ervin-Tripp (1977) found results similar to those reported by McTear. Ervin-Tripp also found that not only the addressee but also the task affected the children's choice of request forms, apparently because the kinds of task tend to vary with addressee. In speaking to other children, for example, O'Connell (1974, cited in Ervin-Tripp, 1977) found that the 'can you ...?' or 'could you ...?' forms were commonly used when children tried to wheedle goods out of other children. Simple imperatives were more common in attempts to control other children's behaviour. Negative imperatives were used in order to stop other children from interfering. In speaking to adults, children used need statements (or statements of personal desire) to obtain desired objects.

One of the most comprehensive studies of role-related request forms has been conducted by Andersen (1978; 1990b). She asked 18 children aged 4;1 to 7;1 to role-play with puppets in three different settings: a family, a doctor's office, and a classroom. Her study suggests that children aged from four to seven years have an internalised knowledge of social status relationship and how people speak in various social contexts. For instance, in the doctor's office, the children playing the doctor addressed twice as many imperatives to nurses as they did to other doctors. In the classroom situation, the teacher's speech to a student most frequently contained imperatives, the 'let's' form, and hints.

Another study of role-related request forms has been done by Mitchell-Kernan and Kernan (1977). The children ranging in age from five to twelve years performed on an improvised stage with puppets in front of their peers. The children in this study used imperatives frequently to equals and those of lower status, but only infrequently to those of higher status. Thus, these children revealed an awareness of the social factors that affect the choice of request forms used.

In summary, the studies concerning variation according to age and role of addressee that we have reviewed here suggest that in both natural and role-playing situations, and across age groups, children use direct requests to younger children, while they make less direct requests to adults. However, with peers and adults, not all the research shows variation in the choice of request forms. Some research shows that children are likely to use imperatives to their peers, while they are more likely to produce indirect request forms with adults. Other findings show that children address peers and adults in much the same manner. Nevertheless, the research does indicate that children by the age of twelve or even much earlier show sensitivity to addressees, and so reflect their awareness of social factors.

2.4.3 A comparison of the requests produced by children and adults

Children acquiring a second language are both cognitively and socially more sophisticated than children beginning their first language acquisition of pragmatics. Since research has not yet uncovered the contribution of either social or cognitive factors to second language pragmatic development, it is not possible to say how its development might differ from that of a first language. The best that can be done at this point is to determine the range of first language pragmatic development from child to adult and by doing so to provide a basis for judging whether second language pragmatic development matches or differs from those in first language development. This requires the examination of the request behaviour of adult native speakers of English.

Whether the requests of L1 children are the same as those of adults is an issue that has also been addressed in the past research. Ervin-Tripp (1977), Gordon and Ervin-Tripp (1984), and Mitchell-Kernan and Kernan (1977) have shown that by four or five years of age children are able to produce all the major request types reported by Ervin-Tripp (1976; 1977) for American English-speaking adults. Ervin-Tripp (1977: 166–7) divided the directives or requests used by adults into six categories:

(1) *Need statements* (e.g. I need a match)
    The addressee is primarily lower in rank.
(2) *Imperatives* (e.g. Gimme a match)
    The addressee is lower in rank, or equal and familiar.
(3) *Embedded imperatives* (e.g. Could you gimme a match?)
    The addressee is most often unfamiliar and/or differs in rank.
(4) *Permission directives* (e.g. May I have a match?),
    The addressee is more often higher in rank.
(5) *Question directives* (e.g. Have you gotta match?)
    The desired act and often the agent of the act are omitted. Because these forms of request can be treated as information questions, it gives the addressee an escape route. This form is most commonly used when the probability of noncompliance is strong.
(6) *Hints* (e.g. The matches are all gone)
    The addressee's options are open as they require inference. Hints are used when speakers rely on shared knowledge. They are generally used in families and communal groups.

As seen in the previous sections, at an early age children become aware of the social features impinging on their language, and they alter the syntactic forms of their requests according to these social contexts.

Camras *et al.* (1985) compared children and adults in their use of request forms and politeness in a variety of situations. Their subjects were 60 first-grade children and 60 university students. Both groups were presented with short stories and asked to supply requests that could be made by the story characters. Half of the stories presented situations where speakers were of higher rank than their addressees and were expected to use imperatives. The other half contained situations where speakers were of lower rank and were expected to use non-imperatives, particularly embedded requests. Camras *et al.* found both children and adults varied their request forms according to the story type, but that children generally produced requests that were somewhat less polite than those produced by adults. They advance two possible explanations for this. Firstly, although much socialisation of language use has already taken place by seven or eight years of age, further development of more courteous indirect forms is still required. Secondly and more generally, children may not feel as compelled as adults to be courteous.

Although children are not as courteous as adults, their use of requests is in other respects similar: They can produce almost all the request forms used by adults, and they can vary the forms of request according to addressee. However, Becker (1982) claims that there is a limit to the kinds of requests children are able to produce: At any given point in his or her development, a child's ability to use requests will be constrained by his or her basic semantic and syntactic abilities.

Furthermore, Ervin-Tripp (1977: 188) notes that the major difference between adults and children is the use by the former of 'systematic, regular, unmarked requests, which do not refer to what the speaker wants'. Since children only gradually learn to conceal the intentions of their requests, hints do not occur often in their repertoire. According to Owens (1992), it is not until adolescence that children approach adult proficiency.

In sum, the use of requests by school-age L1 English speaking children is similar to that of adults. However, their requests are less courteous than are those of adults. Nor do children use hints as often as adults.

2.5 Variation in Relation to Goal

The addressee as a social factor affecting the choice of request forms has been much examined, as documented above, but there are other factors that have been only rarely investigated. Goals, though they are an important variable when accounting for variation in request strategies, are an example. In their study of request behaviour in Hebrew, Blum-Kulka *et al.* (1985) selected the variables of sex, age of addressee, power relationship, social distance or familiarity, request goal, setting, and communication medium; and found that the three most important factors affecting the choice of request strategies are the type of request goal, the age of the addressee, and the power of the speaker relative to the addressee. Their data were collected using an ethnographic approach in diverse situations (e.g. face to face interaction in student dorms). They distinguish four types of goals: requests for action, for goods, for information, and for permission; and report that requests for action were the most direct, and requests for permission were the most indirect. They (1985) claim that with requests for action, it is necessary to formulate requests in the shortest and most explicit way possible, characteristically by the use of imperatives or elliptical forms, while with requests for permission, a person of lower power tends to seek permission from a person of higher power, and therefore these requests are likely to be most indirect. They also found that requests for goods are much less direct than requests for action, with more than half of the requests for goods formulated by conventionally indirect strategies.

Another study in this area is by Cathcart (1986). Her study is related to both goal and addressee. She examined various communicative acts performed in English by eight Spanish-speaking children aged from 5;0 to 5;6 in a Spanish–English bilingual kindergarten. She found that with respect to requests for action, children tended to make longer and more complex requests to an adult than to their peers, while task-related requests with a joint goal became longer and more complex with peers.

As seen earlier, Blum-Kulka *et al.* (1985) have shown that request goal, the age of the addressee relative to the speaker, and the power of the speaker relative to the addressee are the major variables affecting the choice of request strategies and forms. In the world of children, however, one's age as well as role is a mark of power. For instance, mothers have power not only because of age but also because of their role. Therefore, in the children's world, age, power, and role are intertwined when they come to select a request form for an addressee. In sum, it can be said that the goal and addressee are exceptionally important factors when investigating variations in a child's requests.

2.6 Conclusion

The literature on requests reviewed above has shown that the developmental patterns of strategies, variations, and modifications are areas of major concern. This has motivated four research questions that can be framed in the following manner:

(1) What range of strategies and linguistic forms does a child use to realise requests in a second language and what is the pattern of their development?

(2)   What types of request strategies and linguistic devices does a child use in order to achieve varying request goals in a second language and what is the pattern of their development?

(3)   To what extent do a child's linguistic devices and request realisation strategies in a second language vary depending upon the addressee?

(4)   With what frequency does a child use the various types of modification in a second language in relation to requests (1) across phases, (2) in differing strategies, (3) for differing goals, and (4) with differing addressees?

In the next chapter the methodology used in this study is described.

Notes

1. However, as Holtgraves (1986) noted, Gibbs (1979) argues that if there is sufficient context, indirect requests are understood just as quickly as direct requests.

2. Morgan (1978) extends Searle's view and distinguishes between two types of convention in indirectness. One is the *convention of language*, which refers to the literal meaning of an utterance. The other is the *convention of usage*. An example of this is an expression such as, 'can you ...?' as a standard way of indirectly making a request.

3. According to Brown and Levinson (1987: 129), 'negative politeness is redressive action addressed to the addressee's negative face: his want to have his freedom of action unhindered and his attention unimpeded'.

4. DCT is a written questionnaire consisting of an incomplete discourse sequence for the speech act under study. It includes brief situational descriptions. Subjects are asked to complete the dialogue in the way they think suitable for a given context.

5. Blum-Kulka *et al.* (1989a: 289) define grounders as 'reasons, explanations, or justifications for his or her request, which may either precede or follow it'.

6. According to CCSARP (Blum-Kulka *et al.*, 1989a), supportive moves are external to the Head Act, which is the core of the request sequence, and are used to mitigate or aggravate the request.

7. According to Brown and Levinson (1987: 103), positive politeness involves 'S [speaker] claiming 'common ground' with H [hearer], by indicating that S and H both belong to some set of persons who share specific wants, including goals and values'.

8. Much of the L1 literature uses the term 'embedded imperatives' for requests such as 'Can you give me x ...?' while the L2 literature uses the term 'conventionally indirect requests' for the same requests.

Chapter 3
Methodology

3.0 Introduction

This chapter presents the general methodology employed in the study to answer the research questions. It begins with an argument for a longitudinal case study, descriptions of the subject, the data collection procedures, the data sets, and concludes with the classification of request strategies that underpins the analysis of the acquisition of requests by the child second language learner.

3.1 The Longitudinal Case Study

We will argue that the research questions above can be best answered by a longitudinal case study in which records are kept of the learner's pragmatic development from the onset of the language acquisition process. Tarone and Liu (1995: 110) point out that longitudinal data for single individuals are necessary in order to investigate whether 'synchronic variation across situations is related to diachronic change'. A longitudinal case study makes it possible to show synchronic variation within the same individual across different contexts as well as diachronic change. Neither a DCT (Discourse Completion Test/Task) nor a role-play is suitable for a developmental study because a learner's target language has to be good enough from the start to fill in a DCT or engage in a role-play. In fact, Kasper and Schmidt (1996: 151) point out that none of the studies using these methods has subjects at the very first stage of second language development because of their inability to engage in such activities. As indicated in Chapters 1 and 2, there are few longitudinal studies of learners' pragmatic development. There is a substantial literature in learners' pragmatics but most of it consists of cross-sectional studies. According to Bardovi-Harlig and Hartford (1993: 280), cross-sectional studies show what learners of different levels of proficiency know, but they do not show change within individuals. Therefore, there is a gap, a gap that can be filled by longitudinal case studies. Such studies are essential for a clear understanding how the features of pragmatics in the second language actually emerge. It is this task that we have set ourselves.

3.2 The Subject

The subject of this study is my daughter Yao, a Japanese girl, who was seven years old when we began our residence in Australia. Yao had no siblings. Her father remained in Japan during the period of the study. Yao had had no prior training in English. When she was five she had spent three weeks in the United States. During that time, while I was attending a seminar, she had attended a day-care centre for two hours a day for about two weeks. That had been her first contact with spontaneous English. She had, it should be noted, found the time she spent alone with native speakers of English very difficult. It is very unlikely that this brief stay in the United States contributed to her later development in English. In retrospect, Yao, with no further contact with English for the next two years prior to the departure for Australia, said of herself that she learned nothing during that stay, adding that she felt her being more mature was what helped her most. Yao, who had just started her second year of primary school in Japan before she left, was initially hesitant about the move, even if it would be only temporary. A week after her arrival she was enrolled in a primary school in a middle-class community in Melbourne, adjusted rapidly, and soon expressed a preference for school and life in Australia. She received minimal ESL support at school, and initially, although I continued to use Japanese with her, there was no other regular context for Japanese to be used. Three months after her arrival she started attending a Japanese school on Saturdays. I felt that Yao needed the contexts in which Japanese could be used and Japanese writing was learned.

Although I continued to use Japanese, Yao started from the beginning to use English with me. While initially her use of English was restricted to just a few words, she appeared to want to use as much English as she could. For instance, on the third day she called me from the kitchen to watch her doing a cartwheel using the words, 'Come here. Come here.' By the end of the 17 months of data collection, she was using English extensively with me. Both Examples 1 and 2 from the diary were produced in the last month of data collection.

1   **Y:** *mum could you do me a favour?*
     (Yao came to my room while I was studying.)
   M: *naani?*[1]
     (=what is it?)
    Y: *it's only a small favour / could you put up my leotard?/ I'm too short*
     [Diary, 19-10-93]
     (Yao wanted me to put her leotard on the shelf in the closet.)

2   **Y:**   *police mum!/ you'd better be careful but don't get nervous*
      [Diary, 21-10-93]
      (While I was driving her to see the doctor, Yao suddenly noticed
      a police car in front of us. I was a new driver.)

I tried consistently to use Japanese with her except when a native-speaker of English was present. There were times, however, when I unconsciously replied in English to Yao's questions or requests. If I talked to her in Japanese when English speaking people were around even if those people were strangers to her, Yao refused to answer or said to me, 'Mum, use English, please.' By the end of the period of data collection, English became Yao's communicative mode except at her Saturday Japanese school, where it was a rule to use Japanese. Yao seemed quickly to have internalised English as a means of communication.

3.3 Data Collection Procedures

There are two kinds of data in this study. One is the recorded data, on which the major arguments and analyses are based. In addition, there is a diary, which serves as a supplementary source of information.

The recorded data for this study were collected over a 17-month period primarily at Yao's home in Australia within the context of her natural, playtime interaction with three types of interlocutor: a peer, a teenager and an adult. I was always present as an observer, and only spoke with her when she initiated the interaction.

All the peer interlocutors were classmates of Yao's. Her class was a composite of first and second graders during the first year, when she was a second grader, and a composite class of third and fourth graders during the following year. Therefore, some of her classmates were at times one year younger or one year older than she. Many of her classmates, usually one at a time, came to play after school. The peer interlocutors for the analysis were ten different children.[2] There was one peer interlocutor in each session, except for the session of the 17th week in which there were two. These interlocutors were sisters and classmates of Yao's at different times. The teenage interlocutor was a 14-year-old girl named Hannah, who came to play with Yao about once a week on her way home from school, usually staying for dinner. Hannah and her family were the first Australians Yao and I met in Melbourne. The adult interlocutors were Emily and Janice. The interlocutor for the two sessions in the 8th and 10th weeks was Emily, a 19-year-old university student, who was employed as a baby sitter in Sydney, when Yao and I were there for a seminar. From the 15th week to the end of data collection period, the adult interlocutor was Janice, a 33-year-old neighbour. She and Yao met often. Janice and her husband were from New Zealand and had lived in Australia for several years when Yao first met them. Yao was well acquainted with each of her interlocutors before their first recording session.

Yao's interaction with interlocutor was both audio- and video-recorded except for the first few recordings, which were only tape-recorded. A video camera was used after Yao and her interlocutors felt comfortable about being videotaped. The camera was placed in the corner of the room even when it was not used, so that Yao and the others would grow accustomed to it. In fact, they paid little attention to either the tape recorder or the video camera.

Recordings with each type of interlocutor were made approximately once every other week at the beginning, then approximately once every four weeks, and finally once every six weeks. Given approximately one hour of recording per session, a total of some 60 hours of interaction were collected. From this corpus, data from recorded sessions at approximately five- or six-week intervals for each type of interlocutor were selected for analysis, yielding a total of 42 hours of recorded sessions.[3] As we shall see from what follows, this seemed to be the optimum interval. Since there were three types of interlocutor, having recording sessions at approximately five- or six-week intervals for each type of interlocutor meant that there were much shorter intervals between recording sessions and therefore few if any significant stages in Yao's progress would be omitted (see Appendix 3.1). Recording sessions for the data began on the 5th of June 1992 and were completed after 17 months on the 14th of October 1993. The selected data are presented in Table 3.1. The full recording schedule is given in Appendix 3.1.

Table 3.1 Recorded data selected for analysis

Play contexts	Interlocutors (with mother)	Total hours of recordings analysed	Recording commenced (after Yao's arrival)[4]
with peer	10 children	13.5	6th week
with teenager	Hannah	14.5	4th week
with adult	Emily, Janice	14	8th week (Emily) 15th week (Janice)

The activities that Yao and the interlocutors engaged in during the recorded sessions, except for the activities that had to be planned beforehand, such as visiting a science museum, were for the most part spontaneous play, such as drawing, making things with play dough, and various kinds of games. For all sessions, conversations were recorded as they occurred spontaneously. Out of the 43 recording sessions for analysis, all but six sessions took place at home. The six recording sessions which took place elsewhere were:

(1) In the room of a residential college at the University of Sydney (2 sessions) – Playing with Emily [8th and 10th weeks]
(2) At Janice's home – baking cakes [19th week]
(3) At Janice's home – decorating a Christmas tree [29th week]
(4) At Janice's home – playing computer games [44th week]
(5) At a science museum in Melbourne – using various pieces of equipment [32nd week]

The tapes were transcribed as soon as possible following the recording. Out of the 42 hours of tape recordings (covering 43 sessions) selected for analysis, I transcribed 32, which were all checked by a native speaker.[5] The remainder were transcribed by the native speaker and checked by me. The tape transcriptions were orthographic and include all the speech produced by Yao and her interlocutors, including mine. All relevant contextual information is reported.

The recorded data for the present study are supported whenever necessary by a diary, which I kept from the second day of her residence in Australia until the end of the data collection period. As her mother I had an opportunity to see her using English in a variety of ways and contexts. I carried a pencil and paper with me regularly and noted down, whenever possible, Yao's spontaneous use of English, mostly addressed to me. At the end of the day, I transferred this material into the diary, with details of the contexts in which her utterances and comments were made. In order to catch the actual process of her learning, the diary also includes her comments related to her language learning. Some of the features in the diary data throw invaluable light on the recorded data. These implications will be considered in the concluding chapter.

The transcription conventions used for the data in the study are presented in Appendix 3.2.

For the purpose of this study, a notation such as [PL57-46], [H-4-29], [E8-8] or [J38-15] is attached to all the recorded examples cited in the present study. Letters indicate the context of an interlocutor: PL stands for a peer (Linda), PC for a peer (Carol), H for Hannah, E for Emily and J for Janice. The number before the hyphen indicates the week of Yao's residence in Australia. The number after the hyphen indicates the request number in the transcription. For instance, the example below was observed in the 57th week of Yao's residence in Australia in the context with a peer, Linda. The request number is 46 in the transcription. Thus:

could you please help me? [PL57-46]

An additional number 2 after two hyphens, as in [PC75-35-2], indicates the initial request was not complied with and the request was made second time. If the number is 3, the request was not complied with twice.

In the diary data, a notation such as [Diary, 21-10-93] is attached to all the examples. This indicates the date of occurrence.

3.4 Data Sets

There are two subsets of the recorded data which will be discussed in the present study. All the analyses except for the analysis of addressees were based on the total number of requests recorded in the sessions. These analyses involved the larger sample of requests. This data set was used for the chapters on development (Chapter 4), requestive hints (Chapter 5), request goals (Chapter 6), and modification (Chapter 8). The analysis of addressees (Chapter 7) excluded the data from the first 12 weeks where there was inconsistency in the adult interlocutor. As stated earlier, prior to the commencement of recordings with Janice, the adult addressee was Emily, a 19-year-old university student. Only after the 12th week was it Janice, a 33-year-old neighbour. The analysis of addressees also excluded requests made during improvised role-plays. This was done in order to maximise homogeneity in the data and to exclude ambiguity of addressee since a role-play creates potential ambiguity in the perception by the speaker of the addressee. This data set involves the smaller sample of requests.

3.5 Defining Requests

As stated in Chapter 2, requests were defined as 'attempts by the speakers to get the hearer to do something' (Searle, 1976: 11). The focus of this study is on attempts on the part of the speaker to get the addressee to perform some kind of action or to stop an action. Performing an action includes not only non-verbal actions but also verbal actions such as 'say something/ just talk talk' [H20-57]. However, requests to provide information, which could also be seen as a form of verbal action (e.g. 'who did you see Jurassic Park with?' [H73]) were not included in this corpus because their inclusion opens up a whole new range of potential categories for investigation, such as requests for clarification, requests for confirmation as well as 'display questions'[6] and real questions. Requests to get the addressee to give permission were also excluded. Requests for permission (e.g. 'can I go first?' [H32], produced by Yao when Hannah and Yao were playing a game) were excluded because the activity required does not involve services by the addressee but only the granting of permission for the speaker to perform an action. This decision meant that the data sets used for the study were broadly comparable to other sets of data in the literature (e.g. Ellis, 1992).

3.6 Units for Analysis

The unit of analysis for this study is a request. Based on Blum-Kulka *et al.* (1989a), and Blum-Kulka and Olshtain (1984), a request was analysed into the following segments: address term; head act; support move[7] or reiteration.[8] For example, the following request is divided into three parts:

mum[9]/ we want to play here/ so <u>could you</u> please <u>go to your room?</u>[10] [PJ63-62-2]

'mum': *address term*

'so could you please go to your room': *head act with the addition of a conjunction, 'so', and a modifier, 'please'*

'we want to play here': *support move*

The address term is an attention getter which precedes the actual request. The head act is the request proper or the core of the request. Support moves are external to the head act. They can either precede or follow the head act. They support the actual request in order to gain the cooperation of the addressee and lead him or her to perform the desired action. In the above example, all parts, except the core of the request, which is the underlined part, are optional and can be omitted without altering the illocutionary purpose of the request.

3.7 Identifying Requests

In the next stage of the research, all the requests defined in Section 3.5 were identified. Requests, it was found, occurred in several different ways. A single request may occupy an entire turn. Or several requests may occur in sequence in the same turn, or across turns. The following are examples of requests in a turn (or turns):

(1) A single request in a single turn.

   3   *could you please help me?* [PL57-46]
      (Yao and her peer were making things with clay. Yao wanted the peer to help.)

(2) A request adjacent to at least one different request (Example 4) or connected to at least one different request by a conjunction (Example 5) in a single turn.

   4   *I need a rubber[11] mum/ wait just a minute* [H55-22-1,2]
      (The first request was made to me and the second to Hannah. Yao was going to write the word 'autumn' on a piece of cardboard for an autumn leaf collage. She had just asked Hannah how to spell autumn. Hannah started to spell it when Yao discovered she needed an eraser.)

   5   *oh just crack in there/ and put it in* [PJ63-4-1,2]
      (Yao and her peer were making muffins. 'There' referred to a small bowl, and 'put it in' referred to pouring an egg into a mixing bowl.)

(3) Multiple requests in multiple turns. These occur where requests are spread over several turns, after the first request fails to result in compliance.

In the following example, a peer and Yao were making things out of plasticine. Yao was encouraging a peer who had almost given up making a rabbit. After several turns with noncompliance Yao, too, gave up. When looking at the underlined requests, we see that the first [PC75-35-1] could be taken as a suggestion, but for the purposes of this analysis it was taken as a request. It seems to be often the case in children's play that the play is not fun unless both of the participants are happily involved in doing things. Yao wanted both to be happily involved in making animals and that is the reason why she wanted her peer not to give up. Because she did not want her peer to give up, we have coded the utterance as a request not to give up. (The requests are underlined.)

   6   **PC:** *no I can't make it*
      Y: *you can make it if you try* [PC75-35-1]
      PC: *I did*

> **Y:** *you don't have to make uh like mine*
> **PC:** *it looked like a frog/ it did*
> **Y:** *make it again* [PC75-35-2]
> **PC:** *it had these big ears a big body and small legs and uh*
> **Y:** *make it again then* [PC75-35-3]
> **PC:** *no*
> **Y:** *well what will you make – if you don't like that if you don't like it then make other animal* [P75-35-4]
> **PC:** *then I'll show you how it looked/I swear it looked like a frog/ no I can't make it/ just squashed it*
> **Y:** *oh!*

(4) A single request in multiple turns where the other turn(s) consist(s) only of modifications. (The request and its modification are underlined.)

The second turn in Example 7 is classified as a modification to the initial request because Yao elaborates the initial request once she is prompted by Hannah's request for clarification.

> 7 **Y:** *can you do it in fancy writing?* [H73-61]
> (Hannah and Yao were making a zoo from various materials. 'It' refers to the sign Hannah was going to write on the stick.)
> **H:** *I don't know/ you mean bubble writing?*
> **Y:** *any writing/ fancy/ any writing that is fancy*
> **H:** *on that stick/ here we go/okay*
> (Hannah was going to write the word, 'zoo' on the stick.)

3.8 Classification of Strategies

In relation to the classification of request strategies, there have been several important theoretical as well as empirical studies of illocutionary act of requests (Blum-Kulka, 1982; Blum-Kulka & Olshtain, 1984; Blum-Kulka, 1987; Blum-Kulka *et al.*, 1989a; Dore, 1977a; Ervin-Tripp, 1976; Garvey, 1975; Gordon & Ervin-Tripp, 1984; House & Kasper, 1981; Leech, 1983; Liebling, 1988; Searle, 1975). Among those, the Cross Cultural Speech Act Realisation Project (CCSARP) is perhaps the most prominent and comprehensive piece of speech act research done to date because of its extensive coding scheme (cf. Blum-Kulka *et al.*, 1989a). In the CCSARP (Blum-Kulka *et al.*, 1989a: 278), a request strategy is defined as 'the obligatory choice of the level of directness by which the request is realised. By *directness* is meant the degree to which the speaker's illocutionary intent is apparent from the locution.' We have adopted this definition.

Following previous classifications of request strategies on a scale of indirectness (Blum-Kulka, 1982; Ervin-Tripp, 1976; House & Kasper, 1981; Searle, 1975), the CCSARP (Blum-Kulka *et al.* 1989b: 18) identifies nine strategy types ranging from most to least direct, *mood derivables* being the most direct and *mild hints* the least, as in the following:

(1)   mood derivable (e.g. Leave me alone);
(2)   performatives (e.g. I am asking you to clean up the mess);
(3)   hedged performatives (e.g. I would like to ask you to give your presentation a week earlier than scheduled);
(4)   obligation statements (e.g. You'll have to move that car);
(5)   want statements (e.g. I really wish you'd stop bothering me);
(6)   suggestory formulae (e.g. How about cleaning up?);
(7)   query preparatory (e.g. Could you clean up the kitchen, please?);
(8)   strong hints (e.g. You have left the kitchen in a right mess);
(9)   mild hints (e.g. I am a nun).

In the CCSARP, the scale is based on degrees of requestive (or illocutionary) transparency. As you go up on the scale (from 1 to 9), 'the length of the inferential process needed for identifying the utterance as a request becomes longer' (Blum-Kulka *et al.*, 1989b: 18). The most direct or transparent level of requests are marked syntactically as in 1, 2 and 3, where grammatical indicators signal the illocutionary force. The least direct levels of request are those whose interpretation depends heavily on the contexts, such as in hints 8 and 9. Here, utterance 9 makes little sense out of its requestive context. Between these two extremes there are two groups of requests that derive their relative requestive transparency from various means. In 4 and 5 the illocutionary force is directly derivable from the semantic content of the utterance. In 6 and 7, the illocutionary force is signalled by conventional usage. These nine levels are combined into three major levels of directness: *direct strategies* (1–5), *conventionally indirect strategies* (6–7), and *nonconventionally indirect strategies* (8–9) (see Blum-Kulka *et al.*, 1989b). These three major levels of directness on the CCSARP coding scheme are explained as following (Blum-Kulka, 1989: 46–7):

(1)   The most direct, explicit level realized by requests syntactically marked as such, for example, imperatives, or by other verbal means that name the act as a request, such as performatives (Austin, 1962) and hedged performatives (Fraser, 1975).
(2)   The conventionally indirect level: strategies that realize the act by reference to contextual preconditions necessary for its performance, as conventionalized in a given language.

(3)   The nonconventional indirect level, i.e. the open-ended group of indirect strategies that realize the request either by partial reference to the object or element needed for the implementation of the act or by reliance on contexual clues.

This is the coding scheme used in the present study. As detailed below, however, the subcategories were modified somewhat in order to better clarify the data in the present study. The first modification made applies to those utterances which contain reference to 'preparatory conditions' (Searle, 1975: 71–4) for the feasibility of the request. The coding scheme in the present study makes a distinction between two types of 'preparatory conditions' strategy (i.e. statements and queries),[12] while in the CCSARP coding scheme there is only one (i.e. query preparatory). One can make a request by questioning as well as by stating the presence of preparatory conditions, such as 'Could you be a little more quiet?' and 'You could be a little more quiet' (cf. Searle, 1975: 65). These two types of strategy in the present coding scheme are labelled as *stating preparatory* (e.g. you can/you could …) and *query preparatory* (e.g. can you/could you …?)[13] The second modification has been made in relation to *hints*.[14] The CCSARP coding scheme (Blum-Kulka *et al.*, 1989a; Weizman, 1989) identified two types of hints, in terms of the amount of contextual clues provided for their interpretation, i.e. strong hints and mild hints. Weizman (1993) later collapsed these two strategies and reanalysed the requestive hints.[15] Following Weizman's (1993) later category of hints, the present coding scheme combines all the hints into one category. Finally, the categories of performatives and hedged performatives were taken out in the present taxonomy, since these categories do not appear in the data. Nor do there seem to be any instances of these strategies in the data of native English speaking children; neither nursery school children (e.g. Dore *et al.*, 1978; Garvey, 1975) nor school-age children (e.g. Ervin-Tripp *et al.*, 1990; Levin & Rubin, 1983). The two children in Ellis' study (1992) were aged ten and eleven when they began learning English and they did not use performatives or hedged performatives either. Thus it appears that use of those strategies is acquired late. The subjects of the CCSARP were not children, but adult native- or non-native speakers of English. Therefore, it seems reasonable to exclude those categories from the present taxonomy.

In the present data, therefore, seven strategy types are distinguished. All of these categories appear in the present data and their distribution provides information on the relative degree of directness preferred by the subject in making requests. The strategy types are presented in Table 3.2.

Table 3.2 Request strategy types: Definitions and examples

Types and their definitions	Examples
Direct strategies	
1 *Mood derivable*[16] The grammatical mood of the verb signals the illocutionary force of the request. The imperative is the prototypical form. Elliptical imperative structures express the same directness level.	*take off your rings* [J50-2] (Yao and Janice intend to make animals out of the flour mixture. The water has been added to the mixture and become very messy.) *don't move my fish* [H38-68] (Yao and Hannah are playing 'the Little Mermaid' game.) *choco chip, please* [H62-22] (Yao and Hannah are making chocolate chip muffins. Yao wants to eat a chip.)
2 *Obligation statements* The utterance states the obligation of the addressee to carry out the act.	*mum, you have to help us* [PA32-78] (Yao and her peer are playing 'shopping centre'. Before they begin, they have to make mini supermarket packs from the flattened packs provided, which is not an easy task.) *you better stay at our house* [PL69-34-1] (Half jokingly. Yao thinks her peer should stay with Yao to clean up the mess the peer has made.)
3 *Want statements*[17] The utterance states the speaker's personal need or desire that the addressee carry out the act.	*I want a circle* [J44-51] (Yao wants Janice to show how to draw a circle on the computer.) *I need a garbage bin mum* [H11-39] (Yao and Hannah are cleaning up after playing with play dough.)
Conventionally indirect strategies	
4 *Suggestory formulae*[18] The utterance contains a suggestion to do something.	*let's put this over here* [PA32-11] (Yao and her peer are playing store. She is referring to a toy.) *why don't you make a chair?* [PL57-44] (Yao and her peer are making things out of clay.)

Table 3.2 *continued*

Types and their definitions	Examples
5 *Stating preparatory* The utterance contains a reference to preparatory conditions for the feasibility of the request (e.g. ability, willingness, or the possibility of the act being performed). The speaker states the presence of the chosen preparatory condition.	*you could put some blu tack down there* [J74-18] (Janice and Yao are making things out of various materials.) *if you cannot draw a shark you can draw a whale* [H26-25] (Yao first asked Hannah to draw a shark.)
6 *Query preparatory* The utterance contains reference to preparatory conditions for the feasibility of the request (e.g. ability, willingness, or the possibility of the act being performed). The speaker questions the presence of the chosen preparatory condition.	*could you please pass me the glue?* [J54-11] (Yao and Janice are making collages.) *would you please hold this like this?* [H73 35 2] (Yao wants her mother to hold the animal she has been making, so she can put something on the animal's head with both hands.)
Nonconventionally indirect strategies 7 *Hints* The utterance makes no reference or only partial reference to the object or element needed for implementation of the act.	*my hands get sore.* [H55-23-4] (Yao is erasing letters that have been written heavily. She wants Hannah to help her.) *maybe it takes a long time to do it with this one* [J68-34] (Janice and Yao are painting a Mickey Mouse figure on fabric. In order to make Mickey's coat dark enough, Janice suggested that Yao paint over the fabric a couple of times. Yao is reluctant to do this and wants Janice to do it.)

3.9 Conclusion

This chapter has described the general methodology used to answer the research questions. It also established the classification of strategies which was the principal analytical framework for the study. These are the three major strategies and the seven substrategies.

Several different analyses were employed to answer each research question and those analyses will be presented in the following chapters. The next chapter will introduce a framework of phases in which the development of a child's interlanguage pragmatic system can be most effectively interpreted.

Notes

1. The double *a* in the Japanese utterance 'naani' indicates a long vowel.
2. The names of the peer interlocutors have been changed for reasons of privacy.
3. There were 43 sessions for analysis but two of these, those recorded in the 6th week, were 30 minutes long and were, therefore, analysed as one recording. All the other sessions were about one hour in length.
4. The first recording was made in the second week of Yao's residence in Australia with Hannah. However, since this session was only 15 minutes long, while the others were approximately one hour, it was omitted in order to maintain consistency in the recorded data.
5. The native speaker was Janice, an adult interlocutor.
6. Ellis (1988: 97) defines 'display questions' as 'questions which require the learner to demonstrate his knowledge of something'.
7. In Blum-Kulka *et al.* (1989a), and Blum-Kulka and Olshtain (1984) this is labelled as 'supportive moves' but for this study the word 'support' has been chosen instead, because it appears more neutral than the term 'supportive'.
8. Reiteration generally occurs after the request proper. It entails repetition of all or part of a previous head act, or paraphrase or elaboration of a previous head act. Blum-Kulka *et al.* (1989a) do not use the word 'reiteration' but instead use the term 'repetition' which is literal repetition of the request or paraphrase. The term 'reiteration' allows for a slightly wider range of items to be included since it does not require literal repetition.
9. In the actual request of this particular example, the address term 'mum' was not used. It is inserted here, however, to show the possible parts which can occur in a request.
10. The complexity within this example will be explored further in Chapter 8 (Modification).
11. A 'rubber' means an eraser in Australian English.
12. House and Kasper (1981) also distinguish these two types of 'preparatory conditions' strategy.
13. We thank Gabi Kasper for the insight into how to label them (personal communication, May 1996).
14. Hints defined in CCSARP were not always labelled as *hints* in the literature. For example, Ervin-Tripp (1976: 29) referred to requests with question forms 'which do not specify the desired act' as *non-explicit question directives*, while the term *hints* was reserved for statements. Later, in Ervin-Tripp and Gordon (1986), and in Gordon and Ervin-Tripp (1984), statements were referred to as *nonconventional instrumental moves*, or *NCI*. However, in Ervin-Tripp *et al.* (1987), all these three terms were called *hints*. On the other hand, Garvey (1975) and Levin and Rubin (1983) referred to this strategy as *inferred requests*.

15. House and Kasper (1987), which is part of CCSARP, also had one category for *hints*.
16. *Mood derivable* includes not only 'ordinary imperatives' and 'elliptical imperatives' but also 'you + imperatives' and 'formulaic imperatives'. An example of 'you + imperatives' is 'mum, you spin it' [H4-5] in playing a game. An example of 'formulaic imperatives' is 'excuse me' [PL69-30], when it was not used as an attention getter but as a request proper to ask the addressee to move when the addressee was in the speaker's way.
17. According to Gordon and Ervin-Tripp (1984), since *want statements* do not specify what the addressee must do, they may be interpreted as formally indirect, but they are logically direct especially in children's speech because *want statements* underlie assumptions of cooperation in children's speech.
18. In suggestory formulae, what Yorio (1980: 437) calls 'organisational gambits' such as 'it's your (my) turn' in a game were included. He suggests that organisational gambits are formulaic and that their general role is to organise interactions.

Chapter 4
Development of Request Realisation

4.0 Introduction

This chapter is concerned with the development of Yao's request realisation from very early in her English learning as she expanded the range of strategies and their linguistic exponents to express her request intentions over a period of 17 months. The chapter traces the emergence of these strategies and their linguistic exponents employed. In particular, the chapter addresses the following research question:

> What range of strategies and linguistic forms does a child use to realise requests in a second language and what is the pattern of their development?

In an attempt to answer the above research question, this chapter seeks to identify relevant divisions within the period so that contrasts can be made within the developmental process and progress can be charac-terised. The purpose here is to create an analytic framework that will reveal developmental patterns within the request system.

What we describe hereafter does not attempt to test any one particular theoretical model of language acquisition. Instead, we have tried, by carefully examining the present data, to discover and characterise the developmental patterns and sequences of one child's request realisation. Inasmuch as any specific acquisitional framework informs this analysis, the framework that we have drawn upon is a modified version of that proposed by Schmidt (1993). While employing Schmidt's view that 'notic-ing' is an essential component of language acquisition, we do not mean to imply that such noticing must entail understanding. We take as evidence of noticing the inclusion in Yao's request system of features not previously used or not previously used in the same way. Noticing in this way may not be accompanied by evidence of understanding on Yao's part. This notion of contextualised emergence is the same as that which informed the studies of child second language acquisition by Pienemann (1980) and Nicholas (1987). By making use of this approach, we have tried to let the categories of the analysis reflect as openly as possible the features of the data rather than seeking to impose pre-determined categories onto the data. One other consequence of adopting Schmidt's approach is that we define acquisition as an intra-individual phenomenon. No matter how the acquisition process is mediated through interaction, our focus is on the development of Yao's pragmatic abilities even though these abilities necessarily emerge as a result of her engagement within a specific socio-cultural context.

This chapter also provides the background for subsequent chapters.

4.1 Procedures for Analysis

In the present study, the data from three recording sessions, each with one of the three different types of interlocutor, were analysed together as a unit labelled 'Time'. Each Time is three hours long, one hour with each type of interlocutor. There were 14 Times altogether (see Appendix 4.1):

Time 1 (4–9 weeks)	Time 2 (10–12 weeks)
Time 3 (13–16 weeks)	Time 4 (17–20 weeks)
Time 5 (21–25 weeks)	Time 6 (26–31 weeks)
Time 7 (32–37 weeks)	Time 8 (38–42 weeks)
Time 9 (43–47 weeks)	Time 10 (48–53 weeks)
Time 11 (54–61 weeks)	Time 12 (62–66 weeks)
Time 13 (67–72 weeks)	Time 14 (73–75 weeks)

All the three different types of interlocutor, i.e. peers, a teenager and an adult appear from Time 1 (see Appendix 4.1). In each session, I was present as an observer, participating at times in aspects of interaction. Therefore, each Time consists of data from four different interlocutors.

For each Time, the total number of requests produced by Yao was computed. Then each request was analysed according to the three major request strategy types and their seven sub-strategies as presented in Chapter 3.

For inter-rater reliability, two raters, a native speaker of English, and myself examined three transcripts and coded them according to strategy type. The three transcripts were randomly chosen except that each had a different interlocutor. Inter-rater agreement was 97.2%. The items that were not agreed upon were discussed until the raters came to a full agreement on them.

4.2 Results and Discussion

There were 1413 requests produced during the approximately 17 months of data collection. Direct strategies, conventionally indirect strategies, and nonconventionally indirect strategies (*hints*) numbered 918, 458 and 37, respectively (see Appendix 4.2). Nonconventionally indirect strategies (*hints*) are included in the numerical data for this chapter, but will be discussed separately in the following chapter, because they differ in nature from the other two types of strategy. As mentioned in Chapter 2, in direct strategies the propositional content (sentence meaning) and speaker's meaning are identical, while in conventionally indirect strategies, both propositional content and linguistic forms combine to signal the pragmatic force. Therefore, in both there is only a limited range of exponents available. On the other hand, in nonconventionally indirect strategies, as Blum-Kulka (1989) has pointed out (see Chapter 2), the range of possible exponents is virtually unlimited, being open-ended in propositional content, linguistic form, and pragmatic force.

4.2.1 Developmental phases

We will now divide the overall period into phases, with the term 'Phase' used to refer to a period with specific characteristics in the use of requests. This has been done to capture the manner in which changes took place within the entire system.

Figure 4.1 shows the distribution of subcategories of the main strategy types (see Appendix 4.3).

In Figure 4.1, it is possible to identify distinct patterns that appear at the beginning and the end of the data gathering period. Times 1 and 2 are distinctive, as are Times 12, 13 and 14. In Times 1 and 2, there is a rapid decline in the proportion of *mood derivable* and a rapid increase in that of *query preparatory* up to Time 3, after which both go down in favour of other strategies that are developing (i.e. *obligation statements* and *stating preparatory*). After Time 3 the system appears highly unstable, suggesting that this is a point of change. In the last phase (Times 12, 13 and 14), there are significant changes, in that *stating preparatory* leaps and *query preparatory* goes down. The increased use of *stating preparatory* distinguishes the last phase from the earlier parts of the data gathering period. The establishment of the first and the final phases leaves open the question of whether there is a division within the intervening period.

A closer look at Figure 4.1 suggests that there is an additional division in the long, middle period. In Times 3–6, changes are relatively constant, whereas in Times 7–11, there are substantial changes of increase and decreases (i.e. *mood derivable, want statements* and *query preparatory*). Times 7–11 can be characterised by its instability. On the basis of these, it is reasonable to postulate the following four phases:

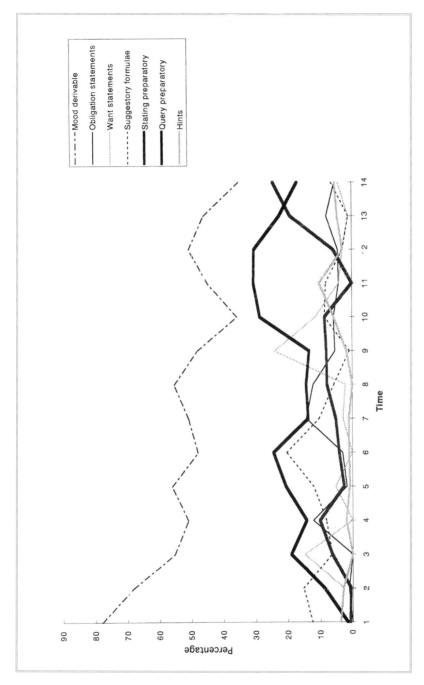

Figure 4.1 Distribution of request strategy types over time

Phase I: Times 1 and 2
Phase II: Times 3, 4, 5 and 6
Phase III: Times 7, 8, 9, 10 and 11
Phase IV: Times 12, 13 and 14

The divisions are, nevertheless, arbitrary and there are no clear boundaries between these phases.

4.2.2 Characteristics of each phase

This section attempts to capture the characteristics or patterns of each phase to show Yao's pragmatic development in L2 in relation to requests. This section focuses on the linguistic forms belonging to each strategy. A look at the linguistic repertoire employed in the strategies used by Yao will enable us to analyse the development of her pragmatic behaviour. Unless otherwise specified, all the detailed data referred to in Sections 4.2.2.1–4.2.2.4 is contained in Appendix 4.4.

4.2.2.1 Characteristics of Phase I

This phase covers approximately the first 12 weeks of Yao's residence in Australia. Frequent use of formulaic utterances in the early acquisition of English as a second language by children is recognised in many studies (e.g. Bahns *et al.*, 1986; Ellis, 1984; Hakuta, 1974; Huang & Hatch, 1978; Krashen & Scarcella, 1978; Rescorla & Okuda, 1987; Vihman, 1982; Wong-Fillmore, 1976). This phenomenon of formulaic use of utterances was frequently observed in Yao's requests in this phase. According to Krashen and Scarcella (1978), formulaic speech can be divided into routines and patterns. Routines are whole utterances that are memorised and unanalysed. Patterns refer to utterances that are only partly analysed, and they include an open slot to be filled in a frame.

Examples 1–9 are all routines (Elements under discussion that appear in a string of more than one utterance are underlined). All the utterances below were produced during a game or as part of play. Examples 1–3 are routines in a game, which Yorio (1980) calls 'organisational gambits', used when one tries to urge another to make or to stop a move. These gambits were used both as a request proper (Examples 1 and 3) and as a modification to give the reason for a contextually elliptical imperative 'don't' (Example 2).

1   *my turn* [H4-31]
     (Hannah, Yao, and Yao's mother[1] are playing a game.)

2   ***don't*/ *it's my turn* [H4-30]

3   *your turn* [H4-12]

4   *come on* [H4-16]
      (Yao wants Hannah to start a game.)

5   *mum / hurry up* [H4-29]
      (Hannah and Yao are ready to play the game. But her mother is still in the kitchen.)

6   **H:**   hey your mother didn't get a go
               (Hannah, Yao and her mother are playing a game. Yao thought it was her turn.)
      M: *oh*
      Y: *oh sorry / no oh no just a minute / I get it / no* [H4-23]
               (A piece has dropped on the floor and Yao tells the others to stop playing while she is trying to get the piece. However, she could not reach it.)

7   *come in* [E8-8]
      (Emily and Yao are playing shopping centre.)

8   *that's enough* [E10-25]
      (Emily and Yao are making a menu together. Emily writes items as Yao says them.)

9   *hang on* [PB12-12]
      (Yao and her peer are making jigsaw puzzles. Yao does not think that the piece her peer is about to use is the right one.)

Yao's utterances above already show an adequate use of routine formulas at the very beginning of data collection (the 4th week of her residence in Australia). This matches the findings of Bahns *et al.* (1986) who found in the data on four German children learning English that their use of formulas was extremely target-like. Routine formulas are rarely replaced by any other non-formulaic expression in English, either by native speakers of English or by non-native speakers. There may be several reasons for the appropriate use of formulas by second language learning children. First, many of those routine formulas are syntactically simple. Secondly, unlike early first language acquisition, the child is already equipped with an ability to memorise large chunks of unanalysed language and has a strong desire and need for social interaction. Thirdly, the routine formulas associated especially with games and play are repeated over and over. According to Peters and Boggs (1986: 84), 'passive listening to regularly repeated utterances can lead to improved perception of the utterances as previously missed or poorly perceived pieces are filled in'. Finally since they are attached to specific situations, they 'follow the here-and-now principle' (Hatch *et al.*, 1979: 275).

Another type of formulaic speech contains patterns such as 'look at ...', 'let's ...', 'can I ...?', 'can you ...?', and 'do you want to ...?', which are discussed below. The open slot in the pattern can be filled by a word or a phrase referring to a range of objects or actions.

The first type of formulaic speech pattern, the ordinary imperative, 'look at ...' (Examples 10–13) was regularly used, especially around the 6th week of Yao's contact with English. This is a device to accomplish initiations which L1 children often use (McTear, 1979) and Yao seems to have used it with a similar function. This device enabled Yao to draw her addressee's attention to something and to help her communicate when she had only a few linguistic devices at her disposal, and it perhaps gave her a sense of control over the activity.

look at ____

10   *look at that* [H6-21]
      (To Hannah. Yao points to an interesting card on the wall.)

11   *look at the little baby* [H6-51]
      (Hannah and Yao are looking at a book of animals.)

12   *close your eyes and then <u>look at this one</u>/ <u>look at this</u>/ <u>look at this</u>/ this is my class and every body and this is my teacher* [H6-48]
      (Yao shows Hannah a picture of her class in Japan.)

13   *<u>look at this Hannah</u>/ this is a veil* [H6-21]
      (Hannah and Yao are drawing pictures. Yao puts a veil on the picture of a girl.)

'Let's ...?' (Examples 14–16) is used to invite the addressee to join in an activity with the speaker. The request in this sense is part of a proposal or suggestion. Compliance requires joining in the activity the speaker proposes. It also sets up a cooperative situation (McTear, 1985; Gordon & Ervin-Tripp, 1984).

let's ____

14   *let's play the game* [H6-26]
      (To Hannah.)

15   *let's clean up here/ you're you're finished ok?/* [H11-40]
      (To Hannah when they have finished with play dough.)

16   *let's go to the mermaid house* [H11-47-2]
      (Hannah and Yao are playing with dolls.)

'Let's ...' appeared for the first time in the 6th week. Towards the end of this phase another form, 'do you want to ...?' was added to her repertoire to achieve the same goal. 'Let's ...' is an indirect strategy, but it still implies that the speaker has control over the addressee. 'Do you want to ...?' (Examples 17 and 18), on the other hand, 'appears to leave matters to the hearer's volition, and avoids the appearance of control' (Gordon & Ervin-Tripp, 1984: 309), since it has the same form as an offer or an information-seeking question.

do you want to _____?

17 *do you wanna play?* [PB12-35]
    (Yao and her peer are playing with dolls. Yao uses her doll to speak to the peer's doll.)

18 *do you want to draw pictures?* [PB12-48]
    (Yao and her peer have finished playing with dolls.)

'Can I ...?' (Examples 19–21) and 'can you ...?' (Examples 22 and 23) are different only in perspective. These two forms emerged at around the same time. However, the degree of imposition on the addressee is different. Since 'can I ...?' is in the form of a permission request, it does not give the appearance of imposing on the addressee as much as does the 'can you ...?'form.

can I _____?[2]

19 *can I have this?* [E8-4]
    (Yao asks for the sweater her mother is wearing. Emily and Yao are pretending to be in a shopping centre and Yao needs clothes for her shop.)

20 *can I use that?* [H11-31]
    (Hannah and Yao are making things with play dough. Yao wants the trimmer that is beside Hannah. Hannah hands it to Yao.)

21 *can I have space?* [PB12-1-1]
    (Yao and her peer come into the living room to play with jigsaw puzzles. There are snacks and juice on the table, so there is hardly any space for the jigsaw puzzle. Yao wants her mother to make some room for them.)

can you _____?

22 *I can't draw / can you draw in? / coffee or ...* [E10-10]
    (Emily and Yao are drawing up a menu.)

23 *can you help me?* [H11-20]
    (Yao wants Hannah to help her to make things with play dough.)

About the same time that 'can I …?' and 'can you …?' emerged, 'I (we) need …' began to be used and appeared to perform the same functions as the other two. In fact, Example 24 appeared as the second request following on from Example 21, 'can I have space?', when the first request was not immediately complied with. Example 25 appeared in the same transcript as Example 23, 'can you help me?'.

24   *we need space* [PB12-1-2]

25   *I need help/ please I need help* [H11-54]
     (Yao wants her mother to clean up after Hannah and Yao have finished with the play dough.)

The use of imperatives was very common in this phase, possibly because their forms are relatively simple (Gillis & Weber, 1976). 'Ordinary imperatives' appeared both in negative and positive forms (Examples 26–32).

26   *clean up/ clean up/ clean up* [H6-25]
     (Hannah and Yao have finished drawing.)

27   *don't clean up here* [H11-41]
     (Hannah and Yao have finished making things with play dough. Hannah is cleaning up.)

28   *colour in here* [E10-29]
     (Emily is drawing a menu for Yao.)

29   *don't colour in* [E10-56]

30   *draw girl picture* [H6-18]
     (Yao wants Hannah to draw a picture of a girl.)

31   *keep going/ keep going* [H11-56]
     (Hannah is playing the piano.)

32   *I need uh yellow/ pass me a yellow please* [H11-43]
     (Yao is putting the play dough in the container.)

'Ordinary imperatives' appeared most frequently in this phase (41.8% of all the forms produced in Phase I), but one of the features that distinguished this phase from others was the frequent use of 'contextually elliptical imperatives' (27.8% of all the forms produced in Phase I but under 8% in the other phases), as in Examples 33–35.

33   *quick/ this one is uh better* [H6-33]
     (Hannah, Yao and her mother are playing a game. Yao points to the stick she thinks is better for her mother to take.)

34 *don't* [H4-22]
(Yao stops Hannah from starting the game.)

35 *one more time/ one more time* [PM6-1]
(Her mother has measured Yao and her peer's height. Yao wants her mother to measure her height again.)

The above forms without verbs are taken as requests. They are appropriately elliptical in nature. Both child and adult native speakers of English use these forms in the contexts where the desired action is obvious. In the early stages of second language acquisition this form seems to be very convenient in that a child can express what is wanted in one or two words without using a verb, but can still be understood as making a request.

'You + imperatives' were not frequent in the data, even though they emerged in the 4th week. 'Imperatives' with the subject 'you' occurred both with a vocative (e.g. mum) and without. 'You + imperatives' had two functions here. The explicit 'you' was useful for specifying her intended audience when three people were playing (Example 36). It was also used when Yao was playing with just one person and in that case, she wanted her addressee to do certain things, implying that she was going to be doing something else (Example 37).

36 *mum/ you spin it* [H4-5]
(Hannah, Yao and her mother are playing a floor game.)

37 *you make this and this* [H11-7]
(To Hannah. Y points to the picture of the Little Mermaid on a play dough box.)

Some non-target-like requests[3] appeared, but only at the very beginning of data collection (Examples 38–40), and there were very few. Example 38 was uttered when Yao wanted to play a game with her mother and Hannah. But her mother and Hannah were busy talking and neglected what she said. So Yao made the second request (Example 39) to draw attention to what she had said previously. 'Everybody' is probably an influence from her classroom teacher. These two examples can be paraphrased as 'let's play this game'. They were uttered in the 4th week, before 'let's ...' first appeared (in the 6th week). By Example 40, Yao probably meant 'I want a one-dollar coin.' The 'I want ...' form (Example 41) emerged in the same transcript as this non-target-like utterance. In Example 41, she started saying 'I'm' and then she corrected it to say 'I want ...' This may indicate that the form is not internalised and is unstable at this point. Therefore, this non-target-like utterance co-exists with the target-like utterance.

38   *this one game* [H4-38-1]

39   *everybody this one game* [H4-38-2]

40   *mum your one dollar* [H4-60]
     (Yao wants a dollar coin to transfer its impression onto the paper
     by rubbing a pencil over it.)

41   *I'm – I want this one* [H4-28]
     (In a game where every player is supposed to have a piece of one
     colour to play with. Yao wants a red one.)

Despite the structural limitations on her English, Yao made use of all
the strategy types (from *mood derivable* to *hints*) in Phase I. The linguistic
forms were limited, and formulaic expressions, either routines and patterns dominated

4.2.2.2 Characteristics of Phase II

Phase II covers the period from the 13th week through the 31st week
of Yao's residence in Australia. Four major features mark this phase. First,
it is marked by a shift from a formulaic use of language at the beginning
of the phase to a non-formulaic use for the rest of the phase. Second, there
is a substantial increase in the frequency of some of the linguistic forms
that emerged in Phase I. These forms are used much more extensively
and with greater ease and fluency than in Phase I. Thirdly, we find a
limited expansion of her repertoire to encompass several new request
forms. Finally, this phase is characterised by an emerging awareness of
the rules and of English grammar.

In reference to the first feature, there was still, at the beginning of this
phase, a reminiscence of the formulaic use of language, as in Example 42.
However, this changed by the end of the phase, as seen in Example 43.
The former example was produced at the beginning of Phase II (the 14th
week) and the latter well into Phase II (the 26th week). Both examples are
very alike in structure. However, Example 42 appears to be formulaic,
while Example 43 is longer, more specific, and non-formulaic. (Elements
under discussion are underlined.)

42   *can I have a look?* [H14-26]
     (Hannah is showing her music paper to Yao's mother. Yao wants to
     see it, too. Hannah hands it to Yao.)

43   *can I have a look at that book please?* [H26-2]
     (Hannah and Yao are drawing animals. Yao wants to see an animal
     book so that she can copy an animal from it. Hannah passes the
     book to Yao.)

At the beginning of this phase, the use of 'can you (I) ...?' may still have been formulaic, although in Phase II the formulaic use of language was dramatically reduced. However, as Bahns *et al.* (1986: 721) point out, 'the borderline between formulaic and non-formulaic strings is obviously not very clear-cut; it seems, on the contrary, best conceptualised as a continuum'. It is, therefore, probably best not to view the use of formulaic speech in an all-or-nothing way. Nonetheless, the non-formulaic use of 'can I ...?', for example, appeared soon after in the 17th week, as in Example 44.

44   *can I have some chocolate?* [H17-21]
     (Yao wants her mother to give her some chocolate ice-cream. There are other kinds available as well.)

Similarly, we can see that the expansion of the lexicon with the 'can I ...?' form continued, as in Example 45, into the 25th week.

45   *can I have some more chocolate?* [PT25-13]
     (Yao wants her mother to give her more chocolate ice cream.)

Compare Examples 44 and 45. They are very similar in situation. The only difference is that in the former Yao has not been given ice cream yet, while the latter is a request for more. She was able to express this difference in her second language.

In reference to the second feature, a significant change from Phase I can be seen in the greater use in Phase II of 'can you (I) ...?' (i.e. 2.9% of all the requests produced in Phase I and 16.5% of all the requests produced in Phase II). This indirect strategy was the second most frequently used form in this phase, while in Phase I a direct strategy, contextually elliptical imperatives, was the second most frequently used form (ordinary imperatives were the most frequently used form in both phases). Compare Example 46 with Example 32 ('pass me a yellow please') in Phase I. Both are requests for goods using the same verb, 'pass'. In Phase I only ordinary imperatives were used to make such requests, but in Phase II *query preparatories* were added.

46   *can you pass the pencil please?* [PT25-61]
     (Yao and her peer are playing school.)

By the end of Phase II, various lexical items were available for the 'can you (I) ...?' form. For instance, Example 47 illustrates that Yao was now able to specify what she wanted by adding 'some more of' to 'these things.' Example 48 shows that the 'can you ...?' form had 'for me' added. According to H. Clark (1979), in English 'for me' is a special marker, which can be used to mark utterances as requests, while the 'can you ...?' form without 'for me' can be a request or a viable information-seeking question asking about the interlocutor's ability to do something. It is doubtful that Yao was at this stage consciously aware of this attribute of 'for me'. However, it is very likely that she was aware that 'for me' could be attached to a request, since she sometimes used 'for me' with the 'can you ...?' form when she was making a request as in Example 48, and she never used it in information-seeking questions.

47 *you can see the ground see/ oh no it's a messy/ <u>can you get some more of these things</u>?* [J29-30]
(Janice is setting up the manger scene at the bottom of the Christmas tree. Yao is referring to the way the straw has been placed on the paper and the tear in the paper. 'These things' are the strands of straws.)

48 *can you do another one <u>for me</u>?* [H21-5]
(Hannah has helped Yao to move the legs of a toy rabbit so it can stand up. Yao asks Hannah to do the same with another animals.)

Although the increase was not as great as that of 'can you (I) ...?', there was a large increase in the use of 'I want/ I want to (wanna)' (Example 49), 'how about/ what about ...?' (Example 50), and 'you can ...' (Example 51). These forms were used just once in Phase I, and in Phase II the number of uses of each form increased.

49 *I wanna play tiggy* [H14-3]
(Yao wants to chase Hannah.)

50 *what about you put this on/ what about here* [J29-29]
(Janice and Yao are putting lights on the Christmas tree.)

51 **Y:** *you can um <u>you can choose a page</u>/ this one/ this one/ this one* [H26-20-1]

    H: *I like....*
       (Hannah cannot decide which shark to choose.)

    Y: *um this one/ this one/ this one/ <u>just choose one</u>/ this one this one/ any one/ this one/ this one/* [H26-20-2]

Example 51 shows that Yao is now able to express the same intention or function in different forms. The situation here is that Yao has asked Hannah to draw a shark. Hannah has agreed to do it, but says that sharks are hard to draw. Yao brings a book in which there are illustrations of sharks, so that Hannah can copy from it. The first strategy Yao used was an indirect strategy ('you can choose a page.'). When Hannah could not decided which shark to choose, Yao used a direct strategy ('just choose one') to urge her.

The third feature of this phase is a limited expansion of linguistic forms. There is at this time the addition of several new forms to her repertoire, which enabled her to make both direct and indirect requests. 'You have to …' (Example 52) and 'you'd better …' (Example 53) were new additions to *obligation statements* (a direct strategy). 'Why don't you …?' (Example 54) was added to *suggestory formulae* (an indirect strategy) and 'do you have …?' (Example 55) was added to *query preparatory* (an indirect strategy). Except for 'you have to …', these forms were infrequent throughout the data.

52 *you have to shut the curtain* [H21-62]
    (It is getting dark and Yao's mother has turned the lights on, but she has not closed the curtain.)

53 *I think you'd better put this* (xxx) [J29-25]
    (Janice and Yao are putting decorations on the Christmas tree.)

54 *why don't you do that?* [H21-9]
    (Hannah and Yao are playing with toy animals. Hannah is about to speak for her animals so that they talk with each other.)

55 **Y:** *do you have ruler-ruler?* [PK13-26-1]
        (Yao and her peer are drawing pictures.)
    PK: *do I have what?*
    Y: *ruler/ I need ruler*
    PK: *here*
    Y: *thank you*

As does Example 51, Example 55 shows that Yao was able to express the same function using different strategies having different forms. Her first request made use of an indirect strategy and the second one a direct strategy.

The final feature of this phase, which appeared toward the end (see Examples 56–59), is the emergence of an awareness of the grammatical rules of English. Yao began to make explicit comments about English and comparisons between English and Japanese. This pragmatic ability can be attributed to a combination of her improved understanding of socio-cultural context and her ability to draw on an expanded repertoire of linguistic resources. Even though Yao's metalinguistic comments are not directly related to requests, they illustrate her understanding of English grammar at this stage. Her understanding of them very likely allowed Yao to use a variety of linguistic resources that are pragmatically more sophisticated. This phase contained a large number of metalinguistic comments. She seemed to have been thinking about these before she made her comments. They would arise suddenly, at the dinner table, for instance, when the conversation between Yao and her mother was on some unrelated subject. Below are a few examples of these comments, all of which are from the diary data. (Comments were in Japanese except for the utterances within quotation marks.)

56 *What are the meanings of 'I would' and 'I wouldn't'? When and how do you use them?* [Diary, 26-10-92]

57 *What is the difference between 'the' and 'a'? I don't know exactly when you are supposed to use 'a' and 'the'.* [Diary, 24-11-92]

58 *The 'gh' of 'light' is a 'silent letter.' The 'e' in both 'house' and 'home' is also a 'silent letter'.* [Diary, 17-11-92]

59 *If you literally translate 'I have an apple' into Japanese, it would be 'watashi wa motte imasu ringo o'.* [Diary, 24-11-92]

Example 56 is a question about an English modal, Example 57 a question about English articles, and Example 58 a comment on the English sound system. Example 59 shows that Yao recognised a difference in the word order between English and Japanese: SVO (I have an apple) vs. SOV (watashi wa (I) ringo o (an apple) motte imasu (have)). Felix (1978) argues:

> Due to his past linguistic knowledge the L2 learner is already familiar with the syntactic principle of natural languages. He knows that words cannot be randomly combined, even if the underlying conceptual or semantic relation is clear. Verbal utterances have to be constructed in accordance with certain grammatical rules.
>
> (Felix, 1978: 477)

Yao's metalinguistic comments reflect her awareness that languages are syntactically constructed and that word order is important. In addition, she seemed aware that modality was important for the expression of communicative meaning. As Ellis (1982) points out, L2 learners utilise their awareness of the contribution of word order to meaning and look for the ways to express communicatively useful modality elements. In fact, in this phase Yao was able to produce in the right order an embedded interrogative, 'do you know <u>what this is</u>?' ([H21-44]) along with a wh-interrogative 'what's this?' ([H21-46]).

Schmidt (1993: 27) argues that 'linguistic forms can serve as intake for language learning only if they are noticed by learners'. Yao's comments cited above on language and language use seem to indicate that she has at this time begun to 'notice' some of the linguistic features and that her conscious reflection upon them have aided her learning. Given the range of features that she has made comments on, it is likely that she has also noticed others, in particular, features relating to requests.

English was, during the phase, quickly becoming Yao's preferred means of communication, not only outside but also at home, without caring about the fact that her mother talked to her in Japanese, except for some occasions when she slipped into English to answer spontaneously one of Yao's questions or requests. After Phase I, the use of English replaced Japanese almost completely, except when Yao felt herself unable to express herself adequately in English.

On the whole, in Phase II the formulaic use of language that marked Phase I was dramatically reduced, and Yao came to produce longer requests spontaneously. She now used the forms that emerged in Phase I much more extensively, with a wider range of lexical items, and with significantly greater fluency. Especially, the use of the 'can you (I) …?' form greatly increased from Phase I to Phase II. There was also a limited expansion of new request forms. However, requests using past tense modals, such as 'could you (I) …?' had not yet emerged, and the use of *query preparatory* was limited to only three types of forms (i.e. 'can you (I) …?', 'do you want to …?', and 'do you have …?'). In addition, this phase is characterised by Yao's developing awareness of the grammatical rules of English.

These changes seemed to have provided the platform for the further development in Phase III.

4.2.2.3 Characteristics of Phase III

This phase covers the period from the 32nd week through the 61st week of Yao's residence in Australia. In so far as many new forms have been added to Yao's repertoire of requests and also a wide range of forms have become available to her for the expression of her intentions, the third phase of the acquisition process can be characterised as one of pragmatic expansion.

One of the new forms which emerged in this Phase was 'you should' in direct strategies (Example 60). It appeared in the middle of the period. All the four types of the form classified as *obligation statements* appeared (Examples 60–64).

60 **Y:** *very good dinosaur/ you <u>should</u> shut uh* [H43-7]
    H: *shut the mouth*
    Y: *mouth*
    H: *okay*
    Y: *so it wouldn't look like a dinosaur*

61   *I think you'd better put this* (xxx) [J29-25]
     (Janice and Yao are putting decorations on the Christmas tree.)

62   **H:** *we would like to present you the fabulous/ the wonderful Yao*
         (Yao is going to do gymnastics on the floor. Hannah as a circus
         master introduces her to the audience.)
     Y: *no you don't need to* [H38-52]
         (=you don't need to introduce me like that.)

63   *you have to comb her hair first* [PE47-55]

   In Example 60 Hannah was drawing a donkey for the game, 'Pin the
Tail on the Donkey' to be played at Yao's birthday party. What Hannah
was drawing looked more like a dinosaur than a donkey. 'You should ...'
is used here more as advice than as an imperative. 'You'd better ...' also
has an advisory function (Celce-Murcia & Larsen-Freeman, 1983), as in
Example 61. Example 62 communicates necessity. There was a substantial
increase in the use of 'you have to (you've got to) ...' (9.0%) over the
previous phase (2.6%). According to Gerhardt (1991),[4] children use 'you
have to ...' to invoke the relevant procedures or conventions that regulate
a particular act. Example 63 exemplifies Gerhardt's point. A peer was
going to put a scrunch on the doll's messy hair without combing it. Yao,
however, wanted the peer to comb the hair first. In order to achieve the
goal Yao invoked the normal procedure, which is combing hair when it
is messy before doing anything else with it. Controlling the addressee's
action by invoking prescribed procedures or conventions seems to occur
often in children's play. Another instance of this is Example 64, which
occurred at the very beginning of this phase. The situation here is that Yao
was a customer and her peer was a sales-clerk in a shopping-centre game.

64   **Y:**   *hello/ you have to say 'hello'* [PA32-103]
     PA: *hello*
     Y: *you have to say 'may I help you?'* [PA32-104]
     PA: *may I help you?*
     Y: *yes please*

   By convention, exchanges between a customer and a sales-clerk conform to the following pattern, which Yao wanted her peer to adhere to:

   Customer: *Hello.*
   Sales-clerk: *Hello. May I help you?*
   Customer: *Yes, please.*

   Yao invoked a 'convention or procedure', if we follow Gerhardt's
terminology in controlling her peer's actions. Since invoking certain

procedures or conventions to regulate an addressee's activity occurred
fairly often in this phase, the 'you have to ...' form was much more
frequently used than any of the other three forms in *obligation statements*.
Apart from the use of 'you have to ...' form, it is worth noting that
Example 64 shows a significant aspect of Yao's perceptual and analytical
development in the application of appropriate social rules. Certain kinds
of content and linguistic forms are expected in situations such an
exchange between a customer and a sales-clerk.[5] Example 64 suggests
that Yao seemed to have observed and internalised this previously. It was
Yao who prompted her peer to perform the utterances that were appropriate to that situation, rather than the other way around.

In indirect strategies, too, there was a great deal of expansion. In the
category of *suggestory formulae*, 'shall we ...?' was added (Example 65).

65   *shall we* play with the doll – dollies? [PC52-35]
     (Yao and her peer have just finished making things with clay.)

Expansion in the range of *query preparatory* is significant especially in
terms of pragmatic development. Three forms emerged for the first time
either at the beginning or close to the beginning of this phase: 'may I ...?',
'will you ...?', and 'could I (you) ...?'. The 'may I ...?' and 'will you ...?'
forms were rare and appeared only in this phase in the recorded data
(Examples 66 and 68, respectively), whereas the 'could you (I) ...?' form,
which is a syntactically modified form of 'can you (I) ...?', now became
available and was used more often than either 'may I ...?' or 'will you
...?', although 'could you (I) ...?' was not frequent in this phase.

66   Y: hello Mr Doggy/ can I – *may I* talk to your children? [H38-15]
          (Hannah and Yao are playing with toy animals.)
     H: I'll just get them for you/ Brownie and Whitie and Daughter Frog

As Ervin-Tripp (1976) points out, 'may I ...?' looks like a request for
permission. Such requests do not anticipate action by the addressee,
while requests for action include the expectation of addressee's action, as
in Example 66. This example is a request for action because when the
child rabbit (Yao) said, 'can I – may I talk to your children?', Mr Doggy
(Hannah) had to go and get them. 'May I ...?' is normally used to
addressees of higher rank. When the child rabbit addressed Mr Doggy,
she changed her request form from 'can I ...?' to 'may I ...?', since Mr
Doggy was her friends' father. This may reveal Yao's knowledge of on-
record polite request forms as being appropriate in certain contexts and
to certain addressees. 'May I ...?' with 'have', requesting goods did not
appear in the recorded data. However, the form was recorded several

times in the diary. These requests were addressed to her mother, usually when Yao wanted some sweet, as in Example 67.

67   *may I have some?* [Diary, 19-12-92]
      (Yao's mother is putting sweets in a container.)

'Will you' (Example 68) also appeared in an improvised role-play.

68   *oh will you just come and put that money?* [PE40-36]

Here the situation is that Yao and a peer are playing a TV game show. Yao as the TV hostess is requesting that her peer as a contestant pay her paper money to begin the game. Fraser and Nolen (1981) report on English native speakers' judgements of the relative degree of deference associated with linguistic request forms. According to them, the 'will you ...?' form was fairly high on the scale of deference. This appears to support the use of 'will you ...?' by a TV hostess to a contestant. The reason why both 'may I ...?' and 'will you ...?' occurred only in this phase may simply be that the context did not encourage their use at other times. In most of her play situations, Yao was playing with her addressee more-or-less as an equal play partner.

The first appearance of the 'could I ...?' form was also observed in an improvised role-play in this phase (Example 69).

69   Y: *could I have another chocolate because my children – I have five*
            children [J38-23]
            (Janice and Yao are playing store. Janice is the sales clerk and
            Yao the customer.)

      J: *five children goodness me yes you can do that/ thank you/ I'll just*
            put it through the cash register/ ten cents

Yao may have observed the protocol between a customer and a sales clerk, since Australian customers seem often to use the 'could I ...?' form. The following is another example of this form with a 'you' subject.

70   *I don't know how to play this/ can you – could you tell me how to play*
      this? [J38-24]
      (To Janice. Yao wants to play her new board game.)

This expansion in the range of *query preparatory* suggests that Yao has developed the capacity to become increasingly sophisticated in modulating her requests depending on her addressees.

The effect of a request may depend on the syntactic elements employed, such as different types of modal verbs (e.g. can/could; will/would) (Blum-Kulka *et al.*, 1989a). More polite requests are expressed with conditional forms (Koike, 1989a), which mitigate the impositive force of a request. The 'could you (I) …?' form, one of the conditional forms, is a syntactically modified form of 'can you (I) …?'. The semantic meaning of both utterances is the same but 'the conditional conveys a certain tentativeness on the part of the speaker' (Fraser & Nolen, 1981: 102). According to Sifianou (1992) and Trosborg (1995), the conditional 'distances' the request by shifting the focus away from the reality. Therefore, the conditional makes it easier for the addressee not to comply and makes the request less imposing.

The expansion of linguistic forms mentioned above indicates that Yao was becoming progressively more sensitive to social contexts and to the linguistic forms available for social use. Further evidence of Yao's understanding of the linguistic forms available for social variation is seen through self-correction, as in Examples 66 and 70. She started with one form and immediately changed to another such as in 'can I – may I …?' (Example 66) and 'can you – could you …?' (Example 70), this being done in spite of the grammatical correctness of her first attempts. This suggests that she was consciously trying to generate socially appropriate forms to mark the variation in addressee.

Acquiring second language pragmatics involves learning the grammatical code. As a result of the general increase of L2 competence, including vocabulary and structures, Yao began, early in this phase, to have a more precise ability to express what she wanted her addressee to do and by the end of this phase her requests became more elaborated, as seen in Examples 71, 72 and 73. In Example 71, the head act (the request proper) is elaborated by additional details. Example 72 is the same, but here, elaboration is achieved through an if-clause. In Example 73, 'can I see it?' is combined with a subordinate clause, 'I can copy it' using the conjunction 'so', which makes the purpose of this request more specific. In these examples, what Yao wants her addressee to do is specified. Specification of requests is an important aspect of Yao's pragmatic development, with her expanded linguistic capacity permitting her to be more precise in her expression of pragmatic purposes. This aspect of linguistic expansion will be taken up in detail in Chapter 8.

71 *you can put some things over here/ I put some here and you put things over here* [J38-6-2]
    (Janice and Yao are playing store. Yao brings small baskets to put the goods in.)

72 *oh just tell me the story I know um/ if I guess it you have to tell me another story okay?* [H55-59]
    (Hannah and Yao are making collages with autumn leaves. As they do this, Hannah tells Yao stories.)

73   *can I see it <u>so I can copy it?</u>* [PE47-47]
   (Yao and her peer are making animals with play dough. The
   peer has just finished making an elephant. The 'it' refers to the
   elephant.)

This phase also saw the emergence of more sophisticated syntactic
structures. These are not exclusively pragmatic. The sophisticated structures derive from Yao's increased ability to manipulate the grammar of
English. Compare Example 74, which was produced in the middle of
Phase III, with Examples 75 and 76 that were uttered in Phase I and Phase
II, respectively. The situations for these three examples were similar in
that Yao wanted Hannah's help in drawing animals. However, it was not
until Phase III that 'can you help me ...?' and the specific designation of
the thing that Yao wanted assistance with were combined to make a
single request (Example 74).

74   *can you help me <u>to draw a donkey?</u>* [H43-1]

75   *can you help me?* [H11-57]

76   *can you draw a dolphin for me?* [H26-3]

Example 74 is qualitatively different from the requests that preceded
it, such as Examples 75 and 76. In 74, the request is certainly expressed in
a more specified way and is therefore more sophisticated than the
requests made without structural expansion. This kind of expansion of
linguistic capacity seems to add an important dimension to the way in
which Yao was learning to use English.

This phase is consequently characterised by Yao's use of a wide range
of linguistic forms. These forms enabled her to express her intentions in
varying ways. One piece of supporting evidence is Yao's differentiated
use of perspectives. Both Examples 77 and 78 were addressed to the same
person (i.e. Janice), had the same request goal (i.e. to have the glue), and
were said in the same recording session, where Janice and Yao were
making collages. The difference is one of perspective: Example 77 is
addressee-based, while Example 78 is speaker-based.

77   *<u>could you</u> please pass me the glue?* [J54-11]

78   *<u>could I</u> please have the glue up here?* [J54-16]

Another piece of evidence is found in her second or third requests
when the first is refused or ignored (Examples 79–82). Second or third
requests are attempts to be more persuasive and gain compliance by
employing the correct tactics. The strategies used in Example 79 are
direct strategies, *mood derivable*. Although the level of directness is the

same, the forms are different: The first and second requests are contextually elliptical imperatives, while the third is an ordinary imperative.

79   **1st:**   <u>*no peeking!*</u>/ *no peeking* [PA32-3-1]
            (A peer tries to guess where Yao's bedroom is. There is no bed in the room, so the peer opens a locker door to have a quick look inside to see if there is a bed in there.)
      2nd: *can you – <u>don't</u> Ann* [PA32-3-2]
      3rd: <u>*don't peek*</u> *please okay?* [PA32-3-3]

After asking someone not to peek a number of times, if he or she is still peeking, the request is normally made more intense by saying something such as 'Don't peek please, okay?'. Yao seemed to be responding appropriately to the pragmatic requirements for such reinforcement. Reiterating a request in different ways means that an addressee cannot easily dismiss the request as 'more of the same'. Consequently, the variation adds to the intensity of the request.

In Example 80, Yao moved from a direct strategy (*mood derivable*) in the first request to an indirect one (*stating preparatory*) in the second. On the other hand, in Examples 81 and 82, she moved from indirect strategies (*query preparatory* for Example 81, and *suggestory formulae* for Example 82) in the first to direct strategies (*mood derivable*) in the second.

80   **1st:**   *just take just <u>take this off</u>* [PE47-15-1]
            (Yao and her peer are playing with a doll. The doll is wearing a pendant. 'This' and 'it' refer to the pendant.)
      2nd: <u>*you can take it off*</u> [PE47-15-2]

81   **1st:**   <u>*can you put glue here and here?*</u> [H48-33]
            (Yao and Hannah are decorating eggs for Easter. Yao wants Hannah to put glue on an egg so the glitter will stick to it.)
      2nd: <u>*put it on here and here*</u> [H48-34]
            thank you/ can you hold it? [H48-35]
            (The first 'it' is the glue and the second is the egg. Yao is going to put glitter on the egg.)

82   **1st:**   <u>*why don't you talk*</u> *with my mum or me?* [H55-54-1]
            (Hannah and Yao are making collages with autumn leaves. Hannah has not said very much. Yao does not like the silence.)
      2nd: <u>*say something*</u>/ *just talk talk* [H55-54-2]

Regardless of whether Yao's second or third request was direct or indirect (there was no systematic pattern), the change of strategy indicates that she was acquiring the means to express her intentions in several ways, without repeating the same forms. Ervin-Tripp *et al.* (1990) report that the tactic used for retries by children up to three and half years old is simply to repeat, while four- and five-year-olds use mitigation and change to more indirect forms. It is interesting to note that in their findings the oldest children, who are between about six and 11 years old, rarely use mitigation or explanation after noncompliance. Ervin-Tripp *et al.* (1990: 329) give a reason for this: Children over six already know that it is 'more effective to escalate pressure, to persuade with urgency'. Examples 81 and 82 may fit their findings.

There is one more strategy to note with respect to this phase: *Want statements* stand out in the middle of the phase (Time 9, see Figure 4.1). However, neither 'I want (to) …' nor 'I need (to) …' forms of *want statements* were used very often, except for the 'I want (to) …' in the middle of Phase III. Nearly all of them in Time 9 were uttered when Yao and Janice were engaged in a computer game (Examples 83 and 84). This was the first computer game Yao had played and at every stage she needed help. By 'I want to …', Yao meant 'I want to do x, so do something for me.' Janice told her verbally how to play the game as she played the game herself.

83   *ok I wanna I want to rub this out* [J44-42]

84   *I wanna put him over here* [J44-48]

Yao's use of 'I want (to)/wanna …' was very much bound to the context of the computer game. This suggests again that contexts determine the sort of language produced by learners.

As for another form of *want statements*, 'I need (to) …?', Mitchell-Kernan and Kernan (1977: 193) argue that this form 'conveys a condition of urgency'. This was also the case with Yao when she used the form 'I need …'. In Example 85, Yao and Hannah were decorating eggs for Easter. She was trying to say something else when she said 'do you think – do you,' and before she said what she wanted to say she suddenly noticed that the egg was leaking.

85   **Y**   *do you think – do you – I need a tub* [H48-53-2]
     H: *what?*
     Y: *tub quick!/ quick*

In addition to this use of 'I need (to) …', Yao used the form when she believed that her request was legitimate and should be complied with or she wanted to state her desire very clearly and firmly (Example 86). The situation in Example 86 is that Janice, Yao, and her mother went to a science museum. Her mother obtained maps from the information counter and gave one to Janice but not to Yao.

86   *well I need one* [J32-1]
      (To Janice.)

According to Ervin-Tripp (1976; 1977), and Gordon and Ervin-Tripp (1984), *want statements* are among children's earliest directives. Ervin-Tripp (1977) observes that they are used by children mostly when they are interacting with adults. In contrast, Garvey (1975), in a study of peer interaction, finds that children do not use them very often. Read and Cherry (1978) suggest possible reasons for these different results. One is that children are not accustomed to having their desires or needs satisfied by peers. Another is that children are aware that *want statements* are effective ways to obtain compliance from adults, especially parents. In this study the situation in which the 'I want (to) ...' form was used most frequently was that of computer games, which were being played with the adult, Janice. However, the situation seemed to contribute more to the frequent use of this form than the addressee's status, since the overall frequency of this form in the entire data is low. The reason for the low frequency of the 'I want (to) ...' and 'I need (to) ...' in this study may be a consequence of the situations being those of playing. In such circumstances, all interlocutors, whether they are children or adults, are play partners and therefore their language takes on a 'child-like' quality. Among play partners, the paucity of these forms may not be unexpected, as Garvey's (1975) study suggests.

A further feature of this phase is the extension of metalinguistic awareness. In this phase, playful manipulation of language, which shows Yao's metalinguistic awareness, was also observed. Yao puns on the meaning of a word 'rich' in the following instance.

87   **M:** *kono chokoreeto 'rich' ne*
             (Yao and her mother are eating the chocolate that Hannah had
             given them for Easter.)
             (=This chocolate is rich, isn't it?)
      Y: *Hannah is rich so she bought it* [Diary, 11-4-93]

On the whole, this phase is marked by pragmatic expansion. Many new linguistic forms were added (i.e. 'you should ...', 'shall we ...?', 'may I ...?', 'will you ...?', and 'could I ...?') and many structurally differentiated requests were observed. The emergence of the 'could you (I) ...?' form, which is a syntactically modified form of 'can you (I) ...?' is significant in terms of pragmatic development. Yao was now, by the use of the conditional, able to mitigate the impositive force of her requests syntactically. However, 'can you (I) ...?' was still far more frequently used than 'could you (I) ...?' (12.7% vs. 2.6%). Also, the conditional, 'could' was used only in a question form (i.e. *query preparatory*) and not in a statement (i.e. *stating preparatory*).

At the end of Phase III, despite these developments, further refinement of Yao's pragmatic system was still required. A key feature of this refinement is the ability to fine-tune the force of her requests, as will be seen in the next section.

4.2.2.4 Characteristics of Phase IV

This phase covers the period from the 62nd week through the 75th week of Yao's stay in Australia. This is a period of sophistication, in which the fine-tuning of the realisation of her requests was observed. Yao's repertoire continued to expand, especially in indirect strategies. Different linguistic forms, including syntactically mitigated forms, became available, allowing for different types of indirect requests. This expansion led to pragmatic sophistication.

All the new forms that occurred in this phase were indirect strategies, specifically *stating preparatory* and *query preparatory*. A very indirect way of making a request, 'is there ...?' (*query preparatory*) emerged in this phase. Three syntactically mitigated forms were also added: 'would you ...?', 'would you like to ...?', and 'you (we) could ....' Types of *query preparatory*, 'would you ...?' and 'would you like to ...?' are mitigated forms of 'will you ...?' and 'do you want to ...?' respectively ('Will you ...?' occurring in Phase III and 'do you want to ...?' appearing in all the previous phases.) One type of *stating preparatory*, 'you (we) could ...', is a mitigated form of 'you (we) can ...', which emerged as early as in Phase I. Furthermore, 'do you have ...?', which appeared in Phase II, was now used more often. The 'could you (I) ...?' which became available in Phase III was now constantly used.

We will now look more closely at the expansion of indirect strategies. The frequent use of the modal verb, 'could' is very salient both in *stating preparatory* and *query preparatory*. In spite of its first emergence in this phase, 'you could ...' (Example 88) was the second most frequently used form after ordinary imperatives. Requests become less forceful and more suggestive with this form.

88   *you could put some blu tack down there* [J74-18]
       (Janice and Yao are making things out of many different materials. The giraffe Janice is making does not stand on the table by itself.)

The use of 'could you (I) …?' (Examples 89 and 90) was also frequent. The frequency of the form greatly increased after Phase III, when this form first emerged (from 2.6% to 8.3%).

89   <u>could you please do that here</u> and then I do the pants [J68-42]
     (Yao and Janice are painting Mickey Mouse on fabric.)

90   mummy <u>could I please have one more biscuit?</u>/ one more each please
     mum? [PL69-2]
     (Yao and her peer have been eating biscuits.)

The forms with the past-tense modals 'you could …' and 'could you (I) …?' were now frequently used along with the forms with the present-tense modals 'you can …' and 'can you (I) …?'. The frequencies of 'you can …' (8.3%), 'you could …' (9.1%), 'can you (I) …?' (8.7%), and 'could you (I) …?' (8.3%) were almost the same. These forms together now appeared in about one third of Yao's requests. As Leech (1983) points out:

> … the past-tense modals signify a hypothetical action by h [the hearer], and so in reply, h can in theory give a positive reply to the question without committing himself to anything in the real world.
>
> (Leech, 1983: 121)

As indicated earlier, Sifianou (1992) and Trosborg (1995) have an interpretation very similar to Leech's. The hypothetical forms being more indirect than the real forms are seen not only in interrogatives but also in declaratives such as 'you could' (Leech 1983).

There are other forms Yao learned to use at this time in order to realise requests in indirect ways. Their frequency, however, was much less than that of 'could you …?' and 'could I …?'. One of those forms, 'would you …?' emerged as in Example 92. Comparing this example with Example 93, which was produced in Phase II, we find that both have an identical clause 'you hold this', but the modal verb is different. Therefore, the level of indirectness is different, Example 91 being more indirect than Example 92 because of the hypothetical nature of 'would'.

91   would you please hold this like this? [H73-35-2]
     (Hannah and Yao are making a zoo out of various materials. Yao asks her mother to hold the animal she is making so she can put something on the animal's head with both hands.)

92   can you hold this please? [H21-24]
     (Hannah and Yao are playing with toy animals. Yao wants Hannah to hold one of them, so Yao as Mrs. Rabbit can give juice to the others.)

Another newly added indirect form, 'would you like to …?' (Example 93) is considered as a mitigation of 'do you want to …?' (Blum-Kulka *et al.*, 1989a), although both forms 'exhibit a protective orientation toward her own face in that she does not take compliance for granted' (Trosborg, 1995: 235).

93   *would you like to play with the play dough?* [H67-25]
     (Yao brings play dough from the other room.)

Towards the end of this final phase, one more indirect form, 'is there …?' emerged (Example 94).

94   *is there any more white* [PJ75-72]
     (Yao and her peer are making things out of plasticine.)

This is a distancing device, to use Sifianou's (1992) term. It is a way of impersonalising requests by avoiding the use of 'I' and 'you' in the expressions such as 'could I have …?', 'could you give me …?', or 'do you have …?'. On the surface the 'is there …?' form refers to the existence of an object and there is no necessary implication that the addressee has it. Therefore, it has a non-coercive connotation. Yao's use of 'is there …?' suggests her recognition of the social nuances of the situation and her possible imposition on the addressee. It also implies that she was framing her requests so that they were only indirectly demanding of her addressee.

Another development in the linguistic forms of this phase is the occurrence of 'do you have …?' as in Example 95.

95   *mum/ have you got a lid?* [PL69-38]
     (Yao and her peer are making things out of various materials. And Yao wants a lid.)

This form already appeared once in Phase II and again in Phase III, but now more frequently in Phase IV. The form, which refers to the possession of an object, is similar to 'is there …?' which refers to the existence of an object. These forms are conventional in asking for goods, but they are different from 'could (can) I have …?' which is highly conventional. The former can be information questions and meant literally, but not the latter. When Yao used the forms, 'is there …?' and 'do you have …?' in such contexts as Examples 94 and 95, she was not using them literally, since she knew or could assume that her addressee had what she wanted although she may not have known for sure. Yao was using these forms as if they were literal questions. Gordon *et al.* (1980) found that among their American subjects from kindergarten through fifth grade, children below third grade (under eight-year-old) rarely used 'is there …?' or 'do you have ...?', while children in third grade (eight-year-olds) and above used them frequently. Gordon *et al.* (1980: 5) suggest that children in third grade and above 'seem to be developing a more complicated sense of speech convention in which forms may be simultaneously conventional in one respect, but must be used literally in another'. They conclude that it is at a later stage of development (eight-years-old and above) that children learn the use of 'conventionalised literal forms' such as 'is there ...?' and 'do you have ...?'. In the present data, during Phase IV, when Yao was eight years old (a third grader), the 'is there ...?' form emerged and the 'do you have ...?' form increased. What Gordon *et al.* suggest for L1 development seems to have began in Yao's L2 pragmatic development during this phase.

In relation to the 'do you have ...?' form, there is another development to be noted: 'Do you have ...?', with a post modifying 'I could use' added, appeared in this phase, as in Example 96.

96 *I need a blu tack/ do you have a blu tack I could use?* [PL69-58]
    (Yao and her peer are making things from materials called 'Oodles'.)

Gordon *et al.* report that their children under eight-years-old never added this qualification. This was also true with Yao. Yao was eight years old when she first added this qualification to the 'do you have ...?' form. Gordon *et al.* speculate that one reason for its use by children is that they want to make sure that their questions are not to be heard as information questions but as genuine requests. The other reason they offer is that children recognise they are imposing upon the addressee and consequently want their requests to sound less direct.

Forms which refer to existence, such as 'is there ...?' and which refer to possession such as 'do you have ...?', especially 'do you have ...?', with its qualification (Example 96) show that Yao senses a potential obstacle in her getting compliance from her addressee. This is very similar to what has been found in the native speaking children of English in the study by Gordon *et al.* It suggests that the pragmatic development of children of L1 and L2 at about eight years of age may be similar. Yao's pragmalinguistic[6] development during this phase is a consequence of both social and linguistic attainments. Once she had at her disposal the grammar necessary to realise requests, she was able to produce different forms to fit different contexts. In addition, she now acquired a sense of social context, which developed rapidly around age eight.

Thus far in this section we have seen that during this phase Yao's pragmatic ability to express her intentions in indirect ways was advancing rapidly. The following instance (Example 97), from the diary data, may further illustrate her pragmalinguistic awareness at this stage. The question about the difference between 'could you ...?' and 'would you ...?' was asked about one month after Yao had begun using the 'would you ...?' form during this phase. (The 'could you ...?' form appeared for the first time in the previous phase and the 'would you ...?' form in this phase.)

97 **Y:** *could you get me a plate, please?*
(Yao is taking some cake out of a container.)
thank you
(Her mother gives Yao a plate.)
mum what's the difference between 'could' and 'would'? [Diary, 8-8-93]
(After a pause.)

M: *hotondo onnaji yo*
(=about the same)

Y: *how come two ways to say it?/ what's the difference*

Yao's question here indicates that she has 'noticed' (Schmidt, 1993) features of English usage that have direct relevance to the expression of her requests.

Another interesting development in this final phase is the growth of persistence, persuasiveness, and a greater engagement with her interlocutors in her attempts to achieve compliance. Now, Yao seemed to be in full control of the forms she had already mastered and was able to elaborate the structural options that were available to her. This perhaps enabled her to engage at greater length with her interlocutors in her attempts to be persuasive. Examples 98 and 99 are from the same interaction with the same addressee (a peer) but they show different aspects of her greater willingness to engage. In Example 98, the utterances are getting longer as Yao tries to achieve compliance. In Example 99, she is engaged with her interlocutor in a way that required greater syntactic capacity (i.e. the conditional 'would'). Although compliance and non-compliance is not at issue here, Example 98 was not complied with, but Example 99 was.

The situation in Example 98 is that a peer is about to give up making a rabbit with plasticine.

98 **PC:** *no I can't make it*
Y: *you can make it if you try* [PC75-35-1]
PC: *I did*
Y: *you don't have to make uh like mine*

PC: *it looked like a frog/it did*

Y: *make it again* [PC75-35-2]

PC: *it had these big ears a big body and small legs and uh*

Y: *make it again then* [PC75-35-3]

PC: *no*

Y: *well what will you make – if you don't like that if you don't like it*
      then make other animal [PC75-35-4]

PC: *then I'll show you how it looked/ I swear it looked like a frog/*
      no I can't make it/ just squashed it

Y: *oh!*

In the first request, Yao gives encouragement and tries to persuade her peer not to give up by saying 'you can make it if you try'. She uses the form, 'you can …' (*stating preparatory* which is an indirect strategy). This does not work. So, Yao moves to a direct strategy, *mood derivable,* and uses ordinary imperatives, which are more forceful. In the third request, she adds 'then' at the end of the imperative form, presumably expecting to get compliance, but doesn't get it. In the fourth request, she suggests making something else. This time she attaches a modification, 'if you don't like it', to the imperative form. After making four requests, Yao finally gives up. After her second request, each time she makes a request, the imperative form becomes more elaborated as follows:

1st request *you can make it if you try*
2nd request *make it again*
3rd request *make it again then*
4th request *if you don't like it then make other animal*

By the end of Phase IV, Yao had developed the capacity to expand what she was saying in order to be persuasive.

The situation of Example 99 is that Yao and the peer are making things out of plasticine.

99   PC: *can you make me a duck?*

Y: *if you want – well if you promise me you would do all the others*
      except for the duck/ would you do all the other things except for the
      duck? [PC75-42]

PC: *(The peer nods.)*

Y: *okay then/ here/ do you want a little one?/ how big?*

PC: *yeah a little one to fit in that pond*

Y: *okay*

PC: *(The peer starts making something.)*

The utterance, 'if you want – well if you promise me you would do all the others except for the duck' is an answer to the request by the peer. Yao's request in turn is 'would you do all the other things except for the duck?' In this example, Yao gets the peer's promise to do what Yao wants her to do by trading off in order to achieve her goal. Her utterance has great syntactic complexity (the use of the conditional sentence, for example) and shows a greater engagement and negotiation than before with the interlocutor in her efforts to achieve compliance with her request.

As we have seen in this phase, Yao's pragmatic ability to express her intentions in indirect ways, especially in *stating preparatory* and *query preparatory*, rapidly advanced. New forms in those strategies, including mitigated forms were added to her repertoire. In addition to the new forms, the 'could you …?' form, which emerged in Phase III, was used with significantly more frequency.

4.3 Summary and Conclusion

It can be said that the development of Yao's requests moved from initial formulaic and routinised forms to progressively more differentiated ones. By the end of the data collection period, when she was eight and a half years old, Yao had begun to produce various indirect forms used by her native-English-speaking contemporaries, as documented in the literature. It seems reasonable to assume that children develop a sense of social context regardless of L1 and L2. Certainly, once Yao had the grammar necessary for request realisation in L2, she was able to produce a variety of indirect forms when she recognised the potential for imposition on the addressee or sensed a potential obstacle to her getting compliance. While not necessarily evidence of a 'conscious awareness' (Schmidt, 1993) on her part that she was selecting one means of expression over another, the fact that Yao had become better able to alternate appropriately between more and less direct requests indicates that she had noticed not only the existence of various request forms (a pragmalinguistic insight) but also how they should be deployed (a sociopragmatic insight).

The following chapters will continue the exploration of Yao's ability to manipulate her English in accord with the features of the context.

For this chapter Yao's employment of *hints* has been included in the numerical data of results, but it has not been discussed. The next chapter will look at Yao's use of *hints*, another strategic resource that was available to her from the beginning.

Notes

1. In the remainder of the thesis I will refer to myself as Yao's mother or her mother when I talk about myself as an interlocutor.
2. Requests for action, for goods, and for permission can take this form. Requests for permission, however, are excluded from this analysis, since they are used to ask an addressee to give permission for the speaker to act rather than to ask an addressee to perform an action. Therefore, the following example, which occurred in this phase, was not considered here: 'can I play with her?' [PB12-34] (Yao and her peer are playing with dolls. Yao speaks through her doll to the peer to get a permission to play with her peer's doll.)
3. Non-target-like requests are found in 'others' in Appendix 4.4.
4. Gerhardt's subjects used '*hafta*' instead of '*have to*'.
5. By using an exchange between a customer and a sales-clerk in Japan, H. Cook (2001: 83–4), too, illustrates that interlocutors need to know the normative expectations of the social role they play in a given situation in a given society – as well as the linguistic features associated with the role in that situation – in order to speak appropriately.
6. The term 'pragmalinguistic' is complementary to 'sociopragmatic'. Both were first used by Leech (1983). The former refers to 'knowing that the linguistic form conveys the right pragmatic purpose' and the latter, to 'knowing that a linguistic form has specific social conditions for appropriate use' (Kasper & Rose, 1999: 98). The distinction between 'pragmalinguistics' and 'socio-linguistics' is explained in further detail in Kasper and Rose (2001: 2–3).

Chapter 5
Requestive Hints

5.0 Introduction

The previous chapter traced the emergence of the strategies and different linguistic exponents that Yao used to realise requests, and it addressed the following research question: What range of strategies and linguistic forms does a child use to realise requests in a second language and what is the pattern of their development?

In an attempt to answer this research question, a detailed examination was made of direct and conventionally indirect strategies. In this chapter, we will focus on Yao's use of nonconventionally indirect strategies, which form a distinct category that we shall refer to as *hints*. As pointed out in the previous chapter, unlike the other two strategies, hints are basically open-ended in propositional content, linguistic form, and pragmatic force. Neither the action to be performed by the interlocutor nor the goal of the speaker is mentioned and therefore the illocutionary force is not explicitly expressed. In hints, the degree of inference is greater than in both direct and conventionally indirect strategies. Hints are for these reasons a more creative use of language than the other strategies.

5.1 Identifying Hints in Context

Because there are no formal limitation on hints, the interpretation of hints depends largely on the context, with the same utterance having a broad range of illocutionary force. If the same utterance can express such different intentions (e.g. a literal meaning and a requestive hint) how can we know which the speaker intends?

Depending on the context, questions concerning location, such as 'where is my pen?', can function also as requestive hints to give the item to the speaker. In such contexts, addressees become aware of the types of goods that they are expected to supply. One of the typical settings is the classroom during group activities, where several children are sitting at a table and sharing things. During such activities in Yao's classroom, we observed many questions concerning location (e.g. 'where are the scissors?'). Those at play regularly heard such questions as requests.

Those utterances were not accompanied by searching by the speaker, and it was always the case that the child who was the closest to the object mentioned handed it to the speaker without comment. In this context, interpreting the 'where' question as a request was frequent, normal, and apparently routinised. In cases such as this, inference from the utterance to its implied intent is rather obvious. If the addressee decided to interpret the question literally for some reason and said, 'it's right here,' without handing the item to the speaker, or did not perceive the implied requestive force of the utterance, it would annoy the speaker. There are general rules here for the 'where' question to be interpreted as a request. Objects on the table in a group activity are usually shared and are handed to the person who wants them. Thus, such 'where' questions regularly have the illocutionary force of requests. The 'where' question then, in spite of its nonconventional form is 'contextually conventionalized' (Weizman, 1989: 78). This feature also applies to the situation where Yao and her interlocutor were doing something together at the table at home (e.g. drawing pictures, making things out of plasticine, etc.), as in Example 1.

1   *where is the rubber?* [H17-54]

The interlocutor acted on the assumption that the 'where' question addressed to her had the illocutionary force of a request and handed the rubber beside her to Yao without further clarification.

However, in other contexts, the identical utterance, 'where is the rubber?' can be solely an information-seeking question. For example, when another interlocutor was showing Yao how to draw different things on the computer, Yao said, 'where's the rubber?' in order to find out where the eraser was on the computer. In this case, Yao's 'where' question was nothing more than an information-seeking question.

The intention of other interrogatives in the data were also obvious, as in Example 2:

2.   *how many times do I have to say it's not* [J50-37]

In this example, Janice and Yao were making things out of bread dough. Janice was trying to guess what Yao was making. She could not think of anything except 'hamburger' and repeatedly mentioned 'hamburger'. Yao was a little annoyed by the repetition, and it is highly unlikely that she seriously intended her question to be given a literal interpretation.

It is not very difficult to infer the implied intentions of the utterances in the foregoing examples. There are, however, some interrogative forms where it is difficult to identify whether they are intended as requests or information questions. For instance, in Example 3, the underlined interrogative form is legitimately interpretable either as a request or as an information-seeking question:

3   Y: *have you seen another one of those?/* there should be one [P69-19]
        (Referring to an ice-cream stick.)
     PL: (The peer looks for it without saying anything.)
     Y: *how come there's not* =
     PL: *= I had one here a moment ago*

In this situation, Yao and her peer are making things at the table out of materials that include ice-cream sticks. The utterance 'have you seen another one of those?/ there should be one' may have been intended by Yao as a request for an ice-cream stick. She may have expected the peer to know where it was, and give it to her. However, mainly because Yao was searching for an ice-cream stick as she uttered this and the peer said, 'I had one here a moment ago' as she searched too, the utterance was treated as an information question.

5.2 Results and Discussion

5.2.1 Low frequency of hints

Out of 1413 requests produced in the data, the total number of hints produced by Yao amounted to only 37 (2.6%), while direct strategies and conventionally indirect strategies numbered 918 (65.0%) and 458 (32.4%) respectively. But the low frequency of hints in Yao's data is not surprising if compared with the use of hints by native speakers. The research cited below illustrates that native speaking adults and children, too, rarely use hints as a request strategy, regardless of their native language.

With regard to children, Garvey's (1975) American subjects, whose ages varied from 3;6 to 5;7, rarely used hints. In Trosborg's (1985: 62) study with Danish children aged three to five, the three- to four-year-olds did not use hints and the five-year-olds produced only a small number (four out of 64 requests). Unfortunately, there is no research directly on requests by Japanese children, but there is related research. Clancy (1985; 1986) finds that the Japanese style of interaction is very indirect, even vague, varying significantly from the interaction of Americans. If she describes accurately the characteristics of Japanese communicative style, then requests made by Japanese should display relatively high frequency of hints. However, several pieces of research report conflicting results. For example, Matsumori (1981) reports, on the basis of research that dealt with directives employed by Japanese and American mothers interacting with their children aged three to six, that the American mothers tended to use conventional indirect request such as 'could you …?', and 'would you …?' more frequently than their Japanese counterparts. As for non-conventionally indirect strategies (i.e. hints), she found no significant difference in frequency. The frequencies of hints for both were fairly low (10% for the Japanese mothers, 14.2% for the American). Although Matsumori's work is not on children but on their mothers, it might be speculated that the frequency of the hints used by Japanese children would reflect the cultural behaviour modelled in their mothers' use of hints. Consequently, it is reasonable to expect Japanese children to use hints relatively infrequent. Rose (1994) also reports results that conflict with the common perception of Japanese interaction being vague and indirect compared, for example, with interaction in American English. For his study, Rose employed an open-ended DCT (Discourse Completion Test/Task) and analysed requests made by Japanese (in Japanese) and American undergraduates (in English). He found that the Japanese undergraduates were more direct than Americans in making requests and that the Americans used hints more frequently than did the Japanese. The average percentage of hints made in the eight situations given in the DCT was low for both languages, with Americans choosing them 9.8% of the time and Japanese choosing them only 3.4%.[1] Based on this study, Rose and Ono (1995: 212) administered DCTs and multiple-choice question-naires (MCQs) to Japanese to elicit requests. They found that hints were more frequent on the MCQ than on the DCT (12.3% vs. 3.2%).[2]

Rose's (1994) and Rose and Ono's (1995) studies were actually designed to address methodological validation in speech act research, which is not the focus of the present study. However, even if the result of the MCQ is more representative of actual face-to-face interaction, which Rose and Ono (1995) seem to claim, the percentage of hints even on the MCQ (12.3%) is still not very high. It is also worth mentioning here the study of Beebe and Takahashi (1989), which is concerned with Japanese learners of English. In their study of face-threatening acts by native English-speaking Americans and Japanese learners of ESL, Beebe and Takahashi (1989: 120) conclude that 'Japanese ESL speakers often do not conform to prevalent stereotypes about their indirectness and their inexplicitness'. The low frequency of hints is also evident in other studies of L1 adults. For example, the use of hints by native speakers of British English, Danish and German varied from 0% to 9.8% depending on the situation (House & Kasper, 1987: 1258–60; Kasper, 1989: 48–9). In the CCSARP (the Cross-Cultural Speech Act Realisation Project) data (Blum-Kulka & House, 1989: 130), the use of hints in five languages (Australian English, Canadian French, German, Hebrew, and Argentinian Spanish) varied between 1.14% and 8.2%. Using an ethnographic approach, Blum-Kulka *et al.* (1985: 121) found that for native speakers of Hebrew only 10.1% of their requests were hints.

In light of these findings, the low frequency of hints in the present data is not surprising. Both the native speakers' use of hints as well as Yao's in the present study are remarkably low. The low frequency in the other data mentioned above may have to do with the nature of hints; since their interpretation depends to a large degree on contextual knowledge rather than on the literal or utterance meaning. The speaker's intentions may not always be correctly interpreted. Therefore, the speaker may avoid taking a risk, and consequently hints may be only rarely reported.

This may also be one of the reasons why Yao's use of hints is low. There are other reasons, however. Yao was using English as a second language, one in which she had limited proficiency. Takahashi and Beebe (1987) report that lower proficiency Japanese ESL speakers were less indirect in their refusals than those with high proficiency, who used a variety of expressions to soften directness. There is still the possibility that the criteria for identifying requests (i.e. the exclusion of the questions which were more likely to be information questions than requests) may have restricted the number of hints in the present data, and this again may be related to the low frequency of hints in the data.

5.2.2 Hints from the beginning

As Table 5.1 shows, Yao was able to make hints from the beginning of her second language experience, although the number was small.

Table 5.1 Distribution of hints over time

Phase		I		II					
Time		*1*	*2*	*3*	*4*	*5*	*6*		
Hints	n	5	5	0	1	1	1		
	%	3.7	2.9	0.0	2.0	0.9	1.0		
No. of requests		136	170	47	49	116	98		
Phase		*III*					*IV*		
Time		*7*	*8*	*9*	*10*	*11*	*12*	*13*	*14*
Hints	n	2	0	2	4	5	2	4	5
	%	1.1	0.0	1.8	5.7	10.2	2.9	4.5	5.3
No. of requests		175	139	112	70	49	69	89	94
Total no. of requests = 1413; Total no. of hints = 37 (2.6%)									

Moreover, she did not use them in any markedly non-standard way. Bates (1976a, b) notes that the ability to interpret conversational implicature (e.g. 'It's cold in here' as a request to close the windows) as proposed by Grice (1975)[3] is acquired fairly early in childhood, but that the production of hints indicating desires without actually mentioning the objective is among the last to develop. Bates (1976a: 293) speculates that a full fledged capacity for hints is established only when the concrete operations described by Piaget (1959) are well-established, which is at around seven to eight years of age, when 'the child is confident and versatile in role-taking skills'. Yao was seven years old when she found herself in the second language environment and in all likelihood by that time her cognition had already enabled her to perform hints in her native language. Since the range of options in L1 requestive hints is already familiar to L2 learners at this age, the pragmatic ability to produce hints does not have to develop conceptually. Fraser *et al.* (1980: 79) argue that 'what [the learner] has learned about the concept of requesting in his first language will carry over to the second'. This seems to suggest that L2 learners do not have to have all the linguistic knowledge of the L2 in order to produce hints. L2 learners seem to be able to use hints to realise requests because they do not need to acquire the strategy anew (Blum-Kulka, 1982; Weizman, 1993). Blum-Kulka (1982) suggests that

> ... the speaker will probably know how to draw pragmatic inferences from context and will be able to assign a variety of functions to one utterance (or form) (depending on context) in a second language almost as well as he does in his own. (Blum-Kulka, 1982: 31)

Since Blum-Kulka's focus here is on L2 adults, her findings may not apply to L2 children. However, the fact that hints appeared from the beginning of the present data suggests that the above applies as well to L2 children over seven or eight years of age. Even if such children are not able to produce some of the elaborate conventionally indirect strategies such as 'could you . . .?' or 'would you mind if you . . .?', they would most likely be able to make simple statements expressing nonconventionally indirect strategies. Simple grammar may be sufficient to guide their language behaviour in producing some hints, although syntactically more complex hints might well develop later. Koike (1989b) states that

> since the grammatical competence cannot develop as quickly as the already present pragmatic concepts require, the pragmatic concepts are expressed in ways conforming to the level of grammatical complexity acquired. (Koike, 1989b: 286)

For this reason, although Yao's ability to use different surface syntactic devices was limited at the beginning, she manipulated the forms she knew in order to hint, sometimes masking both form and content, in achieving her communicative goal. Yao used the conventional indirect request form, 'can you (I, we) ...?' in Phase I, but did not use the more elaborate conventional indirect form 'could you (I, we) ...?' until Phase III. Nevertheless, she produced hints from the beginning of the study. Example 4 shows that in Phase I of her second language acquisition Yao was already able to mask her illocutionary requestive force and still achieve her primary goal, as in the example below. The situation is that Emily, Yao's baby-sitter, was drawing curried rice, as Yao identified the ingredients she wanted Emily to put in her drawing.

4   **Y:**   *and uh meat*
    E: *curried rice doesn't have meat in it*
    Y: *yeah*
    E: *oh does it?*
    Y: <u>*my mum – she put uh meat*</u> [E10-52-2]
    E: *ok we'll put little bits of brown in there too then*

Yao could not think of curried rice without meat. She had to have Emily put some meat in it. So she said, 'my mum – she put uh meat' calmly but firmly. The desired act to be performed ('put meat') is mentioned, but Emily's responsibility for performing the act is not made explicit. However, because of the mutually shared rules, Yao's reference to the way her mother made curried rice sufficed to convey a request. In this particular case, the mutually shared rule is that Yao's mother is her caretaker and is in authority over them. In hints, the interpretation of the speaker's intentions does not rely solely on the literal or semantic meaning of the utterance. Rather, the contextual factors are the basis for inference in hints. Therefore, 'without mutually known rules, hints are not likely to be effective' (Dore *et al.*, 1978: 368). Thus, while the utterance in Example 4 did not have any explicit illocutionary requestive force, Yao's directive intent is certainly implied. In this instance the hint was effective and her request was complied with.

5.2.3 Substrategies of hints

Hints are very indirect, nonconventional in form, and extremely context-embedded. The speaker's intended meaning differs from the surface meaning of the utterance. Therefore, in order to be interpreted, hints require considerable knowledge of the other person, as well as specific background knowledge, although hints are non-transparent, they are 'part of conversational routine and the necessary work of interpretation is a normal part of co-operative conversation, which is generally taken for granted by participants in everyday interactions' (Trosborg, 1995: 193).

There are two dimensions to the lack of transparency in hints: propositional and illocutionary.

5.2.3.1 The propositional dimension

On the propositional dimension, where a speaker specifies the extent to which something is wanted, there can be a range in the explicitness from specific reference to no reference to the desired act. This range is manifested in the present data. The following four substrategies of hints on the propositional dimension were identified.

(a) Specific reference to the desired action

The desired action is explicitly referred to but there is no reference to the addressee's responsibility for its performance, as in Example 5.

5   *I can't put it up there* [H73-57]
     (Yao wants Hannah to put up the sign Yao had made for the tiny zoo they had made.)

(b) Explicit reference to the desired objects

There is explicit reference to the desired object such as 'the rubber' in Example 6, but no reference to the desired action.

6   **Y:** *where is the rubber?* [H4-61]
          (Hannah and Yao are drawing pictures. Yao wants to use the eraser that was supposed to be on the table.)

     H: (Hannah hands the eraser to Yao without saying anything.)

     Y: *thank you*

(c) Reference to related elements

There is here reference to the object related to the desired action, as in Example 7. In this example, the object (a muffin tin) to be put in the oven is referred to but the desired action is not. Unlike the specific reference to the desired action above, the addressee's responsibility is only indirectly referred to in the example below.

7   *you forgot this* [H62-26]
     (To Hannah. Referring to one of the muffin tins to be put in the oven.)

(d) No reference to the request proper

There is no reference to the request proper and the interpretation of the utterance relies heavily on context, as in Example 8.

8   **PC:** *I just wash my hands*
      Y: *okay/oh we're going to make it again* [PC 75-72-1]

The situation here is that Yao and her peer had been making things out of plasticine and the peer was going to wash her hands. Yao's utterance might be paraphrased: 'You are going to wash your hands now but we are going to make things out of plasticine again. So I request that you do not wash your hands yet.' The utterance 'oh we're going to make it again' can be barely interpreted as a request not to wash her hands yet, unless the addressee shares contextual knowledge and can determine for herself what the speaker wants her to do or not to do. In this case, Yao and her peer had played with the plasticine before and it was routine that they washed their hands when they had finished playing with it. By virtue of the peer's (the addressee's) contextual knowledge, Yao's (the speaker's) unexpressed intention seems to have been understood.

5.2.3.2 The illocutionary dimension

In spite of the lack of transparency, there seems to be a certain pattern to substrategies of hints, in terms of the nature of the statements and questions used. This consistent pattern along with the knowledge of specific contexts and situations may be what leads to the appropriate interpretation of the speaker's intentions. In the present data, along the illocutionary dimension, the two main substrategies involve 'stating reasons' and 'questioning feasibility'.

(a)   <u>Stating reasons</u>

By 'stating reasons' the speaker gives reasons or arguments for the performance of the requested act. This category corresponds closely to the category of 'stating potential grounders' by Weizman (1989; 1993) and 'reasonableness' by Trosborg (1995). The following are examples of the category of stating reasons. (A paraphrase of each utterance is underneath.)

9   *I'm hungry* [H48-63]
    (=You take care of my needs and wants. I am hungry. So, I request that you give me something to eat.)

10   *my hands get sore* [H55-23-4]
    (=I have been trying to erase what I wrote, but I pressed too heavily. My hands are getting sore doing it. So, I request that you do the erasing for me.)

11   *I can't put it up there* [H73-57]
    (=I am too clumsy to attach the sign I have made for the tiny zoo we have just made. So, I request that you do it for me.)

12   *oh we're going to make it again* [PC75-64]
     (=You are going to wash your hands now, but we are going to
     make things out of plasticine again. So, I request that you do not
     wash your hands yet.)

(b) Questioning feasibility
    The other category along the illocutionary dimension is that of
'questioning feasibility', a term used by Weizman (1989: 85; 1993: 131).
Such acts challenge, indirectly or partially, some condition for the
feasibility of the act requested. A similar but less broad category is called
'availability' by Trosborg (1995). Examples of questioning feasibility are:

13   *where is the rubber?* [H4-61]
     (=Can you hand me the rubber?)

14   *where is my pencil gone?* [PT25-61-1]
     (=Can you hand me the pencil?)

15   *oh yeah you've got blu-tack haven't you?* [PL69-22]
     (=Can I have some of the blu-tack you have?)

16   *do you need two eyes?* [J74-28]
     (=Can I have one of the eyes you have?
     Janice and Yao are making things out of the material such as
     straws, strings, sticks, pipe cleaners, balls and eyes.)

17   **Y:**   *how come it's not coming out?* [H55-13]
             (=Can you squeeze the glue for me?
             Yao squeezes a new glue container but the glue does not come
             out.)

     H: *here*
             (Hannah removes the inner plug for Yao.)

     Y: *thank you*

    There is a further type of hint, which does not belong to the categories
above. It is a rhetorical question, as in Example 18. This example, as
explained earlier, is a request not to repeat the same thing, but at the same
time it is very close to a complaint about Janice's repeatedly mentioning
the same thing.

18   *how many times do I have to say it's not?* [J50-37]
     (=Don't mention the same thing again, please.)

    Table 5.2 shows the frequency of the illocutionary hint substrategies,
that appear in the present data.

Table 5.2 Distribution of hint substrategies

Stating reasons	Questioning feasibility	Other	Total
23	13	1	37

There is a tendency to prefer the stating of reasons to the questioning of feasibility. This tendency was also observed in the CCSARP data with Canadian French, Australian English and Israeli Hebrew (Weizman, 1993). There are two points that emerge from the figures in Table 5.2. One is that Yao was inclined towards 'the argumentative value of hints' (Weizman, 1993: 90) and seemed to believe that stating reasons could more persuasively convey her requests than questioning the feasibility of the action. However, the responses to her hints indicated the opposite. The number of compliances in stating reasons was 16 out of 23 (69.6%), while the number in questioning feasibility was 10 out of 13 (76.9%). This difference may be very subtle because of the low overall frequency of hints. Nevertheless, the difference seems to indicate that in spite of Yao's preference for the former, stating reasons is less convincing than questioning feasibility. The other point is related to the degree of intrusiveness. A statement is generally less intrusive than a question (Trosborg, 1995; Weizman, 1993), and so hints that include stating reasons are less intrusive than those questioning feasibility.

When the speaker utters a question, he or she cannot pretend never to expect the addressee to respond. On the other hand, when uttering a statement, the speaker can pretend that he or she never expected the addressee to do more than just comment or signal agreement. In this sense, questioning feasibility may be said to have greater elicitative force and therefore be more intrusive than giving reasons. Consequently, stating reasons is less transparent in its illocutionary force than questioning feasibility. Thus, Yao's preference for stating reasons can be explained by both the argumentative value of hints involving stating reasons as well as the less transparent and less intrusive nature of such hints, even though they do not necessarily help in persuading the addressee to do the implied requested act.

5.2.4 Qualitative changes

As described earlier, hints were observed at the very beginning of data collection, and the overall use of hints increased after the middle of Phase III (from Time 10 onwards, see Table 5.1), although their frequency tended to be very low throughout the data. More interesting, however, are the qualitative changes observed. The linguistic means by which Yao made her requests, on both the propositional and grammatical level, developed significantly over the entire period of observation.

On the propositional level, requests that made no explicit reference to either objects or action do not appear in the early data. Examples 19 and 20, which occur as hints in Phase I, refer to objects.

19 *this is a my paper* [H4-45]
 (=Don't use my paper.)
20 *where is the rubber* [H4-61]
 (=Hand me the rubber, please.)

The 'where is + the object sought?' construction was used when Yao asked for things that she and her interlocutor were using while playing. An example of the other kind of hint in the early data is Example 21, whose situation was explained earlier.

21 *my mum - she put uh meat* [E10-52-2]

In this example, also from Phase I, there is no reference to the addressee's responsibility, but there is an explicit reference to the desired act.

It is only in the later stage that Yao produced hints that did not explicitly mention either the action required of the addressee or related objects, as in the following examples produced in the final phase:

22 *doesn't have to be perfect Janet* [PJ63-30]

23 *maybe it takes a long time to do it with this one* [J68-34]

24 *we're going to make it again* [PC75-64)]

The situation of Example 22 is that Yao and her peer are making muffins. Each time the peer put the dough into the muffin tin, she asked Yao if it was the right amount. Yao was a little annoyed by this and wanted her to stop asking. In Example 23, Janice and Yao are painting a Mickey Mouse figure on the fabric. In order to make Mickey's coat dark enough, Janice suggested that Yao paint over the fabric a couple of times. Apparently, Yao was reluctant to do this. In this sense, the utterance could be interpreted not as a request, but as an illocutionary act of refusal. However, from the fact that Yao knew it had to be done to make the Mickey's coat look satisfactory and that she knew Janice always tried to accommodate her, we can safely interpret the utterance as an illocutionary act of request. Yao's hidden intention in this utterance was that Janice would be kind enough to do it for her. Janice inferred Yao's intent and performed the implied act, saying, *'well I'll do/ how about I do/ I'll do that one'.*

The situation of Example 24 was explained earlier (pp. 82–3).

On the grammatical level, Yao used various forms to realise her requestive hints. She used both declaratives and, less frequently, interrogatives. The declaratives included both affirmatives (e.g. *I'm hungry* [H48-63]) and negatives (e.g. *I can't do it* [H55-24-3]). The interrogatives included ones without modal verbs (e.g. *do you need two eyes?* [J74-28]), wh-interrogatives (e.g. *where is my pencil gone?* [P25-61-1]), and tag questions (e.g. *oh yeah you've got blu-tack haven't you?* [PL69-22]). The wh-interrogatives also included rhetorical questions (e.g. *how many times do I have to say it's not?* [J50-37]).

Some forms occurred early as hints and others not until late, although the forms themselves appeared early. Declaratives, both affirmative and negative, appeared as hints from Phase I. Among the interrogatives, 'where' also appeared from Phase I. While Yao had less opaque strategies such as 'can I have …?' at her disposal already, she employed 'where is …?' at times especially when she wished to ask for objects that were there for both she and her interlocutor to use while playing. This form is probably very handy for beginning learners, since it can be used as a formula. A rhetorical question, 'how many times …?' was employed as a hint in Phase III, though the form had frequently appeared from the beginning of Phase II as part of an information question. The interrogatives without modal verbs also appeared from the beginning of Phase II. However, they did not appear as hints (e.g. *do you need two eyes?*) until late in Phase IV. Tags also appeared frequently throughout the data from Phase I onwards, but not as requests. In non-requests, tags functioned most often to signal turn-availability or to appeal to an addressee's benevolent agreement, as in Example 25 and 26:

25　**Y:**　*cold isn't it?* [H6-23]
　　　　　(Hannah and Yao are eating ice cream.)

　　H:　*very*

26　**Y:**　*it looks real funny doesn't it?* [J23-9]
　　　　　(Janice and Yao are drawing things using a vibrating pen. Yao is referring to the drawing she has just made.)

　　J:　*yeah*

However, extending a request by means of adding a tag as a mitigating device was not observed until Phase IV of the present data, and there was only one instance (Example 27). The use of tags for requests seems to be a rather sophisticated device.

27 *oh yeah you've got blu-tack haven't you?* [PL69-22]

In this particular example, Yao and her peer were making things, and since Yao knew that her peer would use her own blu-tack, it was a sensitive issue to ask for her blu-tack. Her reluctance to be explicit may be the consequence of her anticipating noncompliance. The tag was used here to appeal to her addressee's benevolent attention.

The low frequency of tag questions as hints is also reported by Trosborg (1995). In her data, elicited by means of role-plays, Trosborg found that her subjects (native speakers of English, native speakers of Danish, and Danish learners of English) rarely used tag questions in their request strategies. Trosborg (1995: 251) claims that this low frequency of tag questions in requests is due to the tendency that 'tags in English typically occur in fairly direct requests where compliance is anticipated' such as in 'Open the door, won't you?'. This tendency may restrict the applicability of tag questions in situations such as hints, where a speaker may not wish to be explicit because of the anticipation of noncompliance, and explain the low frequency of tag questions in Yao's requests.

In her linguistic realisation of hints, Yao became increasingly elaborate. The following examples show the diverse ways in which she sought her addressee's help by means of drawing attention to her inability:

28 Phase I   *I can't* [H11-58-1]

29 Phase II   *I don't know how to* [J29-11]

30 Phase III *this doesn't come out* [PE47-50]

31 Phase III *you can still see it* [H55-23-2]

32 Phase III *my hands get sore* [H55-23-4]

33 Phase IV   *I can't put it up there* [H73-57]

In Phase I, Yao did not have the appropriate linguistic means to specify what she could not do, leaving it to the addressee to infer the content, and hoping that her addressee would release her from an adverse situation. In Phase II, she was more specific about the content by using the embedded phrase 'how to'. In Phases III and IV, her linguistic means had expanded to the degree that her utterances were more expressive and more concrete. Not only the linguistic means, but also the choice of perspective shows development. While the perspective of the examples in Phase I and II were speaker oriented, in Phase III there were impersonal forms (i.e. 'this', 'you', and 'my hands'). The perspective of an utterance with the pronoun 'you' is also impersonal when it means 'one' or 'people' as in Example 31. Thus, within similar adverse situations, alternatives of perspective had become available to her by the end of Phase III

5.2.5 Why use hints?

According to Searle (1969: 71), requesting is 'an attempt to get a hearer to do something'. The most efficient way to get a hearer to carry out the speaker's intentions is the use of a 'bold-on-record' strategy (Brown & Levinson, 1987: 69, 94–101). This strategy is the most direct, clear, and unambiguous. It also involves features such as the use of an imperative form. With this strategy the speaker can avoid the risk of being misunderstood. In contrast, the use of hints requires the speaker to take a chance with regard to the addressee's correct interpretation. In addition, as shown in Chapter 2, the use of hints does not seem to be motivated by politeness. If both of these observations are accurate, we need to ask why people, especially children, use hints to convey what they mean. In the present data there appeared to be several possible reasons:

(a)   To draw attention to one's inability or discomfort and thereby elicit sympathy.

(b)   To increase the force of one's message.

(c)   To establish the potential for denying one's requestive intention.

While these reasons are interrelated, we will deal with them separately.

(a)   To draw attention to one's inability or discomfort

Children appear to use hints to draw attention to their problems: either their inability to perform a task or their discomfort. The hints they use for this purpose consist of mentioning difficult or uncomfortable conditions that the adult has the capacity to relieve or find a solution for (Ervin-Tripp, 1976; 1977). In the present data, all but one of the hints with this motivation were addressed to Hannah, her mother, or Janice – the one exception being addressed to a peer. Yao relied on older people, including a teenager, to find a solution for difficulties she encountered. Yao presumably sensed that grown-ups are in a position to notice and fulfil a child's needs and desires. In Examples 34, Yao hinted for help by drawing attention to her inability, while leaving the pragmatic interpretation to Hannah and hoping she would identify and help solve Yao's problem.

34   *I can't put it up there* [H73-57]
     (Hannah and Yao are making things out of various materials. Yao wants Hannah to put up a sign Yao made for the tiny zoo they are making.)

A different example of problem statements (Example 35) draws attention to one's discomfort.

35   *I'm hungry mum* [H48-48]
     (Yao and Hannah were about to finish decorating Easter eggs.)

Yao addressed Example 35 to her mother when dinner was later than usual and she wanted to urge her mother to hurry.

(b)   To increase the force of one's message

Thomas (1995: 144) claims that one can increase the impact of one's message by using indirectness. This is true of jokes, irony, sarcasm, and menace. One can make a request in a very impolite and threatening tone as the following dialogue between Janice and Yao illustrates.

36   J: *you're not giving me many clues here/ I think it's a hamburger*
     Y: *no/ it's **not**/ how many times do I have to say it's not?* [J50-37]
     (The word in bold letters was uttered emphatically.)

The question form here is rhetorical and used to imply a desire with almost threatening sarcasm. Yao did not tell Janice directly that she should not mention 'hamburger' again but left Janice to interpret her intention from the context and her harsh tone of voice. By saying 'how many times do I have to say it's not?', Yao took the risk that the addressee might be offended. She could have taken a more modest approach, such as 'could you try to think of something else?', since at this stage the 'could you ...?' form was already in her repertoire. Since Janice was a very familiar person and an adult who accommodated her in many ways, Yao perhaps went as far as she could in using this strategy. Nevertheless, the utterance was effective in getting her message across. Janice's reaction to Yao's utterance was, 'well it's just not looking like anything else so far except a bun/ or uh a cake?'

(c)   To establish the potential for denying one's requestive intention

Weizman (1989; 1993) suggests that a hint bears 'a deniability potential' and explains it as follows:

Hints are the most efficient way for the requester to make a request while at the same time securing the possibility of legitimately denying some of its illocutionary and propositional components ... the requester may plausibly deny having made a request. (Weizman, 1993: 125)

What Weizman suggests can be illustrated in Example 37[4] which took place in a gym.

37 **Speaker:** *are you in the Circuit?*
   Addressee: *I'm sorry*
   (As he moves to another piece of equipment.)
   Speaker: *thanks*

In the gym certain equipment was being used for the specific kind of exercise known as the 'Circuit'. Several people who were not participants in the Circuit, however, were using some of the equipment reserved for those who were. In this situation, the speaker (who belonged to the Circuit) said to the addressee, 'Are you in the Circuit?' The utterance is a yes–no question in form, but what the speaker meant was: 'This equipment is being used only by us. Please move to another.' The addressee understood what the speaker intended, because he said 'I'm sorry' and moved. However, the speaker could have denied having made a request by saying, 'Oh, I just wanted to know if you were in the Circuit. I never asked you to move.' The addressee himself could also have pretended to take it as an information question, by saying, 'I'm not but why?' Therefore, hints have deniability potential for both a speaker and an addressee.

Although Weizman's suggestion is based on adult data, and Example 37 comes from adults as well, the deniability potential has also been observed in the present data. The situation of the following dialogue between Yao and Janice (Example 38) is that they are making things out of various materials. Janice was making a pair of glasses. Yao was making something that turned out later to be a boa. When Yao said, 'do you need two eyes?', Janice at first failed to recognise Yao's intentions and took her utterance as a question to obtain information. Yao made the implied request a second time and said 'do you need them?/ two of them?', still masking the illocutionary force. She did not specify the goal and left the interpretation to Janice. This time Janice made the proper inference from the contextual clues and concluded that Yao was also making an object and she wanted to use some eyes. Janice identified Yao's utterance as a hint and deduced the intention of her utterance.

38 **Y:** *are you gonna decorate it?*
   (Yao is referring to the glasses Janice is making.)

J: *yeah*

Y: *and I think you're gonna put uh eyes/ I knew you were gonna do
that/ oh no there's none*

J: *yeah I got two-two eyes*

Y: <u>*do you need two eyes?*</u> [J74-28]

J: *no I got this – there're two eyes here*
(Janice is referring to the eyes she has.)

Y: <u>*do you need them?*</u> [J74-29]

J: *yeah=*

Y: *=<u>two of them?</u>*

J: *do you want some eyes too?/ you can take the eyes off there*
(Janice has two eyes on something she had previously made.)

Y: *oh yeah okay*

Janice believed that Yao did not intend to convey the literal, semantic meaning of the utterance but rather the pragmatic, hidden, or implied meaning,[5] Yao might have meant to convey both the literal meaning and hidden intentions. Hints can be multifunctional. Although Janice did not give up the eyes she was going to use, instead, she offered two eyes from a previously constructed thing. In the end, without mentioning the desired act, Yao was able to cause 'an action to happen, and at the same time avoid assuming responsibility for it' (Weizman, 1989: 72). In a way, Janice was put in a position where she had the opportunity to comply with Yao's implied request. When Janice offered the eyes, Yao could have legitimately denied having made a request, basing her denial on the literal, semantic meaning of her utterance, and if she wanted, she could have said, 'I did not mean to ask for the eyes. I just wanted to know if you needed to use them.' As Kasper (1995: 65–6) suggests, a hint is 'a prime candidate for metapragmatic comments of the type *that's not what I meant*', and therefore, it is 'a good thing for speakers to have handy when they don't wish to commit themselves to a particular course of action or seek to avoid accountability'.

On the whole, Yao used hints to draw attention to her inability or discomfort, to increase the force of her message, or to establish the potential for denying her requestive intention.

5.3 Summary and Conclusion

Yao produced hints from the very beginning of her second language experience. Although their frequency was low throughout the study, their use increased noticeably after the middle of Phase III.

Qualitative changes in the use of hints were also observed on both the propositional level and the grammatical level. On the propositional level, the hints Yao produced in the early stages made specific reference to the desired objects or actions, although there was no reference to the addressee's responsibility. It was not until the later stages, mostly Phase IV, that Yao produced hints that masked both requested objects and the action required. On the grammatical level, by the end of the final phase, Yao used a variety of syntactic forms to realise her hints.

Since there are no formal limitations in hints, the interpretation of hints depends to a large degree on context. Therefore, the speaker takes the risk of being misunderstood. In spite of this, Yao made effective use of hints. Her reasons for using them seemed to draw attention to her inability or discomfort, to increase the force of her message, or to establish the potential for denying her requestive intention. Yao's use of hints appears to be independent of other strategies.

This chapter and the previous chapter have traced the developmental patterns of Yao's requests. In next two chapters we will look at the variation in her use of requests. Since goals and addressees are among the most important factors to account for variation in request situations (Blum-Kulka, 1985), we will now turn our attention to the extent to which Yao's requests varied with respect to these factors.

The following chapter attempts to determine whether there is an observable relationship between the goals of requests and their realisation.

Notes

1. The average frequency for all the situations combined was calculated from Rose's Table 1 on p. 4.
2. The average frequency for all the situations combined was calculated from Rose and Ono's Table A-1 on p. 212.
3. Grice proposed four conversational maxims to explain how interlocutors interpret conversational implicature: The maxim of quality (be true); the maxim of quantity (be brief); the maxim of relevance (be relevant); the maxim of manner (be clear). Conversation proceeds according to a principle that reflects these maxims. Grice called this the *co-operative principle*.
4. This example is from the field notes, taken by me in the gym of La Trobe University in August, 1997.
5. G. Cook (1989: 29) defines semantic meaning as 'the fixed context-free meaning', and pragmatic meaning as 'the meaning which the words take on in a particular context, between particular people'. We use his definitions here.

Chapter 6
Variation in Use: Request Goals

6.0 Introduction

As observed in previous research (see Chapter 2), speakers vary their strategies and their use of linguistic forms in performing requests. The actual choice of request strategy is influenced by a number of social factors. According to Brown and Levinson (1978; 1987), there are three major social factors: the relative power of the hearer over the speaker, the social distance between the speaker and the hearer, and the degree of imposition involved in performing the act. Claiming that these three are not the only relevant factors that affect the choice of strategies, Blum Kulka *et al.* (1985) select the variables of sex, age of addressee, power relationship, social distance or familiarity, request goal, setting, and communication medium, in order to investigate the variation in requesting behaviour in Israeli society. They find that the most important factors in accounting for variation in request strategies are the type of request goal, the age of the addressee, and the relative power of the speaker (see Chapter 2).

As shown in Chapter 4, Yao deployed all seven types of request strategies. This and the following chapter investigate the extent to which Yao's requests varied with situational contexts, in particular, request goals and addressees, which are two out of the three most important variables identified by Blum-Kulka *et al.* Specifically, these two chapters ask whether there are any observable relationships between the goals of requests and their realisation, and between addressee and request realisation. This chapter is concerned with the following research question.

> What types of request strategies and linguistic devices does a child use in order to achieve varying request goals in a second language and what is the pattern of their development?

6.1 Types of Request Goal

Requests are purposeful. Speakers have goals they want to achieve. They select strategies appropriate to the achieving of those goals. As Blum-Kulka *et al.*, 1985: 118) states, 'the notion of "goal" relates to the relationship between the speaker's intention and the hearer's compliance ...'. A goal is achieved when the speaker's intention is complied with. However, the identification of a goal does not depend on the interlocutor complying with the request. There are four types of goals that can be distinguished in the present data:

(1) Requests for goods

These are the prototypical requests; the speaker is asking for goods. There are two contexts in which utterances such as *'could I please have one choc chip?'* [H62-21] are used. One is where the addressee is requested to deliver a chocolate chip to the speaker. The other is where the addressee is being asked to grant the speaker permission for the taking of a chocolate chip. The present study deals only with the requests for the actual delivery of goods. Compliance, then, requires the handing over of the requested object.

(2) Requests for the initiation of action

These requests typically anticipate non-verbal action on the part of the addressee, as with *'could you please go to your room?'* [PJ63-63-1], but they can be used to ask for verbal action as in utterances such as *'say something/ just talk talk'* [H20-57]. Compliance requires the addressee to act in response to such utterances. Compliance to requests for information, which might be taken as a form of verbal action, as with *'did you have a big birthday party?'* [H67] is not dealt with here. To some extent, requests for goods might be subsumed under requests for the initiation of action. However, the two are here distinguished because requests for the initiation of action focus on performance and not on the object itself.

(3) Requests for the cessation of action

Such requests have as their goal the stopping of an on-going action, the preventing of its recurrence or in certain instances the restraint of an anticipated occurrence of an action, as in *'don't move the table okay?'* [PA32-81]. Compliance is achieved by cessation or restraint on the part of the addressee.

(4) Requests for joint activity (or invitation to join in an action)

These requests invite the addressee to join in the activity with the speaker, as in such utterances as *'shall we play with the doll-dollies?'* [PC52-35] and *'let's clean up'* [H11-40]. The request in this sense takes the form of a proposal. Compliance is achieved by the addressee's joining in the activity.

6.2 The Distribution of Request Goals

Table 6.1 shows the distribution of request goals, as established on the basis of all the 1413 requests in the data.

As these figures make obvious, Yao made extensive use of requests that were related to action. Requests for the initiation of action and for the cessation of action together amount to 82.2% of the total. The remaining two types of request goals (i.e. requests for goods and requests for joint activities) are approximately equally distributed. The high frequency of requests concerning actions (i.e. requests for the initiation of action and for the cessation of action) can be interpreted as a reflection of Yao's need (or desire) to control her interlocutor's act. Or it could be just a feature of the activities in which she is engaged. Other research in naturalistic settings, however, indicates findings very similar to those of the present data. Among parental request goals in family discourse in Hebrew, the frequency of the action goal is as high as 84% (Blum-Kulka, 1990: 275). Among children's request goals in American English, requests for action were also the dominant type (Ervin-Tripp *et al.*, 1990: 317).[1] The high frequency of the request goals concerning action is probably a general tendency found among requests in every day interaction, particularly interaction involving children, rather than a tendency unique to the present data.

In the present data as well as in Blum-Kulka's study, request for the cessation of action were the most frequent type after request for the initiation of action. In the study by Ervin-Tripp *et al.* (1990), too, requests for the initiation of action were the most frequent type regardless of context. The next most frequent type in their study, however, depended upon the context. Among activities with objects, requests for the cessation of action were the second most frequently used type. Most of the

Table 6.1 Distribution of request goals

Type of goals	*n*	*%*
Goods	123	8.7
Initiation of action	853	60.4
Cessation of action	308	21.8
Joint activity	129	9.1
Total	1413	100.0

activities in the present data involve the use of objects: drawing, making cookies, making things out of play dough, games, etc. These kinds of object related activity may have contributed to the frequency of requests for the cessation of action being the second highest. This finding also concurs with those of Ervin-Tripp *et al.* (1990) and Blum-Kulka (1990).

6.3 The Choice of Strategy Types

In this section we will look at the developmental patterns in the choice of strategies according to the request goal, first with respect to the choice of the main strategies and secondly of their subcategories.

6.3.1 The main strategy types

Table 6.2 shows a cross-tabulation of each request goal with three levels of directness (see Chapter 3). This analysis is based on all the requests (n = 1413), regardless of the Time or Phase in which they were produced.

The type of request goal was found to be related significantly to the choice of request strategies ($\chi^2 = 311.985$, $df = 6$, $p < 0.0001$). There seems to be a difference in the choice of major strategy types between the request goals concerned with action (the initiation of action and the cessation of action) and the others (goods and joint activity). With requests for the initiation of action and for the cessation of action, the direct strategy was the most frequent, while with requests for goods and for joint activity, the conventionally indirect strategy was dominant.

Table 6.2 Distribution of main categories of request strategies by request goal

	Goal							
	Goods		*Initiation of action*		*Cessation of action*		*Joint activity*	
Strategy	*n*	*%*	*n*	*%*	*n*	*%*	*n*	*%*
Direct	44	35.8	573	67.2	279	90.6	22	17.1
Conventionally indirect	65	52.8	263	30.8	23	7.5	107	82.9
Nonconventionally indirect	14	11.4	17	2.0	6	1.9	0	0.0
Totals	123	100.0	853	100.0	308	100.0	129	100.0

Requests for the initiation of action comprise the largest category in the data. About two thirds of all the requests in this category were formulated directly (67.2%) and nearly all of the remaining third expressed conventional indirectness (30.8%). There are two possible reasons for the relatively high frequency of directness in this category. One is the need for efficient communication (Brown & Levinson, 1987: 282). In order to achieve goals in a situation where quick compliance is desired, requests may be made in the shortest, most direct, explicit, and unambiguous way possible, such as by the use of imperatives. The other explanation has to do with a co-operative activity in which the speaker and addressee were engaged and where the action requested was easy to carry out. Most of the situations in the data were of this sort. The use of direct imperatives in such situations is quite normal in adult speech (Gordon & Ervin-Tripp, 1984: 299).

Requests for the cessation of action had an even higher frequency of directness (90.6%). This goal is to stop an on-going action or to prevent an action. There is a need for urgent co-operation in such a case. It is likely that the best tactic for achieving this goal would be the use of explicit, direct strategies.

Requests for goods were uttered much more indirectly than requests for the initiation of action and for the cessation of action. Approximately two thirds of all the requests for goods were formulated indirectly. Conventionally indirect strategies and nonconventionally indirect strategies together formed 64.2% of all the requests for goods. In general situations, goods requested can range from goods of small value such as a salt shaker at the dinner table, to goods of as high a value as a financial loan. We can easily speculate that in the latter case where the request is unusual, indirect strategies, including additional modifications may be used to mitigate the impact of the request. As for small goods, the study by Blum-Kulka *et al.* (1985) involving speakers of Hebrew, which was concerned with requests for objects such as pens, erasers, and salt shakers, also found that conventionally indirect strategies were used the most. The findings of the present study are very similar to theirs.[2] Requests for goods in this study were also concerned mostly with small items such as erasers, crayons, and play dough, and the most used strategy type was conventionally indirect strategies, mostly realised by *query preparatory* (e.g. *'could you please pass me the rubber?'* [J54-29]).

There are three possible reasons for Yao's choice of indirectness in requesting goods. One is that requesting goods involves some form of change to break the shared activity in which the focus is on the action. In the case of requests for the initiation of action or for the cessation of action, the activity currently going on is not broken, but the request occurs in the same activity frame, and the request refers to the actions currently underway, as in Examples 1 and 2.

Initiation of action

1	**Y:**	*this is for you Hannah*
(Yao gives Hannah a piece of cardboard for making a collage.)

	H:	*okay*

	Y:	*just put it here* [H55-20]

Cessation of action

2	*don't put that there* [H32-5]
(Hannah is putting a can of peaches on the table for playing shopping centre.)

On the other hand, in requesting goods, the speaker often steps outside the on-going activity, as in Example 3:

3	*could you please pass me the rubber?* [J54-29]

The situation in this example was that Janice and Yao were each busy making a collage from autumn leaves. Requesting a rubber in such a situation interrupted what Janice was doing and shifted her attention to a different kind of activity, if only temporarily. In this sense a request for goods might be more intrusive than a request with another goal. The second possible reason for this has to do with imposition. Borrowing small items such as an eraser and a crayon is at a low cost to an adult addressee under normal circumstances. However, in the world of children, those items are not always considered small and asking for them is much more of an imposition on the addressee than it would be on an adult. In the present data those goods often had to be shared, and in order to achieve her goal, Yao had to ask 'nicely':

4	*can I please use this blu tack?/ you're my best friend* [PL69-57]
(Yao had used up her blu tack in making things.)

Sometimes Yao and her interlocutor, especially when her interlocutor was a peer, wanted the same thing. For example, in the following, yellow was a popular colour for colouring in a book and Yao had to make sure she would have a turn to use it.

5	**PJ:**	*Yao can I use that?/ for a second/ Yao can I use that?*
(A peer wants to use the yellow magic marker that is right beside Yao.)

Y: *Yeah/ can I please have that after you?* [PJ63-48]

Thus, requests for goods can be more intrusive and more of an imposition than other request goals, especially for children. Finally, informal observation of conversations between young English speaking children and their parents suggests that the children seem to be explicitly trained to make use of conventional indirectness when they ask for goods. Food is a prototypical good and comprise a prototypical area of exchange between children and parents. A young child is often prompted by his or her parents, after saying 'juice', to say something closer to 'can I have some juice, please?' Such food exchange contexts allow the child to practise this use of conventionally indirect strategies. Moreover, the use of preparatory strategies is 'heavily routinised' in English request behaviour (House & Kasper, 1987: 1261), and so we may expect a very routinised way of asking for goods. The native speaker norm is perhaps more routinised for goods than it is for other goals. Considering the fact that Yao was in school, living in an L2 learning environment and mixing with children from the neighbourhood, she would probably have learned to use conventional indirectness when asking for goods. It seems safe to say that she was following the norm for children who are native speakers of English.

Requests for joint activity were expressed most frequently through conventional indirectness (82.9%). The goal was to set up a cooperative situation, and therefore requests were in a way part of the proposal to do a particular activity together such as selecting a certain form of play (e.g. 'would you like to play with the play dough?' [H67-25]) or cleaning up after a play (e.g. 'let's clean up' [H11-40]). Therefore, direct strategies may not have been used very much in an effort to avoid the appearance of control.

6.3.2 Subcategories of the main strategy type

In order to see in greater detail the relationships between the goals and strategies, which are displayed in Table 6.2, the analyses that follow will be based on the seven strategy types that make up the subcategories of the three main strategy types. Table 6.3 shows a cross-tabulation of each request goal with the different strategies.

With respect to Table 6.3, the type of request goal was found to be related significantly to the choice of request strategy ($\chi^2 = 650.87$, $df = 18$, $p < 0.0001$). The type of request goal clearly affected Yao's linguistic behaviour.

Table 6.3 Distribution of request strategies by request goal

	Goods		Initiation of action		Cessation of action		Joint activity	
Strategy	*n*	*%*	*n*	*%*	*n*	*%*	*n*	*%*
Direct								
Mood derivable	22	17.9	474	55.6	260	84.4	5	3.9
Obligation statements	0	0.0	56	6.6	19	6.2	7	5.4
Want statements	22	17.9	43	5.0	0	0.0	10	7.8
Conventionally indirect								
Suggestory formulae	0	0.0	59	6.9	10	3.2	61	47.3
Stating preparatory	0	0.0	75	8.8	9	2.9	12	9.3
Query preparatory	65	52.8	129	15.1	4	1.3	34	26.4
Nonconventionally indirect								
Hints	14	11.4	17	2.0	6	1.9	0	0.0
Totals	123	100.0	853	100.0	308	100.0	129	100.0

(The computer program rounds numbers up or down automatically, and therefore the column might add up to slightly more than or less than 100%. This applies not only to this table but to all others.)

The fairly high frequency of direct strategies in requests for initiation of action is largely composed of the use of *mood derivable* (55.6%) such as:

6   *take off your shoes* [H26-48]
     (Playing a game called Twister.)

Mood derivable was an even more dominant strategy in requests for the cessation of action (84.4%) such as:

7   *don't look until I'm finished ok?* [J50-46]
     (Yao wants Janice to guess what she is making with bread dough.)

A *query preparatory* such as Example 8 was the most frequently deployed type of strategy (52.8%) for requests for goods and was the only type of conventionally indirect strategy chosen for this goal:

8   *can I have one more eye?* [PL69-3]
     (Yao and her peer are making things out of 'Oodles', which is a mixed set of items, such as straws, sticks, eyes, etc.)

Preference for conventional indirectness in requests for joint activity resulted predominantly from the use of *suggestory formulae* (47.3%) such as Example 9 and *query preparatory* (26.4%) such as Example 10.

9   *shall we make something?* [J50-27]
     (Yao wants to make things out of bread dough.)

10   *do you want to play outside?* [PE40-25]
     (Yao and her peer have almost finished drawing pictures, and Yao wants to play outside.)

As can be seen in Table 6.3, instead of resorting to using a variety of directness levels for each goal, Yao tended to concentrate on one or two directness levels in her requests.

Tables 6.2 and 6.3 reveal that the strategies Yao uses differ according to goal, and that the overall patterning of the relationships between goals and both the main strategy type and its subcategories is systematic. Yao seems, therefore, to have developed a system by which she pragmatically made her choice of strategy. Furthermore, the choice of strategy she employed for each goal does not seem to be unusual. Indeed, they do not seem to be very different from those of child native speakers of English. There is no baseline data from an equivalent Australian native speaking child of the same age, and therefore this is only speculation. However, it is reasonable to assume that she took on the behavioural patterns of those around her.

Much of the literature conceives of requests as a single kind of act, especially the studies done within the framework of the CCSARP data, studies which revealed that the most frequently used main strategy type was a conventionally indirect strategy. Across Australian English, Canadian French, Hebrew, and Argentinian Spanish, the range of conventional indirectness 'varies from 58.6% in Hebrew to 82.4% in Australian English, representing the most frequently used level of directness' (Blum-Kulka, 1989: 47). Blum-Kulka (1990: 272) states that '[conventional indirectness] represents the socially normative discourse on non-involvement, and is unequivocally polite on all accounts'. This may explain the reason for the prominence of conventional indirectness as a highly favoured choice within the framework of the CCSARP. The most prevalent realisation of conventional indirectness in the CCSARP data is *query preparatory* such as 'can/could you (I) …?/ could you (I) …?' The findings of House and Kasper (1981) and of Trosborg (1995) using role-play data also showed a clear preference in adult native speakers of English for preparatory strategies. Kasper (1989) gives the following reason for the predominance of preparatory strategies:

> Preparatories ... strike a convenient balance between the conventional maxim of clarity and marking for politeness, i.e. the requestive force is brought out unambiguously while at the same time social requirements for face-saving are observed. (Kasper, 1989: 47)

This is also in accord with the notion proposed by Fraser and Nolen (1981) that *query preparatory* gives the addressee the option of accepting or rejecting the implied request. These are reasonable explanations for *query preparatory*. In a study conducted by Blum-Kulka *et al.* (1985), using an ethnographic approach rather than a DCT with speakers of Hebrew, however, they report that more than half of the strategies were direct and that the conventionally indirect strategy was the second largest category, which is different from the results found within the CCSARP framework for speakers of Hebrew, where a DCT was used. In the present data, *mood derivable* (n = 761) was the predominant strategy type followed by *query preparatory* (n = 232) (see Appendix 4.3). As for main strategy type, the predominant type was direct strategies (n = 918), followed by conventionally indirect strategies (n = 458) (see Appendix 4.2). However, the above analysis reveals that different strategy types are used with different request goals. Consequently, it is possible to suggest that learners do not learn to make 'requests' as a single category, but rather learn to make requests that are differentiated by goals.

Consistent with this study and, as noted above, Blum-Kulka *et al.* (1985) and Blum-Kulka (1990) find that the choice of request strategy varies according to goal: for requests for action, a direct mode is predominant, while for requests for goods, conventionally indirect forms are most frequently used. Similar patterns of variation are found in the present data. There are other studies, which lend further support to the findings of the present study. Examples are Garvey (1975) and Trosborg (1985). In Garvey's investigation, which is based on the spontaneous speech of 36 dyads of American children aged from 3;6 to 5;7, the majority of the requests produced are direct (n = 575), with conventionally indirect requests far fewer (n = 57).[3] Nonconventionally indirect requests (*Hints*) are rarely used. On the other hand, in Trosborg's study of requests made by native speaking Danish children aged from three to five years conventionally indirect requests are more frequent than direct requests (42.5% vs. 29.8%).[4] Nonconventionally indirect requests (*Hints*) are rare (2.3%). The remaining 25% of the utterances are what Trosborg calls primitive speech acts, which are differentiated in her study from full-fledged adult speech acts.[5] The difference between the findings of these two studies seems to be the result of the different request goals occasioned by the situation. Although Garvey's data is taken from peer interactions observed in a laboratory, it represents spontaneous speech without adult facilitation and provides a sample of those interactions that occur in naturalistic settings. The activities are playing with toys, play acting, and holding conversations. The literature mentioned above (Blum-Kulka, 1990; Ervin-Tripp *et al.*, 1990), as well as the present study, reveals a high frequency of requests for action. These studies are in naturalistic settings rather than in experimental settings, where subjects are asked, for instance, to request a specific item. It can be speculated that in Garvey's study there are more requests for action than requests for goods,[6] since the study represents spontaneous interactions in naturalistic settings, allowing the direct mode to dominate in her data. Trosborg's data (1985), on the other hand, consist of only requests for goods. The researcher told the children that they could have some cake and lemonade but first that they had to request it. The most frequently used strategy type in her data is that of conventionally indirect requests. Thus, the results of both Garvey's and Trosborg's studies suggest that different request goals produce different results. This lends further supports to the results of the present study.

We have so far looked at the choice of main strategy types and their subcategories in relation to goals. We will now examine whether or not there is any pattern in the choice of the linguistic exponents of a strategy type. *Mood derivable* will be analysed, since it is the most dominant strategy type in the data when all the goals are collapsed (n = 761, 53.9% of all the requests). Unlike all the other strategies except *query preparatory*, *mood derivable* was used for all the request goals, but to different extents for different goals (see Table 6.3). Table 6.4 shows the distribution of linguistic exponents of *mood derivable*.

Table 6.4 shows that like the pattern for strategies themselves the distribution of linguistic exponents of *mood derivable* differs according to the goals of the request. The type of goal was found to be related very significantly to the choice of the linguistic exponents of *mood derivable* ($\chi^2 = 97.97$, $df = 12$, $p < 0.0001$). Requests for goods were achieved most frequently by elliptical imperatives such as:

11   *yellow please* [H67-28]
     (Hannah has just opened for Yao a plastic bag containing pieces of different coloured plasticine.)

Imperatives are usually formed with a verb. However, 'in situations where the necessary action is obvious, it is common to produce elliptical forms specifying only the new information – direct or indirect object' (Ervin-Tripp, 1976: 30). It is consistent with this that in the present data ordinary imperatives such as Example 12 were rare with the goal of requesting goods.

Table 6.4 Distribution of linguistic exponents of *mood derivable* by request goal

	Goal							
	Goods		*Initiation of action*		*Cessation of action*		*Joint activity*	
Exponent	*n*	*%*	*n*	*%*	*n*	*%*	*n*	*%*
Ordinary imperatives	3	13.6	334	70.5	195	75.0	5	100.0
You + imperatives	0	0.0	49	10.3	0	0.0	0	0.0
Contextually elliptical imperatives	19	86.4	80	16.9	65	25.0	0	0.0
Formulaic imperatives	0	0.0	8	1.7	0	0.0	0	0.0
Others	0	0.0	3	0.6	0	0.0	0	0.0
Totals	22	100.0	474	100.0	260	100.0	5	100.0

12   *I need uh yellow/ pass me a yellow please* [H11-43]
(Hannah and Yao are cleaning up after playing with play dough. Yao is putting the dough back in the container. Yellow refers to the type of dough.)

Requests for the initiation of action were again achieved in more diverse ways than other goals. There were five exponents for this goal, while there were only one or two for the others. However, the majority of requests for the initiation of action appeared as ordinary imperatives such as:

13   *make an easy one Linda* [PL69-46]
(Yao and her peer are making things out of different materials.)

Three quarters of the requests for the cessation of action also appeared as ordinary imperatives, such as Example 14, and one quarter as contextually elliptical imperatives, such as Example 15.

14   *don't eat too much because you might get tummy ache* [PJ63-16]
(Yao and her peer are making muffins. Yao tastes the dough and then she offers the dough to the peer to lick.)

15   *don't/ it's my turn* [H4-30]
(Hannah, Yao, and her mother are playing a game. Her mother thought it was her turn and was going to go.)

Most of the contextually elliptical imperatives in the requests for the cessation of action occurred during games when Yao wanted an action of the addressee stopped immediately. The form 'don't' tended to be used when Yao was reacting to the other's action quickly and forcefully, and it was uttered loudly for emphasis, as in Example 15. Otherwise, *'just a minute/ my turn'* [H4-31] or an ordinary imperative form, *'hang on'* [PB12-12] was used. A vocative, such as the one used in Example 16, also served as a means to stop the interlocutor's action immediately and forcefully.

16   *Alice!* [PA17-35]

The situation of Example 16 was that in the playing of a game called 'Pick-up-sticks' a peer, Alice, picked up the special stick she was not supposed to touch, and Yao stopped her. Such a vocative can be a modification when it occurs with the head act. However, when it stands alone in the absence of a head act as in Example 16, it has the status of a request. *Mood derivable* was rarely used for requests for joint activity. The only exponent used was an ordinary imperative such as:

17   *my mum can do it/ come on mum* [J23-1]
     (Janice and Yao are about to play a game. They need three people. Yao asks her mother to join in.)

In this section we have looked at the relationship between the request goals and strategy types used by Yao: both the three main strategies and the subcategories of those strategies. In addition, the relationship between the request goals and linguistic exponents of *mood derivable* has also been looked at. The result of all of these analyses indicates that the choice of strategy type varies according to request goal. Yao seems to have conceptualised and analysed these different request goals in quite different ways. She appears to behave in a situated manner. Her linguistic behaviour responded to the situation and she was able to situate the request strategy type according to her goal. In making requests she differentiated requests depending on the goal. Yao used predominantly one strategy type for one goal. Thus, in her acquisition of requests, she approached requests employing different strategies for different goals.

6.4 The Choice of Strategy Types Over Time

In the previous section, the significant relationships between the choice of strategy types and request goals were discussed without taking into consideration the developmental process. This section considers whether development or change occurred in the choice of strategies in relation to goals,[7] first with main strategies and then with their subcategories. We will look at these patterns by phase. To do this, all the requests under each goal have been divided into the four phases (see Chapter 4). First the main request strategies and then their subcategories in the four phases will be looked at.

6.4.1 Main strategy type

The following four figures (Figures 6.1–6.4) show the distribution of the main strategies (i.e. direct strategies, conventionally indirect strategies, and nonconventionally indirect strategies) employed for each request goal over the four phases (see Appendix 6.1 for the data used for these figures).

Two generalisations can be extracted from these figures. First, a single form is dominant for each goal in Phase I. This is the use of the direct strategy, which dominates except with requests for joint activity where the conventionally indirect strategy is used most frequently. Second, the developmental pattern differs depending upon the goal, with the developmental pattern varying in the following ways. In requests for the cessation of action and for joint activity, there is hardly any observable change in the frequency of the main strategy types. In requests for the cessation of action, direct strategies are dominant from the beginning to the end of the study. Direct strategies constituted about 90% of the requests in each phase. In requests for joint activity, conventionally indirect strategies were the dominant type, amounting to about 80% of the requests in each phase.

However, requests for goods and for the initiation of action show considerable change over the course of Yao's L2 learning. In requests for goods, a considerable change took place between Phase I and Phase II. In Phase I about two thirds of the requests made use of direct strategies, whereas only about 20% of the requests made use of conventionally indirect strategies. In contrast, from Phase II onwards conventionally indirect strategies were used for nearly two thirds of the requests. This increase in indirectness reflects Yao's increased ability to differentiate her contexts. Likewise, with requests for the initiation of action, substantial changes took place. Between Phase I and Phase II, the use of conventionally indirect strategies more than doubled. In Phase IV, the difference in proportion between direct strategies and conventionally indirect strategies became much smaller (53.0% vs. 45.2%, respectively) than in any other phase. The big leap in the use of conventionally indirect strategies between Phase I and Phase II, observable in both requests for goods and for the initiation of action, indicates that Yao was learning how to ask for goods and ask for actions in more indirect ways.

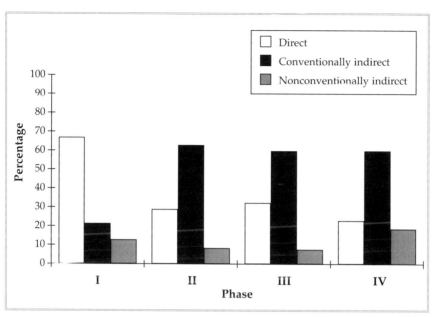

Figure 6.1 Requests for goods

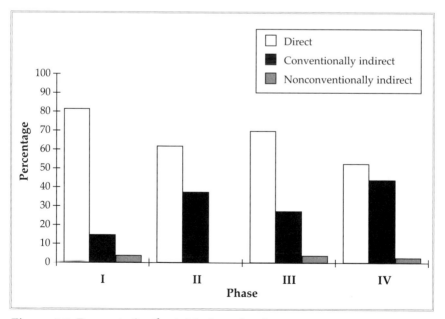

Figure 6.2 Requests for the initiation of action

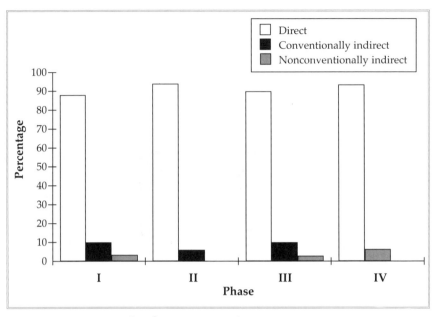

Figure 6.3 Requests for the cessation of action

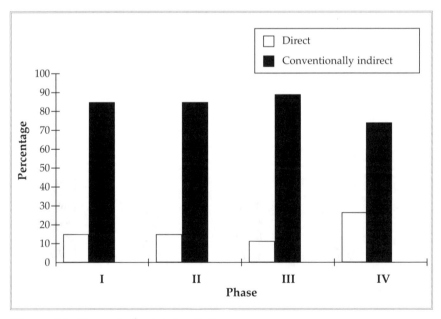

Figure 6.4 Requests for joint activity

6.4.2 Subcategories of the main strategy

So far we have looked at the developmental patterns in the main strategies according to phases. We will now look at them in terms of the subcategories. (Figures 6.5–6.8).

Figures 6.5–6.8 show the strategies deployed for each request goal (see Appendix 6.2 for the data used for these figures).

The first observation to emerge from the data in Figures 6.5–6.8 is that the request goals determine significantly Yao's choice of strategies. In making requests for goods, *query preparatory* is always the largest after Phase I, amounting to approximately 60% of each of the three succeeding phases. *Mood derivable* is dominant only in Phase I for this goal. For requests for the initiation of action, *mood derivables* are frequent. However, they tend to decrease over time. In contrast, *query preparatory* is used fairly frequently after Phase I (17.3–20.8%) for this goal. In requests for the cessation of action, *mood derivable* is the single most frequent strategy type. In requests for joint activity, except in Phase IV, *suggestory formulae* are dominant, amounting to about 52–54% of each of the other three phases. In Phase IV, *stating preparatory* and *obligation statements* overtake *suggestory formulae*. *Suggestory formulae* can be formulaic. However, *stating preparatory* and *obligation statements* require non-formulaic use of language, and consequently, sufficient linguistic resources are needed to be able to produce non-formulaic utterances. Once learners have these resources, they deploy those strategies more effectively. Of the remaining strategies, *query preparatory* is fairly frequent throughout all the phases (21.4–30.8%), but *mood derivable* is rarely observed for this goal.

The second observation is that the overall repertoire of Yao's request strategies expands in Phase III. The number of categories of strategy type is the largest in Phase III (requests for the cessation of action and for joint activity) or is at least no less than in any other phase (requests for goods and for the initiation of action).

The third observation is that further refinement took place in Phase IV. There was in this phase a growing differentiation for all goals, especially for requests for the initiation of action and for joint activity. For these *stating preparatory* becomes an increasingly important part of the repertoire and a reflection of a growing capacity for differentiation. Thus, the data suggest that the choice of strategy type and their distribution in Phase IV reflect the emergence of a greater sense of optionality and of the ability to handle grammatical as well as sociopragmatic complexity.

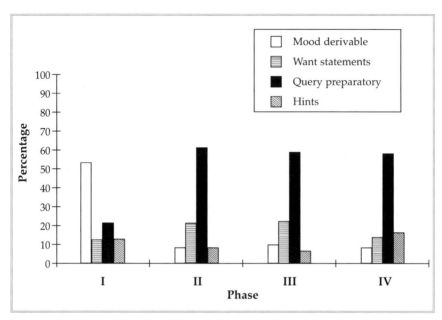

Figure 6.5 Requests for goods

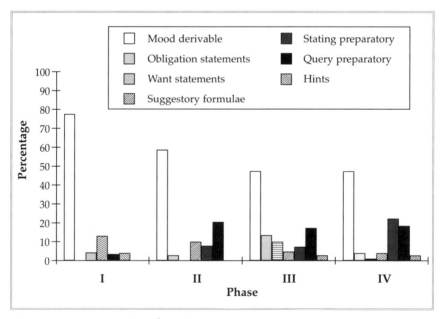

Figure 6.6 Requests for the initiation of action

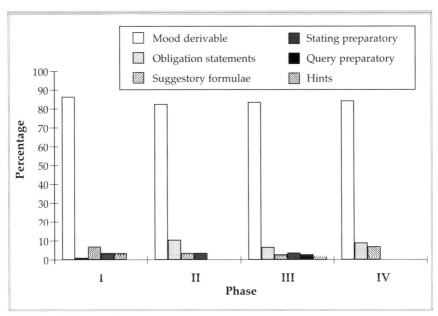

Figure 6.7 Requests for the cessation of action

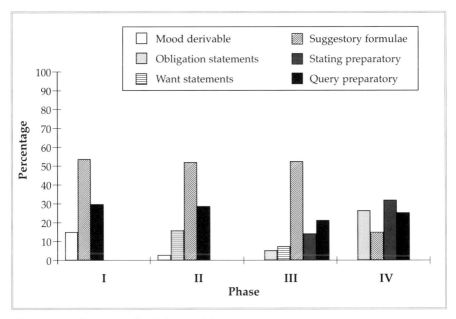

Figure 6.8 Requests for joint activity

6.5. Request Perspectives

Apart from strategy types, another dimension observed for request goals is the variation in the perspective of requests. The perspectives in the present data were coded according to the schema used by Blum-Kulka (1989) and Blum-Kulka *et al.* (1989b), who divided request perspectives into the following four categories according to role:

(1) Speaker dominance in which the role of the speaker as the recipient is emphasised (e.g. *can I have some more chocolate?* [PT 25-13]);
(2) hearer dominance in which the role of agent is emphasised (e.g. *could you please help me?* [PL57-46]);
(3) both speaker and hearer dominance, where the inclusive 'we' is emphasised (e.g. *shall we play with doll-dollies?* [PK52-35]); and
(4) the impersonal in which explicit mentioning of the recipient and the agent is avoided (e.g. *is there any more white?* [PC75-72]).

6.5.1 The choice of perspectives

Table 6.5 provides information on Yao's choice of perspectives according to goal.

The type of request goals were found to be related significantly to the choice of perspectives ($\chi^2 = 971.92$, $df = 9$, $p < 0.0001$). The choice of perspectives varied according to goal. The preferred choice for making requests for goods is speaker oriented (55.3%). This is in accord with the findings of Trosborg (1985). On the other hand, in requests for both the initiation and for the cessation of action the perspective is hearer oriented (86.5% and 92.5%, respectively). In requests for joint activity the perspective is both speaker and hearer oriented (61.2%).

Table 6.5 Choice of perspectives by request goal

	Goal							
	Goods		*Initiation of action*		*Cessation of action*		*Joint activity*	
Perspective	*n*	*%*	*n*	*%*	*n*	*%*	*n*	*%*
Speaker	68	55.3	68	8.0	3	1.0	9	7.0
Hearer	37	30.1	738	86.5	285	92.5	36	27.9
Inclusive 'we'	6	4.9	14	1.6	0	0.0	79	61.2
Impersonal	12	9.8	33	3.9	20	6.5	5	3.9
Totals	123	100.0	853	100.0	308	100.0	129	100.0

The focus on the role of the speaker in requests for goods reflects the preponderance of *query preparatory* utterances having the form 'can (could) I ...?', such as Example 18.

18   *can I have some more chocolate?* [PT25-13]
      (Yao wants her mother to give her some more chocolate ice cream.)

On the other hand, the emphasis on the role of the hearer in requests for the initiation of action reflects the predominance of *mood derivable* utterances such as Example 19 and *query preparatory* utterances in the form of 'can (could) you ...?' such as Example 20.

19   *oh just give me another story* [H55-62]
      (Hannah tells a story while she and Yao are making collages.)

20   *could you please put that in?* [J62-6]
      (Yao and Janice are making muffins and Yao wants Janice to pour the flour into the cup Yao is holding.)

The focus on the role of the hearer in requests for the cessation of action also reflects a preponderance of *mood derivable* utterances, such as Example 21.

21   *don't say anything anymore* [PA32-11]
      (Yao wants to concentrate on doing a back-flip.)

Requests for joint activity emphasised the role of the speaker and the hearer, reflecting the use of *suggestory formulae* such as in Example 22.

22   *let's play a game* [PH28-47]
      (Yao and her peer have just finished playing with dolls. Yao now wants to play a game.)

Not only is there variation in perspective according to goal, as manifested through different strategies, but there is also variation in perspective that manifests itself through the use of similar grammatical structures (within a specific strategy). When we look at some of the linguistic exponents of *query preparatory*, 'can (could) I ...?', 'can (could) we ...?' and 'can (could) you ...?', a different choice of perspective according to goal is apparent (see Appendix 6.3 for details). In requests for the cessation of action and for joint activity, very few utterances employed the 'can (could) ...?' form. Requests for the cessation of action used only a hearer perspective as in Example 23, while requests for joint activity used only an inclusive 'we', as in Example 24.

23   *could you **please** stop write* [= writing] *my name?/ please Esther please/ I'll rub it out if you write* [PE40-21]
      (Yao does not like the picture of her a peer has drawn. The peer is going to write Yao's name on it, and Yao wants her not to.)

24　*could we play um snakes and ladders?* [H62-31]
　　(Yao and Hannah have just made muffins. While waiting for the
　　muffins to get done, Yao asks Hannah to play 'Snakes and Ladders'.)

On the other hand, many requests for goods and for the initiation of action were realised through the 'can (could) …?' form. For requests for goods, utterances with the 'can (could) …?' form encoded the speaker perspective, as in Example 25, much more frequently than the hearer perspective, as in Example 26, while with requests for the initiation of action utterances were more hearer dominant, as in Example 27, than speaker dominant, as in Example 28.

25　*can I have one of those?* [H32-315]
　　(Hannah and Yao are playing store. Yao is a customer. The word
　　'those' refers to pencils.)

26　*could you please get me a pencil?* [J54-22]
　　(Yao and Janice are making collages.)

27　*can you hold this please?* [H21-24]
　　(Hannah and Yao are playing with dolls. Yao wants Hannah to
　　hold one of the dolls so she, as Mrs Rabbit, can give juice to a
　　baby.)

28　*can I see it so I can copy it?* [PE47-47]
　　(Yao and her peer are making animals with play dough. The peer has
　　just made an elephant. After Yao's request, the peer shows it to her.)

As noted by Blum-Kulka (1989: 59), the 'choice of perspective affects social meaning'. Requests asking for an object, such as 'can I have …?', are in the form of requests for true permission. 'True permission requests imply that the addressee has control over the speaker, and that the speaker's wishes are subject to the hearer's approval' (Gordon & Ervin-Tripp, 1984: 308). Although asking for something in the permission form suggests an action on the part of the hearer, it is in fact a way of 'avoiding the appearance of trying to control or impose on another' (Gordon & Ervin-Tripp, 1984: 308). Therefore, the speaker perspective in 'Can I have some more chocolate?' is more polite than the hearer perspective in 'Can you give me some more chocolate?' Yao learned how to reduce the degree of her imposition through what she learned about manipulating the speaker perspective and the hearer perspective.

The inclusive 'we', which is one way to achieve what Brown and Levinson (1978; 1987) call 'positive politeness' and R. Scollon and S. Scollon's (1983) 'solidarity politeness', includes both the speaker and the hearer in the activity and emphasises friendliness and solidarity (Scarcella & Brunak,

1981). If we compare the following pairs of examples, 29 and 30 on one hand and 31 and 32 on the other, we see in both pairs an alternation between pronouns 'we' and 'you'. As the literature cited above suggests, in utterances with the 'we' perspective (Examples 30 and 32) Yao had acquired the ability to display her sense of solidarity as well as her skill at avoiding the impression that she was being coercive.

29   *why don't you put uh his eyes and noses – nose and mouth?* [PK52-25]
     (Yao and her peer are making things out of clay.)

30   *so why don't we just put white and orange together* [PC75-28]
     (Yao and her peer are making things out of plasticine.)

31   *you could put some blu tack down there* [J74-18]
     (Janice and Yao are making things out of many materials. The giraffe Janice is making does not stand by itself on the table.)

32   *maybe we could paint it in this colour* [J68-19]
     (Janice and Yao are fabric painting.)

The impersonal perspective (e.g. *'is there any more white?'* [PC75-72] and *'it's not allowed'* [H4-2]) functions as a means of distancing the speaker and hearer by deliberately avoiding 'I' and 'you' (Scarcella & Brunak, 1981; Lee-Wong, 1993). This perspective is neither speaker oriented nor hearer oriented. Blum-Kulka (1989: 59) suggests that 'avoidance to name the hearer as actor can reduce the form's level of coerciveness'. The perspective of an utterance with the pronoun 'you' is also impersonal when it means 'one' or 'people' as in Example 33.

33   *you can still see it* [H55-23-2]
     (Yao has erased what she wrote on the cardboard but there are still traces left, since they were heavily written.)

The fact that Yao used all four different perspectives implies that she attached some degree of social meaning to these perspectives. In the L2 data of both child speakers (Ellis, 1992) and adult speakers (Scarcella & Brunak, 1981), an inclusive 'we' or impersonal perspective either occurred rarely or was absent. This is in contrast with L1 adult speakers of English (Scarcella & Brunak, 1981). In fact, Scarcella and Brunak note that adult L2 learners acquire inclusive 'we' quite late. A substantial number of utterances in the present data, on the other hand, used the inclusive 'we' or the impersonal perspective. They are, however, much less frequent than the speaker or the hearer perspectives in all uses except those for requests for joint activity, where, not surprisingly, 61.2% of the utterances contained an inclusive 'we'.

6.5.2 The occurrence of perspectives in each phase

The following analysis examines according to goal the perspectives that occur in each phase. Table 6.6 shows that depending on the type of goal, requests differ with respect to the pattern of the perspectives.

Not all the request perspectives appeared from the beginning with all the request goals. Only those for the initiation of action had all the four from the beginning. The reasons for this may be that requests for the initiation of action are most frequently made and therefore many different activities are involved and more opportunities are provided to negotiate with the interlocutors using different perspectives.

We will illustrate the development that took place in relation to perspective by using requests for goods, since the pattern is revealed most clearly in request having this goal. The following are examples of the perspectives that occurred in each phase. In Phases I and II there are three perspectives for this goal (i.e. the speaker, hearer, and impersonal perspectives), and in Phases III and IV there is in addition the inclusive 'we' perspective.

Table 6.6 Occurrence of perspectives in each phase

Goal	*Perspective*	*Phase*			
		I	*II*	*III*	*IV*
Goods	Speaker	+	+	+	+
	Hearer	+	+	+	+
	Inclusive 'we'			+	+
	Impersonal	+	+	+	+
Initiation of action	Speaker	+	+	+	+
	Hearer	+	+	+	+
	Inclusive 'we'	+	+	+	+
	Impersonal	+	+	+	+
Cessation of action	Speaker			+	
	Hearer	+	+	+	+
	Inclusive 'we'				
	Impersonal	+	+	+	+
Joint Activity	Speaker		+	+	
	Hearer	+	+	+	+
	Inclusive 'we'	+	+	+	+
	Impersonal		+	+	

(The '+' mark indicates the occurrence of the designated perspective.)

Phase I: *speaker + hearer + impersonal*

34 *can I use that?* [H11-31]
(Hannah and Yao are making things with play dough. Yao wants the trimmer beside Hannah. Hannah hands it to Yao.)

35 *I need uh yellow/ pass me a yellow please* [H11-43]
(Yao is putting the play dough in the container.)

36 *where is the rubber?* (As a hint.) [H4-61]
(Hannah and Yao are drawing.)

Phase II: *speaker + hearer + impersonal*

37 *can I have some more chocolate?* [PT25-13]
(Yao wants her mother to give her some more chocolate ice cream.)

38 *can you pass the pencil please?* [PT25-61-2]
(Yao and her peer are playing school.)

39 *where is my pencil gone?* (As a hint.) [PT25-61-1]

Phase III: *speaker + hearer + inclusive 'we' + impersonal*

40 *could I please have the glue up here?* [J54-16]
(Janice and Yao are making collages)

41 *could you please pass me the glue?* [J54-11]

42 *have you got any leftovers?* [PC 52-34]
(Yao and her peer are making things out of clay.)

43 **Y:** *can you – can we have some more ...* [J50-42]
(Janice and Yao are making things out of bread dough.)

   J: *some more flour*

   Y: *more flour*

44 *paper where's paper?* (As a hint.) [H32-52]
(Hannah and Yao are playing school.)

Phase IV: *speaker + hearer + inclusive 'we' + impersonal*

45 *could I please have one?* [H62-40]
(The muffins Hannah and Yao are making are ready to be taken out of the oven. The reference is to one of the oven gloves.)

46 *could you please pass me that bowl?* [H62-28]
(Hannah and Yao are making muffins.)

47 *have we got any blu tack left?* [H73-51]
    (Hannah and Yao are making things out of many materials.)

48 *is there any more white?* [PC75-72]
    (Yao and her peer are making things out of plasticine.)

With regard to the speaker and hearer perspectives in the above examples, 40 and 41 in Phase III were both addressed to the same addressee (i.e. Janice) in the same situation (i.e. collage making) asking for the same thing (i.e. some glue) in the same session. However, the former utterance encoded the speaker perspective and the latter the hearer perspective, showing that Yao had both perspectives at her disposal. The hearer perspective was sometimes used as a second request in the same episode, when Yao did not get compliance in the first request using the impersonal perspective, a perspective where explicit mention of the speaker and the hearer is avoided. Examples 38 and 39 in Phase II provide evidence of this. Yao uses Example 39 first, which is a requestive *hint* for a pencil, with an impersonal perspective. However, her peer is too much involved in what she is doing to pay attention to Yao. A *hint* is an implicit way of making a request and is not always taken as such by the addressee (see Chapter 5 for requestive hints). Yao has seen her pencil and she makes a second request, with Example 38, in which she is more explicit and more coercive. This time her peer hands her the pencil. The hearer perspective in this sense is an explicit way of achieving compliance. This episode indicates that Yao is able to handle the hearer and impersonal perspectives interchangeably and appropriately.

In the first three phases, the use of the impersonal perspective tends to be concentrated in *hints* (i.e. where ...?), but in Phase IV another way of using the impersonal perspective, to ask for goods, emerged (i.e. is there ...?). Thus, as Yao acquired a larger repertoire, other forms of requests within the same perspective became more prevalent.

With respect to the inclusive 'we' perspective, it appears in Example 47 in Phase IV. Yao could have approached the request using the hearer perspective as she did in a very similar situation in Phase III (i.e. Example 42). She might also have said, 'I want (need) some blu tack' using the speaker perspective. The reason for Yao's employing the inclusive 'we' rather than the speaker or the hearer perspective might be that by using an inclusive 'we' perspective she was mitigating the request by avoiding coerciveness in order to seek co-operation. Overall, her choice of perspectives suggests that she had developed a better grasp of the social meanings associated with different perspectives.

6.6 Summary and Conclusion

This chapter has demonstrated how the types of request goal affected Yao's linguistic behaviour. First, request goals were found to be related significantly to the choice of request strategies. Secondly, the developmental pattern of the request strategies was further found to differ according to goal. Finally, the relationship between request goals and request perspectives was examined. Again it was found that the choice of perspectives varied according to goal.

Thus, Yao developed different ways of handling requests with different goals. For much of the period of observation, there are quite different patterns of request realisation according to goal. Requests for goods, for the initiation of action, for the cessation of action, and for joint activity all emerge as distinct areas of learning and behaviour.

Further, the data suggests requests may emerge as differentiable not only by goal, but also by addressee. The next chapter will examine the question of whether there are any observable relationships between addressees and request realisation.

Notes

1. However, this claim has to be treated with caution. Ervin-Tripp *et al.* (1990) call request for action 'directives', which are classified as one type of what they call control acts. In their classification, requests for goods may be included in requests for action (in their terminology 'directives'), although this is not specifically mentioned.
2. In Blum-Kulka *et al.* (1985), the data was obtained from native speakers of Hebrew using an ethnographic approach. In their study requests for action were the most direct, while requests for goods were less direct; most of the latter fell into conventionally indirect strategies.
3. This was recalculated for the purpose of the present study.
4. This too was recalculated for the purpose of the present study.
5. According to Trosborg (1985), primitive speech acts take the form of rudimentary propositions and incomplete requests, such as 'this', 'red', and 'red lemonade'. Their illocutionary force has to be inferred from the situation. As the child's linguistic knowledge expands, the primitive speech act develops into fully adult speech acts.
6. In Garvey's study, requests for goods are included in requests for action.
7. In Chapter 4, we looked at the development in the choice of strategies without considering the influence of goals.

Chapter 7
Variation in Use: Addresses

7.0 Introduction

This chapter asks whether there are any observable relationships between addressees and request realisation. Specifically, this chapter is concerned with the third research question:

> To what extent do a child's linguistic devices and request realisation strategies in a second language vary depending upon the addressee?

This chapter deals with Phases II to IV. It excludes the data of Phase I (the first 12 weeks) because the adult addressee in Phase I was different from the adult addressee in the rest of the phases. The adult addressee in Phase I was 19 years old and in a sense both an 'adult' and a 'teenager'. The adult addressee in the remaining phases was 33 years old. The analysis in this chapter also excludes improvised role-play requests in order to maximise homogeneity in the data and to exclude the ambiguity of addressee since a role-play creates a potential ambiguity in the perception by the speaker when addressing a fictional character. Therefore, the chapter involves the following four categories of addressee: Yao's classmates as peers, Hannah as a teenager, Janice as an adult neighbour, and Yao's mother (see data collection procedures in Chapter 3 for details on the addressees).

7.1 Requests with Varying Addressees

Table 7.1 shows the frequencies of requests made to each addressee after Phase I, with the improvised role-plays removed. The total number of requests was 978. The number of requests made to the adult was much smaller than those made to peers and teenagers. This may be a consequence of the adult's being more accommodating than the others. When Yao made requests to Janice, she did not have to negotiate to any great extent, while with her peers and the teenager sometimes second and third requests were needed before compliance was achieved. While Yao's mother was present in every session, she was not actively involved in interaction unless Yao initiated a conversation with her. This contributed to the low frequency of requests made to her mother.

Table 7.1 Distribution of requests by addressee

Addressee									
Peer		Teenager		Adult		Mother		Totals	
n	%	n	%	n	%	n	%	n	%
347	35.5	323	33.0	208	21.3	100	10.2	978	100.0

7.2 Results and Discussion

We will first discuss how her addressees influenced Yao's choice of strategies, and then we will examine whether or not there is any observable relationship between the linguistic form of her requests and the addressees.

7.2.1 Request strategies according to addressee

In order to examine the relationship between strategies and addressees, the total number of requests produced by each addressee (i.e. Table 7.1) was broken down for each strategy. Table 7.2 shows the request strategies according to addressee.

Table 7.2 Distribution of request strategies according to addressee

	Addressee							
	Peer		Teenager		Adult		Mother	
Strategy	n	%	n	%	n	%	n	%
Mood derivable	189	54.5	163	50.5	86	41.3	45	45.0
Obligation statements	28	8.1	23	7.1	9	4.3	7	7.0
Want statements	7	2.0	13	4.0	38	18.3	4	4.0
Suggestory formulae	24	6.9	18	5.6	16	7.7	2	2.0
Stating preparatory	45	13.0	29	9.0	16	7.7	1	1.0
Query preparatory	46	13.3	68	21.1	38	18.3	36	36.0
Hints	8	2.3	9	2.8	5	2.4	5	5.0
Total	347	100.0	323	100.0	208	100.0	100	100.0
Total number of requests: 978								

There were significant differences among addressees depending upon the strategy ($\chi^2 = 109.30$, $df = 18$, $p < 0.0001$). Several noteworthy points emerge from this table. First, *want statements* were addressed to the adult much more frequently than to others. The high frequency of these exponents to Janice is partly the consequence of the context, a computer game, as in Example 1. This activity was shared only with the adult.

1   *I wanna put him over here* [J44-48]
     (This is the first computer game Yao has played, and at every stage she needs help.)

However, the occurrence of this strategy with the adult, even when we consider only the requests outside the computer game, made the adult different from others with respect to the use of *want statements*. There seems, therefore, to be another explanation for the frequent use of this strategy with Janice. She, the adult interlocutor, was one of Yao's play partners. But at the same time she was, in a sense, a caregiver in that she had the ability or willingness to accommodate Yao's wants and needs in the activity they were engaged in, even though she did not belong to the same class of caregivers as did Yao's mother. This is probably the reason why Yao produced *want statements* to Janice much more frequently than to others.

Secondly, the frequency of *stating preparatory* increases progressively from her mother to the adult, the teenager, and finally the peers. This seems to show that the closer Yao and her interlocutors were in age, the more Yao was able to make suggestions concerning their capacities, as in Example 2.

2   *you could put a cloud with this white* [PC75-52]
     (Yao and her peer are making things out of plasticine.)

Finally, Yao's linguistic behaviour with her mother differs from her behaviour with the other addressees. Her mother received two contrasting strategies: *obligation statements* (a direct strategy) and *query preparatory* (an indirect strategy) at the same time. *Obligation statements* were addressed to her mother nearly as frequently as to peers and to the teenager. On the other hand, *query preparatory*, as in Examples 3, was directed to her mother much more frequently than to others.

3   <u>*preheat oven to moderately hot 190c*</u>*/ could you do that mum?* [H63-1]
     (Hannah and Yao are making muffins. Yao reads the underlined part from a recipe.)

The high percentage of *query preparatory* directed to her mother may be the result of the fact that most of the time she was not directly involved in the activities Yao and her interlocutor were engaged in, and so Yao had to interrupt her when she wanted to make a request. During the recording sessions, her mother was sitting close by, either reading the newspaper or pretending to be studying, while actually taking notes about their activities, or cooking in the kitchen from where she was able to observe what they were doing. Yao, who was between seven and eight years seven months at the time of data collection, was aware of what her mother was doing and seemed to want to show sensitivity when disrupting. This explanation is consistent with the research done by Ervin-Tripp and Gordon (1986) and Gordon *et al.* (1980). They report that children around eight years old show such sensitivity when asking for something to be done by a busy adult (see Chapter 2 for details). According to the data from Ervin-Tripp and Gordon (1986), when children interrupted an activity of the other, their use of imperatives dropped from 60% to 27%. As noted above, Yao was acquiring ways of mediating her intrusions by expressing herself less directly.

At the same time, she used a direct strategy, *obligation statements*, with her mother as frequently as with the teenager and peers. Yao could be quite direct to her mother, perhaps because of the greater intimacy of the mother–child relationship. Mothers are assumed to provide help. On the basis of their experiments with requests by Norwegian children dealing with families, playmates, and strangers, Hollos and Beeman (1978) report that a child's interactions with their mothers are quite direct, though interactions with others are generally indirect. Ervin-Tripp *et al.* (1984: 117) observes that though a parent seems to have absolute power over children, there are many occasions when children control the parent, 'exerting power in the form of demanding the attention and goods to which a helpless dependent is entitled'. This trait was also observed in the present data as in the following dialogue.

4   **Y:**   *mum you have to help us* [PA32-78-1]

    M: *do I have to?*

    Y: **you just don't watch!** / *you have to help us*

The situation in Example 4 is one in which Yao wanted her mother to help construct grocery boxes out of flattened miniature packets and to pile them up, so that she could play shopping centre with a peer. This was not an easy job and took time. Yao became irritated and was very direct to her mother, almost bossing her around. She used forceful language, expressed in the form of a direct request ('you have to ...'), further she made an elaboration to the request with a strong voice (**'you just don't watch!'**), and finally reinforced it by repetition. Children are sometimes rude and even make threats in order to gain their mothers' compliance. Ervin-Tripp *et al.* (1984: 130) give the following example: 'if you don't give some now, I won't want any later'. However, they can be indirect as well. Andersen's role-related studies using puppets (1978; 1990a,b, see Chapter 2 for details) show that requests produced with parents by children around seven years old contain not only many direct strategies (i.e. *want statements*) but also indirect strategies (i.e. *query preparatory*).

Requests made to her mother by Yao tended to be both indirect (i.e. *query preparatory*) and direct (i.e. *obligation statements*). They were indirect because her mother was outside of the interaction and Yao was intruding on her, while at the same time they could be direct because Yao was intimate with her mother.

7.2.2 Linguistic forms according to addressee

This section examines Yao's speech behaviour with the four different interlocutors in terms of her choice of linguistic forms. Since her choices are exemplified most clearly by the exponents of *query preparatory*, we use them to illustrate the point. Further, since the differences are subtler than can be captured by statistical analysis, our discussion will be purely descriptive.

Yao's relationship with the various interlocutors and the resulting speech behaviour can be explained in terms of Wolfson's Bulge theory (1986; 1988; 1989). The theory posits that there is a qualitative difference between 'intimates, status-unequals, and strangers, on the one hand, and with non-intimates, status-equal friends, co-workers, and acquaintances, on the other' (Wolfson, 1986: 694). This difference has to do with the relative certainty of the relationship with the first group, as compared with uncertainty and the instability of the relationship with the other. It is the members of the latter group with whom one is likely to negotiate. Since the two extremes of social distance in the first group are seen as fixed, the speaker easily knows what to expect, and therefore, no negotiations is needed. In the present study the adult (status-unequal) and the mother (intimate) seem to fit into the first category. In contrast, peers (status-equal friends) seems to fit into the latter, while the teenager (a status-unequal friend) can belong to both.

Table 7.3 Distribution of exponents of *query preparatory* by addressee

	Addressee							
	Peer		Teenager		Adult		Mother	
Exponent	n	%	n	%	n	%	n	%
can I ...?	15	32.6	13	19.1	8	21.1	12	33.3
can you ...?	11	23.9	42	61.8	16	42.1	8	22.2
could I (we) ...?			4	5.9	1	2.6	4	11.1
could you ...?	3	6.5	1	1.5	11	28.9	8	22.2
would you ...?	1	2.2	1	1.5			2	5.6
do you want to ...?	10	21.7	4	5.9	2	5.3		
would you like to ...?	1	2.2	1	1.5				
do you have ...?	4	8.7	1	1.5			2	5.6
is there ...?	1	2.2	1	1.5				
Total	46	100.0	68	100.0	38	100.0	36	100.0

Table 7.3, which shows the distribution of exponents of *query pre-paratory*, indicates that there was a clear difference in the choice of an indirect form, 'could you (I, we) ...?' between two groups: one consists of the adult (31.5%) and the mother (33.3%) and the other peers (6.5%) and the teenager (7.4%). This form was produced with the former group over four times more frequently than the latter.

With respect to the teenager, Yao's relationship with her seemed unstable. The teenager was a status-unequal friend. In this sense she fit into both categories. For instance, as shown in Table 7.3, Yao's behaviour with the teenager is closer to her behaviour with her peers rather than with the adult (e.g. in the use of 'could ...?'), while in other circumstances it is closer to the adult (e.g. in the use of 'do you want to ...?'). This ambivalent relationship with the teenager is also reflected in the difficulty of negotiating with her as in Example 5. The situation is one in which Yao and Hannah were each making their own collage of autumn leaves. Hannah did not feel like talking very much and there was silence for a short time. Yao broke the silence.

5 **Y:** *do you know what I'm doing?*
       (Yao refers to the collage she is making.)

   H: *no*

   Y: *why don't you talk with my mum or me?* [H55-55]

   H: *me/ what am I going to say?*

   Y: *anything*

   H: *anything/ okay Mary had a little lamb/ her fleece was as white as snow/ and every where that Mary went the lamb was sure to go/ did you like that?*

Yao's first utterance 'do you know what I'm doing?' is a rhetorical question to 'solicit a listener's acknowledgement to allow the speaker to continue' (Dore, 1977b: 145). Yao might have expected Hannah to respond to this rhetorical question with something more like 'no, what?' or 'no idea/what are you doing?' or 'are you making a rabbit with those leaves?' rather than just 'no'. In such a context, Yao would have had the opportunity to comment on what she was doing and could have developed a conversation. Instead, Yao was a bit annoyed by Hannah's indifference and said to her, *'why don't you talk with my mum or me?'* Hannah still did not show any interest in either Yao's request or what she was doing. Yao became more distressed and said, *'anything'*. Then Hannah quickly recited the nursery rhyme, still without trying to co-operate.

The ambivalent relationship with the teenager seems to be reflected also in the prominent use of 'can you ...?' (see Table 7.3) as in Example 6:

6 **Y:** *thank you/ that's very good/ can you draw a sea?* [H26-10]
       (Hannah and Yao are drawing. Hannah has just drawn a dolphin.)

   H: *the sea you want the sea around it?*

   Y: *yeah*

The 'can you ...?' form can be ambiguous. It can be either a request or an information-seeking question about the interlocutor's ability to do something, and so may have been a good solution to the problem when making requests to the teenager, especially one whose responses Yao could not predict.

Yao's relationships with peers were also unstable and her requests were inherently at risk. Consequently, there was the need for negotiation, as was observed in Example 7.

7 **PE:** *mm your face is a little bit fat in this drawing/*
(A peer is drawing a picture of a person who is supposed to be Yao.)

   Y: *mm sort of/ ... but don't write my name* [PE40-14-1]
(Yao does not like the picture. The peer is going to write Yao's name on it.)

   PE: *I will too*

   Y: *don't please* [PE40-14-2]

   PE: *you wrote my name*
(Yao had drawn a picture of the peer earlier and written the peer's name on it.)

   Y: *okay I'll rub it out*

   PE: *you can't rub it out*

   Y: *I go just cross it out*

   PE: *uh I'm writing your name under this*
(The peer is still going to write Yao's name on the picture.)

   Y: *could you please?* [PE40-14-3]

   PE: *you can cross it out afterwards but I don't care/ you don't love my drawing do you/ doesn't look much like you*

(A little later. PE is still drawing the picture of Y.)

   Y: *could you **please** stop write* [=writing] *my name?/ please Esther please/ I'll rub it out if you write* [PE40-21]
(The peer is going to write Yao's name on it. The word in bold was uttered emphatically, with a pleading tone.)

   PE: *you can't rub it out*

   Y: *I mean cross it out*

   PE: *I don't care/ oops something wrong spelling*

(A little later.)

   Y: *I'm going to cross out my name*
(The peer had completed writing the name.)

   PE: *okay do nice cross outs though*

In Example 7, to stop the peer from writing Yao's name on the picture the peer was drawing, Yao made four requests, each time in a different way.

1st time	imperative	*... but don't write my name* [PE40-14-1]
2nd time	imperative + please	*don't please* [PE40-14-2]
3rd time	could you + please	*could you please?* [PE40-14-3]
4th time	could you + please (emphatic)/ please (repeated)/threat	*could you **please** stop write* [=writing] *my name?/ please Esther please/ I'll rub it out if you write* [PE40-21]

In spite of this multiplicity of strategic forms, compliance was not achieved. The peer wrote Yao's name on the picture she had drawn. In the end she let Yao cross it out. Such an absence of social pressure toward courtesy between peers is noted in Mitchell-Kernan and Kernan (1977), where they point out that adults usually comply with requests that have little cost, while children often do not even with simple ones. Moreover, even when requests are made politely, compliance is not guaranteed.

In contrast to her relationships with the teenager and with peers, Yao's relationships with the adult and with her mother were stable in that Yao and these interlocutors knew more precisely where they stood with each other. Therefore, the kinds of negotiations between Yao and the teenager (e.g. Example 5) and between peers and Yao (e.g. Example 7) were not observed with the adult or with the mother.

When all of the above observations are brought together, it can be argued that Yao showed an awareness of at least some of the social meanings that help to decide the appropriate forms of request (e.g. the more frequent use of 'could you (I, we) ...?' with the adult and her mother than with her peers and the teenager). There were differences depending upon addressees, but they were subtle. There are three possible explanations for the subtlety. One is that Yao had not yet developed a target-like, sociolinguistic competence with which she could systematically vary her use of request forms according to addressee. Given the changes in her interlanguage, this explanation seems unlikely. Secondly, the literature reviewed has consistently shown that there are differences in the choice of request forms made to children who are younger than the speaker as opposed to adults. However, the literature suggests no consistency for peers vis-à-vis adults. It could be speculated that the differences are small, because no consistent differentiation is made by language speakers. However, given the differentiations recorded in Yao's

English, this explanation also appears less than likely. The third explanation has to do with the nature of the context (or the activity). The setting was that of supportive play in which Yao and her interlocutor were doing things together. The addressees were all very familiar with Yao. Supportive play sets up a context where little face-work is needed. Therefore, within the setting of supportive or mutual play, interlocutors are treated for the most part as one kind of addressee. This is such an influential factor that even the large differences in age and status between peers and the adult was substantially reduced. Moreover, in such settings, an addressee (except for her mother) has a similar role, that of a play partner. The setting overwhelms individual addressees. It is not so much that Yao was not a sophisticated user of English, but rather that in terms of addressees there was little motivation for variation. Ellis (1992) has a similar view. Neither of the two child learners of English in his study in a classroom setting varied their request forms according to addressee. As an explanation for this, he observes that a classroom environment with all familiar people did not create the need for face-work. This view is consistent with the findings of Walters (1981), whose subjects were bilingual children aged from seven years seven months to eleven years four months. His results show that the age of addressees (peers or adults) had no significant effect on the choice of request forms, while the setting had the strongest. This suggests that in Yao's data, sensitivity to the 'real' addressee was in conflict with sensitivity to the addressee as defined within the play situation. The more appealing explanation for the relatively subtle distinctions between addressees is that there exits a tension between the strong pressure to regard all addressees on the one hand as supportive partners (and hence 'the same'), and on the other the lesser pressure to acknowledge their age-differentiated status.

7.3 Summary and Conclusion

This analysis has explored the relationships between addressees and request realisation. There were variations according to addressee with regard to request strategies and some of their exponents. Yao's varied speech behaviour reflects the different relationships she had with each addressee.

The distinctions, however, were relatively subtle, perhaps because of the supportive play setting, where interlocutors are treated for the most part as the one specific kind of addressee (i.e. play partners except her mother) and no great amount of face-work is called for.

In Chapters 4 through 7, which focused on the choice of strategies and linguistic forms, we have examined the development of request realisation and their variations according to goal and addressee. However, requests are not only realised by strategies and linguistic forms but also by the way they are modified. In the next chapter the focus will be shifted to this dimension of request realisation.

Chapter 8
Modification

8.0 Introduction

All requests can be modified to modulate their impact upon the addressee. Modification is achieved along several dimensions:

(1) Different request strategies varied according to a level of directness:
Direct strategies: *mood derivable; obligation statements; want statements*
Conventionally indirect strategies: *suggestory formulae; stating preparatory; query preparatory*
Nonconventionally indirect strategies. *hints.*

(2) Different syntactic forms within or across the strategy:
Modals (e.g. 'can you help me?' vs. 'could you help me?');
Conditional (e.g. 'would you like to play outside?');
Interrogatives (e.g. 'can you draw a dolphin for me?') vs.
Declaratives (e.g. 'you can draw a dolphin for me') or
Imperatives (e.g. 'draw a dolphin for me').

The two dimensions above were examined and discussed in Chapters 4–7 in terms of development of Yao's request realisation (including *hints*) and its variations according to goal and addressee. The force of a request, however, does not depend only on the choice among strategies or syntactic forms. Modifications can be further achieved by:

(3) Lexical and phrasal choices.

(4) Reiterations that occur after the request proper, or support moves,[1] elements that precede or follow the request proper.

In this chapter we will focus on factors (3) and (4), which contribute greatly to the force of a request. Reiterations, as in (4), are one of the categories that either has been omitted from the literature or classified as a subcategory of something else. This analysis, however, will demonstrate that it is a much more significant category than previously considered.

The function of modification is to vary the impact of a request. The force of the request can be modulated to different degrees. The literature discusses two opposing directions in which the modulation can occur. For example, Faerch and Kasper (1989) using DCT and Trosborg (1995) using role-play data employ the terms 'downgraders' and 'upgraders'. The former refers to the elements used to mitigate the impositive force of a request and the latter refers to those that emphasise the degree of coerciveness. In the naturalistic setting of our data, however, there was a further set of elements that reinforced the illocutionary force of a request, usually without adding aggravation or coerciveness. This is especially true of reiteration, which may appear as repetition, paraphrase, or elaboration. We will call elements whose function is to modulate the impact of a request *mitigators, reinforcers* or *aggravators*. According to Fraser (1978: 13), *mitigators* are defined as elements that soften or ease the force of the request intentionally. *Reinforcers* are defined as elements that increase the force of the request but without adding to the degree of aggravation. *Aggravators* are defined as elements that modulate the request in the opposite direction of mitigation (Blum-Kulka, 1982: 35).

Using these categories and distinctions, this chapter addresses the fourth research question:

> With what frequency does a child use the various types of modification in a second language in relation to requests (1) across phases, (2) in differing strategies, (3) for differing goals, and (4) with differing addressees?

8.1 Categories of Modification

The classification adopted here is based on Blum-Kulka *et al.* (1989a), Blum-Kulka and Olshtain (1984) and Edmondson (1981). The categories aim to capture pragmatic functions realised by the various linguistic elements used in requests.

Although segmentation of a request has already been presented in Chapter 3 (Methodology), it is repeated here in more detail for a clearer understanding of the classification below. Based on Blum-Kulka *et al.* (1989a) and Blum-Kulka and Olshtain (1984), a request was analysed into the following segments: *address term; head act; support move* or *reiteration*. For example, the following request is broken down into three parts:

> Hannah/ let's pretend this is Safeway/ because I've got a Safeway plastic bag [H32-10]
> 'Hannah': *address term*

'let's pretend this is Safeway': *head act*
'because I've got a Safeway plastic bag': *support move*

The *address term* is an attention getter that precedes the actual request. The *head act* is the request proper or the core of the request. *Support moves* are external to the *head act* and modify the impact of the request. In the above example it is possible to insert an appealer such as 'okay?' as in the following:

Hannah/ let's pretend this is Safeway okay?/ because I've got a Safeway plastic bag

The 'okay' is a *modifier* that operates internally within the request utterance proper (linked to the Head act) (Blum-Kulka *et al.*, 1989a) and modulates the impact of the request.

The *lexical/phrasal modifiers, reiterations* and *support moves* that are the focus of the analysis here are detailed and exemplified below. (The underlined parts of the examples are the aspects of modification that are the focus of the particular example.) The categories presented below represent a comprehensive list of these means of modification in this corpus. Although framed within categories of modification presented in the general literature, it is yet to be determined by further research if these categories represent all possible means of modification. Each type of modification outlined below can occur in isolation or in a combination.

For all of the categories identified below it is possible to have either a mitigated, reinforced or aggravated impositive force. In the classification below *reiterations* are placed between *lexical/phrasal modifiers* and *support moves,* which are clausal, because *reiterations* can be either phrasal or clausal.

8.1.1 Lexical/phrasal modifiers

Through specific lexical and phrasal choices a number of devices are available that reduce or increase the impositive force of a request.

(a) Please
By adding an optional element, 'please', to a request, a speaker can signal politeness and elicit cooperative behaviour from his or her addressee, as in Example 1.

1   *could you please help us mum?* [PJ63-3]
    (Yao and her peer are mashing bananas to make muffins. They
    are not finding it easy.)

In other words, 'please', functions as a politeness marker that softens the imposition of the request. In addition to this primary function, 'please' seems to have at least three other functions. First, as in Example 2, in its emphatic function, 'please' can be an emotionally loaded expression to beg for cooperative behaviour from an addressee.

2   *could you **please** stop write* [=writing] *my name?/ please Esther please/ I'll rub it out if you write* [PE40-21]
     (Yao does not like the picture of her a peer has drawn. The peer is going to write Yao's name on it, and Yao wants her not to.)

In Example 2 the request is modified by the emphatic use of 'please' with a pleading tone, followed by similarly repeated 'pleases'. Secondly, 'please' can be used as a request marker. As Searle (1975: 68) observes, the addition of 'please' to an utterance 'explicitly and literally marks the primary illocutionary point of the utterance as a directive'. Insertion of 'please' helps a speaker to convey the intended meaning clearly to the addressee. This is especially true with the 'can you …?' form which can be ambiguous as to whether it is a request or a question to ask about the addressee's ability to do something. Example 3 can be ambiguous in the absence of a specific context. It can be a request or a literal question to ask about Hannah's ability to draw a big shark. In this particular situation, prior to this utterance Hannah had already consented to draw a shark for Yao and was just about to draw it when Yao specified the size of the shark. Therefore, it is unlikely that this is a literal question. In other circumstances, it could be an ambiguous utterance and the insertion of 'please' would make it unambiguous. Finally, 'please' can be used to emphasise what a speaker says. The 'please' in Example 4 functions as a *reinforcer* rather than as a *mitigator*.

3   *can you draw a big shark?* [H26-19]

4   *no/ don't please* [H26-16]
     (Yao's mother has started telling Hannah something about what Yao did. Yao does not want her to do so.)

(b) Appealer
     By adding a tag at the end of a sentence, a speaker can appeal to the addressee's understanding and elicit consent (Blum-Kulka *et al.*, 1989a; Sifianou, 1992; Trosborg, 1995), as in Examples 5 and 6. Therefore, the impact may be softened. However, the impositive force of 'okay?' could vary substantially according to speaker's intonation and tone of voice. They may function to coerce and also as *aggravators*.

5   *don't move the table <u>okay</u>?* [PA32-81]
    (Yao is trying to pile up miniature grocery packs on the table in order
    to play shopping centre. They might fall over if a peer moves the table.)

6   *oh yeah you've got blu-tack <u>haven't you</u>?* [PL69-22]
    (Yao and her peer are making things from different materials such
    as sticks, straws, and pipe cleaners, etc. Yao wants to use some blu-
    tack, but it is not near her. She knows the peer has it. This utterance
    was used as a hint.)

(c)   Toner

   Toners are adjectival or adverbial modifiers that are used to reduce or
increase the impact of a request. They also include phrasal verbs such as
'come on'. As has been noted by Sifianou (1992: 172), 'their function is to
tentativise what speakers say, thus allowing them not to fully commit themselves to what they are saying'. Typical modifiers to reduce the impositive
force in this category are 'just', 'maybe', 'any', 'or something', 'a little', 'a
bit', etc. 'Just' and 'maybe' may be used by a speaker to tone down the
impact the request might have on the addressee as in Examples 7 and 8.

7   *<u>maybe</u> you should hold that side* [J68-9]
    (Janice and Yao are painting on a piece of tracing paper for fabric
    painting. The paper moves while they are trying to paint.)

8   *can you <u>just</u> wait* [H43-25]
    (Yao is colouring in the letters Hannah is outlining. Yao wants
    Hannah to wait before Hannah outlines the next letter, so that she
    would have enough room to work.)

   However, as Sifianou (1992: 173) also observes, 'just' can also be used
to emphasise a speaker's utterance and 'seems to contribute necessary
information for the correct understanding of the utterance', as in
Example 9. In this case, 'just' is not a toner.

9   *give me your hand/ oh <u>just</u> one hand* [H67-67-2]
    (Yao has made small pieces out of red plasticine. She is putting the
    pieces on Hannah's fingernails. Hannah holds out both hands.)

   'Any', which is a 'non-assertive item' (Quirk, 1985: 1092), is used when
a speaker does not wish to give precise specification to a certain aspect of
a request in order to avoid potential refusal as in Example 10.

10 *it wouldn't be very nice if I just use this/ can you give me <u>any</u> colour just
    to put this in?* [PC75-27]
    (Yao and her peer are making things out of plasticine. Yao has
    yellow and wants to mix it with another colour.)

Instead, the use of 'any' by a speaker gives the addressee freedom to specify it. Thus, it softens the impositive force of a face-threatening act. Expressions such as 'a little' and 'a bit' are means by which a speaker can minimise some aspects of the proposition as in Example 11.

11   *please move this a bit* [J68-32]
     (Janice and Yao are painting on a piece of tracing paper for fabric painting. Yao wants Janice to move the paper to make more room.)

A request appears to be of no great cost when minimisation is literally expressed with 'a little' or 'a bit'. Thus, the impact of the request is softened. However, there are some toners that can be intensifiers capable of aggravating the impact of a request. They are intensifiers such as 'now' and 'quick' or 'quickly' requesting immediacy and 'come on', as in Example 12.

12   ***come on*** [J44-10-2]
     (Janice and Yao are playing a computer game. Janice is supposed to guess the word. It is taking her a long time, and Yao is getting impatient. The words are in bold letters to indicate a strong, emphatic voice.)

Such examples can have elements of irritation and function as *aggravators*. 'Quick' or 'quickly' may be used by themselves without verbs and 'come on' without other verbs. Note that they are *aggravators* only when they are uttered emphatically. A speaker's intonation and tone of voice differentiate the level of the impositive force of requests with those expressions. Further toners consist of words such as 'stupid', which when said emphatically function as an *aggravator*.

(d) Subjectiviser
     A speaker can reduce the assertive force of the request by adding subjective opinions about the proposition of the utterance, as in Example 13.

13   *I think* we need a bit more water [J50-4-1]
     (Janice and Yao are making animals out of bread dough.)

(e) Attention getter
     Attention getters are used to alert the addressee to the ensuing request. This category includes not only formulaic elements such as 'excuse me' and 'hey' but also vocatives in the initial position such as an address term or a role name. When they are used with a positive attitude, they connote the speaker's wish to have a pleasant encounter with the addressee while making a request, as in Examples 14, 15 or 16. On the other hand, when

they are used negatively, they contain elements of irritation or annoyance as in Example 17, and increase the impositive force of the request.

14 *excuse me* this is Marmite?[2] [J38-22]
(In playing shopping centre, Yao, the customer, is asking Janice, the shop-keeper, about a product.)

15 *hey* look/ oh it doesn't matter [H11-37]
(Hannah has just made a nice mermaid out of clay. Yao wants her mother to look at it. But the mermaid falls over.)

16 *mum* can you put it uh in my room? [J54-32]
(Janice and Yao have just made collages. 'It' refers to Yao's collage.)

17 *Esther!* don't do that [PE40-2]
(A peer, Esther, tries to cross out her name on the picture of the person she has just drawn.)

8.1.2 Reiterations

Reiterations are subdivided into repetition, paraphrase, and elaboration. *Reiterations* are for the most part external to a head act, occurring after it. They can be phrasal or clausal. They entail repetition of all or part of a previous head act, paraphrase, or elaboration. *Reiterations* can mitigate the impact of the request, but in general they intensify its force and function either as reinforcing devices or, under very restricted circumstances, aggravating devices.

(a) Repetition
Repetition involves the literal reproduction of all or part of a previous head act, as in Example 18. It also includes repetition of an element within a single utterance, though this is very rare, as in Example 19.

18 *that's enough/ that's enough* [PA32-90]
(Yao and her peer are playing shopping centre. The peer is buying many things and it is taking a long time.)

19 just don't **don't** **_don't_** do it any more please [PC75-21]
(Yao and her peer have finished making things out of plasticine and are now collecting half-used colours. The peer has mixed different colours though Yao had asked her not to. The peer, however, continues.)

(b) Paraphrase
Paraphrase involves a different lexical choice of a synonymous expression, as in Example 20 or a structural reformulation of the previous head act, as in Example 21.

20   *oh don't do that/ don't throw it* [H38-20-1]
     (Hannah and Yao are playing with miniature animal dolls. Hannah
     throws one.)

21   *just put over here/ can you put ducky* [H38-12-1]
     (Hannah and Yao are playing with miniature animal dolls.)

(c) Elaboration

Elaboration involves expansion of a head act by supplying additional
elements in order to clarify and specify the illocutionary point. This can
be done with or without a stimulus (i.e. a response) from an addressee as
in Examples 22 and 23, respectively. An elaboration may take several
turns in sequence.

22   *Janet just put butter on the thing/ you just put here like that* [P63-18]
     (Yao and her peer are greasing tins with butter to bake muffins. The
     'thing' refers to the paper towel and 'here' refers to the muffin tin.)

23   **Y:** *can you do it in fancy writing?* [H73-61]
          (Hannah and Yao are making a zoo from sticks, straws, pipe
          cleaners, etc. 'It' refers to what Hannah is going to write on the
          sign.)

     H: *I don't know/ you mean bubble writing?*

     Y: *any writing/ fancy/ any writing that is fancy*

8.1.3 Support moves

Support moves are optional clauses that support the actual request in
order to gain cooperation from the addressee and lead the addressee to
perform the desired action. *Support moves* are external to a head act. They
can either precede or follow a head act. Unlike *lexical/phrasal modifiers* and
reiterations, they have a separate propositional content and illocution from
those of a head act. The following support moves are distinguished.

(a) Preparator

Prior to making an actual request, a speaker prepares the addressee for
it. A speaker can do this in several ways. One way to prepare the addressee
is to announce that he or she is to anticipate a task, as in Example 24.

24   **Y:** *um I know what you could do/ I know what*
          (Yao and her peer are making muffins. The peer is having a
          hard time putting the sugar in a measuring cup.)

     PJ: *yeah*

     Y: *put your cup here* (Pointing to a bowl)/ *just hold it up/ then I could
          just put it in* [PJ63-22]
          (The first 'it' refers to the cup and the second to the sugar.)

The second way is to check on the potential availability of the addressee to perform the request or to try to get some kind of pre-commitment from him or her in order to avoid a potential refusal, as in Example 25.

25[3] **Y:** *mum <u>could you do me a favour?</u>*
     (Yao comes to her mother's room while she is studying.)

   M: *naani?*
     (=what is it?)

   Y: *it's only a small favour/ could you put up my leotard?/ I'm too short*
     [Diary, 19-10-93]
     (Yao wants her mother to put her leotard on her closet shelf.)

In this example Yao is ensuring that the addressee is willing to carry out the request. The addressee could respond either positively or nega-tively. At this point in the discourse, the addressee can either reject the preparator with an expression such as 'Not now, maybe later', or indicate encouragement by saying something such as 'Sure. What is it?' If the response is 'It depends', the speaker has to think carefully about what to say next. The third way of preparing the addressee for the actual request is by making disarming statements, as in Example 26, where the speaker tries to remove the possibility of refusal.

26 **Y:** *<u>sorry to interrupt you but</u> I have one question*
     (Yao comes into her mother's room while she is studying.)

   M: *naani?*
     (=what is it?)

   Y: *have you checked that?* [Diary, 5-10-93]
     (Yao had asked her mother earlier to check her homework. She does not think she has checked it and wants her to look it right away. Yao is hinting.)

   M: *gomen/ ima mirune*
     (=sorry/ I will look at it now)

This is what Edmondson (1981) and Blum-Kulka *et al.* (1989a) call 'dis-armers'. In a sense, disarming statements convey a speaker's awareness that the request might be an imposition.

(b) Option giver
A speaker explicitly indicates that carrying out a request is at the addressee's own volition by adding a clause such as 'if you want to/ don't want to', as in Example 27, or 'you don't have to do what I say, but you can', as in Example 28.

27 *you can make it if you want to* [PA32-64-4]
(Yao wants her peer to make packets from flattened miniature grocery packets so that they can play shopping centre.)

28 **Y:** *you could put a cloud with this white* [PA75-52]
(Yao and her peer are making things out of plasticine. Yao suggests that the peer should put clouds in the background.)

PC: *oh okay*

Y: *you don't have to do what I say but you can*

(c) Reason

Since a request is potentially a face-threatening act, the speaker must be able to justify his or her desired act. By stating reasons for a request, as in Example 29, the speaker hopes to accomplish this and make the addressee more willing to comply. In other words, the addressee 'is led to see the reasonableness of S's FTA' (Brown & Levinson 1987: 128). Reasons are typically causal clauses and may either precede or follow the request. Reasons are termed 'grounders' elsewhere of the literature (e.g. Blum-Kulka *et al.,* 1989a; Edmondson, 1981; Sifianou, 1992).

29 *Hannah let's pretend this is Safeway because I've got a Safeway plastic bag* [H32-10]
(Hannah and Yao are going to play shopping centre. Yao goes to get a plastic bag.)

(d) Other

Threats have been put in this category, since they appeared only once in the data. A threat makes explicit a negative manifestation of a consequence. Example 30 is a threat, though it is a reasonably mild one. The fabricated Example 31 is a stronger threat. These examples express the speaker's negative attitude. On the other hand, a speaker can express a positive attitude and increase the possibility of compliance by promising a reward or a benefit upon the fulfilment of the requests, as in the fabricated Example 32.

30 *could you **please** stop write* [=writing] *my name? / please Esther please/ I'll rub it out if you write* [PE40-21]

31 *If you dare to write that, then I'm going to rub it out immediately* [Fabricated]

32 *If you don't write my name, I'll give you a chocolate* [Fabricated]

8.2 Analysis

All modifiers in this study have been classified according to the above taxonomy, with the focus on the kinds of modification available to the child. Therefore, we did not count separately the repeated uses of the same kind of modifier. In the case of toners in *lexical/phrasal modifier*, however, different words, such as 'maybe', 'just', 'any', 'a bit (a little bit)', and 'quick (quickly)', were regarded as different kinds of toners and were totalled as such.

Lexical/phrasal modifiers operate generally within the request utterance proper. However, they can occur in *support moves* or *reiterations*, and they may affect the force of the request. Therefore, those *lexical/phrasal modifiers* that occurred in *supportive moves* or *reiterations* were also identified and counted.

Since our attempt has been to chart the expansion of Yao's pragmatic repertoire, this analysis has focused on the types of modification that occurred, rather than on their total number. Therefore, when the same modifier was repeated, it was counted as one repetition regardless of the number. For instance, in Example 2, the first 'please' (in the bold type) was classified as a *lexical/phrasal modifier* 'please' and the second and third as one repetition of the first.

The *modifiers* identified in the above manner were first crosstabulated for phases, strategies, forms, goals, and addressees. Second, requests containing modifiers were examined to determine whether the impositive force of the modifiers mitigated or reinforced or aggravated their impact. To determine whether a modifier in a particular instance has such an effect, the instance was looked at in context and judged according to the normal pragmatics of that expression.

For inter-rater reliability, a native speaker of English and I independently examined three transcripts and coded them according both to types of modifiers and to whether the instance was a *mitigator*, a *reinforcer*, or an *aggravator*. The three transcripts were randomly chosen except that each of the three transcripts had a different context with respect to the interlocutor. Inter-rater agreement for the *modifier* type was 93.8% and with respect to whether the *modifier* was an instance of a *mitigator*, a *reinforcer*, or an *aggravator* was 93.3%. Examples where the raters disagreed were discussed case by case until consensus was achieved.

8.3 Results and Discussion

In this section we will first examine each type of request modification individually by phases. Then, we will investigate the data to determine whether there is a systematic relationship between the choice of type of modification and the strategies, goals, and addressees. Finally, we will look at the extent to which each modifier serves to mitigate, reinforce or aggravate the impact of a request. The total number of requests in the data is 1413, and this will serve as the data base for this chapter except for the section on addressees. The analysis of that section excludes the data from Phase I and the improvised role-play (see Chapter 7 on Addressees). Therefore, the total number of requests for the section on addressees is 978.

8.3.1 Modification over the phases

8.3.1.1 Distribution of requests with and without modification

Table 8.1 shows the frequencies of requests with and without modifiers over the phases.

The proportion of requests with modifiers drops between Phase I and II (from 31.7% to 22.9%) and then continuously increases to peak in Phase IV (42.9%). The destabilisation occurring between Phase I and II can be interpreted as an indication that Phase I is a formulaic stage, where there are some formulaic resources such as chunks and repetitions; while Phase II is a beginning-to-learn stage, as will be seen in the increase of toners from Phase I to Phase II, in Section 8.3.1.3.

Table 8.1 Distribution of requests with and without modifiers in relation to phase

	Phase									
	I		*II*		*III*		*IV*		*Total*	
Request	*n*	*%*	*n*	*%*	*n*	*%*	*n*	*%*	*n*	*%*
Without modifiers	209	68.3	239	77.1	360	66.1	144	57.1	952	67.4
With modifiers	97	31.7	71	22.9	185	33.9	108	42.9	461	32.6
Total no. of requests	306	100.0	310	100.0	545	100.0	252	100.0	1413	100.0

8.3.1.2 Lexical/phrasal modifiers, reiterations and support moves

Table 8.2 provides information relating to *lexical/phrasal modifiers, support moves*, and *reiterations*. At the beginning, in Phase I, there is a high proportion of *reiterations*, which decrease by almost half by Phase IV, whereas *lexical/phrasal modifiers* double and *support moves* more than triple by this phase. This seems reasonable. At the beginning Yao did not know how to modify requests other than by repeating herself or by using her limited number of *lexical/phrasal modifiers*. Over time she learned further ways to modify. The fact that *lexical/phrasal modifiers* only double while *support moves* more than triple by Phase IV can be explained by their discourse structural characteristics. *Support moves* are clausal and require a separate structure with their own propositional content, while *lexical/phrasal modifiers* occur as part of the head act and are shorter. In addition, because

Table 8.2 Distribution of categories of modifiers in relation to requests in different phases

	Phase									
	I		II		III		IV		Total	
Modifier	n	%	n	%	n	%	n	%	n	%
Nil	209	68.3	239	77.1	360	66.1	144	57.1	952	67.4
Lexical/phrasal modifiers	46	15.0	42	13.5	113	20.7	77	30.6	278	19.7
Reiterations	56	18.3	30	9.7	65	11.9	25	9.9	176	12.5
Support moves	12	3.9	17	5.5	49	9.0	35	13.9	113	8.0

(The table is based on multiple modifiers per request. Percentages are calculated in relation to the total number of requests for each phase. Therefore, as requests can have more than one modifier, total percentages for modifiers may add up to greater than 100%.)

they have their own propositional content, *support moves* require more careful and extensive processing compared to *lexical/phrasal modifiers* which often have the status of routinised fillers. Consequently, *support moves* involve 'conscious planning decisions on the part of the speaker' (Faerch & Kasper, 1989: 244), and therefore, are difficult to produce especially at the beginning, while *lexical/phrasal modifiers* are easier and consequently found in all the phases.

8.3.1.3 Modifiers

Let us now look at specific types of *lexical/phrasal modifiers, reiterations* and *supportive moves* to see whether or not there are any observable changes over time. Table 8.3 presents the distribution of specific types of modification.

First, the types that were found to be predominant either in a particular phase or several phases will be discussed: repetitions; attention getters; toners; reasons; and 'please'. Then the less frequently occurring types will be discussed: appealers, subjectivisers, paraphrase, elaboration, option givers, and preparators. The underlined segments in the utterances indicate the part under discussion.

(a) Repetitions

Repetitions were the predominant type of modification in Phase I. Their percentage decreases over time and in Phase IV there were only a few. At the beginning Yao's resources were limited so she used many repetitions. Clearly there were some other resources available, such as providing reasons and elaborating on what she was doing. She also used attention getters quite frequently. However, the dominant, and presumably the easiest and the most readily available resources were repetitions as seen in Example 33.

Table 8.3 Distribution of modifiers in relation to requests in different phases

Modifier	Phase									
	I		II		III		IV		Total	
	n	*%*	*n*	*%*	*n*	*%*	*n*	*%*	*n*	*%*
Nil	209	68.3	239	77.1	360	66.1	144	57.1	952	67.4
Lexical/phrasal modifiers										
Please	9	2.9	12	3.9	28	5.1	27	10.7	76	5.4
Appealer	5	1.6	2	0.6	20	3.7	2	0.8	29	2.1
Toner	4	1.3	25	8.1	44	8.1	41	16.3	114	8.1
Attention getter	27	8.8	2	0.6	19	3.5	5	2.0	53	3.8
Subjectiviser	0	0.0	1	0.3	2	0.4	2	0.8	5	0.4
Reiterations										
Repetition	36	11.8	14	4.5	33	6.1	4	1.6	87	6.2
Paraphrase	5	1.6	7	2.3	5	0.9	5	2.0	22	1.6
Elaboration	16	5.2	9	2.9	27	5.0	16	6.3	68	4.8
Support moves										
Preparator	0	0.0	1	0.3	0	0.0	5	2.0	6	0.4
Option giver	0	0.0	0	0.0	5	0.9	6	2.4	11	0.8
Reason	12	3.9	14	4.5	40	7.3	29	11.5	95	6.7
Other	0	0.0	0	0.0	1	0.2	0	0.0	1	0.1

(The table is based on multiple modifiers per request. Percentages are calculated in relation to the total number of requests for each phase. Therefore, as requests can have more than one modifier, total percentages for modifiers may add up to greater than 100%.)

33　*look at this mum/ <u>look at this</u>* [H6-31]
(Yao has made a square with the sticks she had won in the game she was playing with her mother and Hannah.)

(b)　Attention getters

Attention getters, which include initial vocatives, were the second most frequently used modifiers in Phase I. They were robust only here and seem to have several functions. One of the functions is to call attention to the fact that Yao wanted to ask or tell her interlocutors something. Often the interlocutors were not paying attention to the game, as in Examples 34 and 35. Another function, especially of initial vocatives, is to signal the intended interlocutor when there is more than one potential addressee, as in Example 36. Besides these functions, both vocatives and other attention-getting words such as 'hey' are used as devices to initiate a conversation (McTear, 1979).

34 *Hannah your turn* [H6-44]
    (Yao, her mother, and Hannah are playing a game.)

35 *mum hurry up* [H4-29]
    (Her mother meant to join Yao and Hannah in a game, but she is
    still in the kitchen.)

36 *mum you spin it* [H4-5]
    (Yao, her mother, and Hannah are playing a game.)

Attention getters can have either a mitigating effect or sometimes
an aggravating effect. In Phase I, however, Yao may have used them
as a place holder rather than as a *mitigator* while she was trying to
make an ensuing request, as in Example 37. It may be only after Phase I
that she used them as a *mitigator*, as in Example 38, which was from
Phase II.

37 **Y.** *Hunnuh*
           (Yao is trying unsuccessfully to draw the kangaroo on the
           Australian one-dollar coin.)

    H: *mm-hmm*

    Y: *please*

    H: *mm-hmm what do you want me to draw? a kangaroo?*

    Y: *yes* [H4-62]

38 *Hannah let's pretend this is Safeway because I've got a Safeway plastic bag*
    [H32-10]

(c) Toners
    Toners were the most frequently selected means of modification from
Phase II through IV. Their number rises quite dramatically from Phase I
to IV (from 1.3% to 15.9%), showing an increase in language sophistication. As was seen in Table 8.1, the overall proportion of requests with
modifiers drops from Phase I to II (from 31.7% to 22.9%) and subse-
quently increases. This decrease from Phase I to II is in large part due to
the decrease in repetitions and attention getters after Phase I. By Phase II,
Yao was learning new ways to modify. The increase from Phase I to II in
the use of toners (from 1.3% to 8.1%), complementing the reduction in
repetition and attention getters, shows Yao was beginning to acquire
other sources of modification at this time.
    The actual range of toners over the phases is worth noting. Table 8.4
shows the distribution of the various toners over the phases.

Table 8.4 Distribution of various toners in relation to requests in phases

Toner	*I*		*II*		*III*		*IV*		*Total*	
	n	*%*	*n*	*%*	*n*	*%*	*n*	*%*	*n*	*%*
A little bit	0	0.0	3	1.0	1	0.2	2	0.8	6	0.4
Any	0	0.0	2	0.6	2	0.4	3	1.2	7	0.5
Maybe	1	0.3	1	0.3	0	0.0	18	7.1	20	1.4
Just	3	1.0	18	5.8	37	6.8	18	7.1	76	5.4
Quick	0	0.0	1	0.3	4	0.7	0	0.0	5	0.4

(The table is based on multiple modifiers per request. Percentages are calculated in relation to the total number of requests for each phase: 306, 310, 545 and 252 for Phase I, II, III and IV respectively.)

The kinds of toners used initially were limited to only two kinds, while from Phase II onwards the range of toners increased to four or five. The most frequently used toner was 'just' and the next most frequently used one was 'maybe'. Though, both 'just' and 'maybe' are deployed 'to downtone the impositive force of the request' (Trosborg, 1995: 212), 'maybe' was rarely used before the last stage (Phase IV), while 'just' appeared in every phase and increased over the phases. Finally, in Phase IV, the frequency of 'maybe' and 'just' become the same (n = 18), suggesting that 'maybe' is more difficult to acquire than 'just'. Its use seems also to require a greater conscious effort than 'just', being less routinised in utterances. Furthermore, a request with 'maybe' attached manifests a modest approach by the speaker in that he or she is uncertain about the addressee's future act and therefore suggesting that the addressee is less obligated to the act. This new tendency in Phase IV to tone down the impact of a request through the use of 'maybe' is evidence that Yao has found a new dimension to her modifications. The following examples of 'maybe' and 'just' were produced in Phase IV.

39　*maybe you should hold that side* [J68-9]
　　(Janice and Yao are fabric printing. The tracing paper on the fabric moves when they try to iron it.)

40　*just bring it over here* [H62-14]
　　(Hannah and Yao are making muffins. The mixing bowl is on the breakfast table, which is too high for Yao. She wants Hannah to place it on the stool.)

(d) Reasons

'Reasons' were the second most frequently used modification from Phase II onwards and they steadily increased.

The majority of the reasons in the data were objective though a few were subjective. For instance, in Example 41 the reason refers to a future plan and is logical, while the reason in Example 42 is subjective since some desire or need on the part of the speaker is expressed.

41 *wash your hands/ we go outside* [PE47-56]
    (Yao and her peer have finished playing with play dough. Their hands are sticky. They are going outside to play.)

42 *I need a blu-tack/ do you have a blu- tack I could use?* [PL69-58]
    (Yao and her peer are making things from material called 'Oodles'.)

'Reasons' were the most frequently selected means of all the *support moves*. The findings of other studies concur (e.g. Faerch & Kasper, 1989; House & Kasper, 1987; Trosborg, 1995).[4] The reason for the high frequency in the present study, as well as the others, may be due to the fact that 'it is psychologically most plausible to make the addressee understand the reason(s) behind a request' (House & Kasper, 1987: 1281). In addition, it reduces the threat to the addressee's face. Therefore, it is 'an efficient mitigating strategy' (Faerch & Kasper, 1989: 239). As noted in Section 8.3.1.2, *support moves* are clausal and require a separate structure. Therefore, they are more difficult to produce than other types of modification. It follows from this that as Yao's grammatical competence increased, her reasons increased.

As noted in our review of the literature, the results of other studies concerning children's ability to give reasons for their requests vary. In Garvey's (1975) study, requests made by American children ranging in age from 3;6 to 5;7 involved a good many reasons, while in Trosborg's (1985) work on requests in three- to five-year-old Danish children no reasons were supplied. In the work by Ervin-Tripp *et al.* (1990) on requests of American children whose ages ranged from two to 11, they reported that giving reasons developed with age. All these studies are concerned with L1 acquisition. In Ellis' study on L2 acquisition, the two subjects aged ten and 11 years gave few reasons.

In the present study the fact that Yao used 'reasons' to some extent even at the beginning (e.g. Examples 43 and 44, in the fourth and the tenth week respectively), may indicate her awareness of the importance of giving specific reasons to help the addressee understand why the request is being made. In Example 43, Yao is justifying her request based on the invasion of her rights by the addressee; and in Example 44 she is stating her lack of ability as a reason for the request.

43   **don't/** *it's my turn* [H4-30]
      (Yao's mother thought it was her turn in a game.)
44   *I can't draw/ can you draw in?/ coffee or....* [E10-5]
      (Yao is trying to draw a cup of coffee for the menu that she and
      Emily are making.)

(e) Please

'Please' consistently increased, emerging in Phase IV as the third most
frequently used type of modification after toners and reasons. The use of
'please' changed in character in two ways. The first is in the relationship
between request strategy type and the use of 'please'.

Table 8.5 presents the distribution of requests for each request strategy
type containing 'please' in each phase.

In Phase I, 'please' occurred only with direct strategies (i.e. *mood derivable* and *want/need statements*), as in Examples 45 and 46. From Phase II on,
'please' occurred more frequently with a conventionally indirect strategy
(i.e. *query preparatory*) than with direct strategies. The conventionally
indirect strategy with 'please' increased and in Phase IV it occurred 3.5
times more frequently than the direct strategies with 'please'.

At the beginning of Yao's language acquisition, 'please' was added to the
early acquired basic request form (i.e. the imperative), not to the conventionally indirect forms. Examples 47 and 48, which occurred in Phase III, are
of a conventionally indirect strategy with 'please'. Example 47 is especially interesting. Yao was about to use a direct form (an imperative) but
self-corrected it and deployed instead a conventionally indirect request
(*query preparatory*) with 'please'. This may suggest that she had become
aware of the different linguistic devices available for social use.

Table 8.5 Distribution of 'please' by strategy type in relation to requests
in phases

Strategy	Phase									
	I		**II**		**III**		**IV**		**Total**	
	n	*%*	*n*	*%*	*n*	*%*	*n*	*%*	*n*	*%*
Direct										
Mood derivable	8	2.6	5	1.6	11	2.0	5	2.0	29	2.1
Want/need statements	1	0.3	0	0.0	0	0.0	1	0.4	2	0.1
Conventionally indirect										
Query preparatory	0	0.0	7	2.3	17	3.1	21	8.3	45	3.2

(The table is based on multiple modifiers per request. Percentages are calculated in relation
to the total number of requests for each phase: 306, 310, 545 and 252 for Phase I, II, III and
IV respectively.)

45   *I need uh yellow/ pass me a yellow* <u>*please*</u>
     [H11-43-4]
     (Hannah and Yao are putting the play dough back in the container
     after the play.)

46   *I need help/* <u>*please*</u> *I need help*
     [H11-42-4]
     (Hannah and Yao have finished playing with the play dough. Yao
     wants her mother to help clean up the mess.)

47   *oh bottles!/* <u>*get the – can you get the bottles please?/*</u>
     over there on the ground
     [H38-39]
     (Hannah and Yao are playing with animal dolls. The bottles fall off
     the box that is a bedroom, onto the table that is the ground.)

48   <u>*could I please*</u> *have the glue up here*
     [J54-16]
     (Janice and Yao are making collages.)

These findings seem to match those of Liebling (1988) and Nippold *et al.* (1982). As reviewed in Chapter 2, in reference to requests with 'please', Liebling[5] reports that first-grade students' choice was direct requests softened with 'please', while older students (third- and fifth-graders) had gradually shifted to conventionally indirect requests, frequently softened with 'please'. Nippold *et al.* obtained similar results. They found that query preparatory modified by 'please' increased with age (three-, five- and seven-year-olds) as the use of imperatives modified by 'please' decreased. The findings of the present study show a developmental sequence very similar to that of Liebling (1988) and Nippold *et al.* (1982) and as noted above illustrate a shift in the choice of strategy type with 'please' from Phase I to II.

Another development in the use of 'please' is seen in the shift from its main use at the very beginning of her language acquisition as a request marker to a means to indicate politeness. Particularly at the very early stage, in Phase I, when Yao's grammatical and lexical ability was limited, 'please' was not necessarily used as a politeness marker but more likely to indicate that a request was being made. For instance, the 'please' with a vocative only (e.g. Example 49, uttered in the 4th week) or with the name of an object only (e.g. Example 50, uttered in the 8th week) served essentially as a cue for the addressee to perform the desired action, although those uses of 'please' also had a mitigating effect. This, at least, seems to have been the interpretation of the interlocutor, who performed an appropriate action.

49 **Y:** *another coin*
           (Hannah is making a rubbing from a coin.)

     H: *another coin?*

     Y: *yeah/ Hannah please* [H4-63] =

     H: = *you got another coin/ the twenty cents okay*

50 *(coloured) pencil please* [E8-27-1]
     (Yao wants Emily to use a coloured pencil when drawing a picture
     for her.)

Compare these examples with Example 45, which was produced in the
11th week. In Example 45, 'please' is used only as a politeness marker. In
this utterance 'please' is attached to an imperative, and therefore even
without it the utterance contains requestive force and does not need a
marker.

Thus far only the major types of modification have been discussed (i.e.
repetition, attention getter, toner, reason, and 'please'.) We will now deal
with the types of modification that occurred less frequently (i.e. appealer,
subjectiviser, paraphrase, elaboration, option giver, and preparator).

(f) Appealers
     'Appealers' occurred in every phase, but infrequently. They were all
'okay?' (Example 51) except one 'question tag' (Example 52).

51 *don't peek please okay?* [PA32-3-3]/ *and you look after her so she doesn't
     peek okay?* [PA32-3-4]
     (A peer tries to open a locker door in Yao's room to have a quick look
     inside. The former utterance is made to the peer. The latter is
     addressed to the mother when Yao was going to go to the toilet.)

52 *oh yeah you've got blu-tack haven't you?* [PL69-22]
     (Yao and her peer are making things from sticks, straws and pipe
     cleaners, etc. Yao wants to use some blu-tack. This utterance was
     used as a hint.)

It was not that a question tag did not appear as an appealer because
it could not be grammatically constructed. In fact, many question tags
appeared from Phase II on, but not in requests. This observation is
in agreement with Trosborg's findings (1995), in which no instances of
requests containing tags were observed either in Danish learners of
English or in the two native speaker groups of Danish and English.
Trosborg attributes this to the limited possibilities of occurrence of tags
with requests. They co-occur with imperatives and statements, but not

with question forms. This may be the reason why there was only one tag in connection with requests in the present study.

There are two complementary explanations for the low frequency of 'okay?' in the present data. One has to do with power relations and the other with low risk situations. Dore (1977b) reports that teachers in his study often used 'okay?' in their requests addressed to children. This leads to a speculation that 'okay?' is generally used by a more powerful speaker to an addressee who is less so. The reason why there are not many uses of 'okay?' – and then mostly with peers – may well be that Yao couldn't talk down to other addressees. Trosborg (1995) identifies low risk situations. In her data 'okay?' hardly ever occurred in requests. She argues that this is because of the tendency for 'okay?' not to occur in low risk situations where compliance is anticipated. This may also explain the low frequency of 'okay?' in the present data. Since most of the situations here are play situations, it is generally understood by all the parties that they are expected to comply with each other's requests. There are of course also times when they do not. These two factors taken together seem to explain why Yao used of 'okay?' infrequently.

(g) Subjectivisers

'Subjectivisers', which add the speaker's personal opinion to the request were very rare (Example 53). This is consistent with the literature. 'Subjectivisers' were observed very infrequently with adults in other studies (e.g. Faerch & Kasper, 1989; Trosborg, 1995). Some did not even find a need for the category (e.g. Sifianou, 1992). This type of modification does not seem to occur generally in requests.

53   Y: *I think we should make it a bit more lighter* [H67-54]
          (Hannah and Yao are making things out of clay. They are mixing several colours to make the desired shade.)
     H: *okay then*

(h) Paraphrase

'Paraphrase', which is a type of *reiterations*, was not frequently observed, although it appeared in every phase (Example 54). In her study of fifth grade American children, Cook-Gumperz (1977) also reports that paraphrasing is very rare.

54   *oh hang on/ wait a sec* [PL69-18]
     (Yao and her peer are making things out of 'Oodles'. Both of them need 'eyes'. Yao wants her peer to wait until she finishes counting all the eyes.)

(i)   Elaboration

Contrary to 'paraphrase', 'elaboration', which is another type of *reitera-tion* was reasonably robust in Phase IV. Of the three types of *reiterations* used from Phrase I through III, 'repetition' is the most frequent. However, in Phase IV 'elaboration' was observed much more frequently than the other two types. One of the functions of *reiterations* is to give sufficient information to allow the addressee to understand what the speaker wants. 'Paraphrase' (Example 54) and 'repetition' (Example 55) are, however, somewhat different from 'elaboration'. The first two give essentially redundant information (Examples 54 and 55), while the last gives more specific, detailed, additional information (Examples 56 and 57). The increase of 'elaboration' in Phase IV reflects Yao's attempts at specificity and clarity. She may also have discovered that 'more detail is better communication' (Cook-Gumperz, 1977: 117).

55   *can I have space?/ can I have space* [PB12-1]
      (Yao and her peer are working on jigsaw puzzles on a table where
      there are some snacks. Since there is hardly any space to work, she
      addresses this utterance to her mother.)

56   *um could you please help me?/ um could you please do the bottom?* [J68-3]
      (Janice and Yao are painting on fabric. It is not an easy task. Yao
      wants Janice to paint the bottom part of the fabric.)

57   **Y:**   *oh just give me another story*
             (Hannah has started to tell a story that Yao did not want to hear.)

      H: *just give me another story*
             (Hannah repeats what Yao has said while trying to think of a
             story.)

      Y: *there's a famous story like three little pigs and uh ....* [H55-62]

(j)   Option givers

'Option givers' (Example 58) did not appear until Phase III and their number was small. Through 'option givers', a speaker expresses explicitly that carrying out a request is left to the addressee's own volition. Leaving the decision to the addressee and not being able to be in control may be psychologically difficult for a child and thus contribute to the small number. Wide use of this type of modification is probably a late accomplishment.

58   *maybe you could make that if you want to* [PL69-11]
      (Yao and her peer are making things out of 'Oodles'. Yao points to an
      example on the Oodles sheet and wants her peer to make it.)

(k) Preparators

Support moves (i.e. reasons, option givers and preparators) involve a 'conscious planning decision on the part of the speaker' (Faerch & Kasper, 1989: 244). 'Preparators' require this more than the others. They are calculated. In the recorded data, only a few preparators were observed, mostly in Phase IV. However, there were significantly more in the diary data for Phase IV, as seen in Examples 25 and 26 in Section 8.1.3. The situations where preparators appeared in the diary data most frequently were when Yao's mother was occupied with studying in her room and Yao was in the living room or in her own room. So, before she addressed her mother, she had already primed herself for the making of a request. On the other hand, in a play situation, which was the case in the present data, this sort of planning does not happen.

The context of the play situation is an immediate one, where the speaker and the interlocutor are engaged in quick conversational exchanges. The reason 'preparators' were limited in the present data is not that Yao was not able to produce them, but that the context did not allow for their occurrence. From this observation it is worth noting that request behaviour is bound to a temporal context, and that the present study is concerned with a specific kind of temporal context, that is, immediate need satisfaction. In addition to this situational constraint, Yao's use of 'preparators' with her mother, which appeared in the diary data, may have been motivated by her desire to appear competent as a speaker of English.

8.3.2 Choice of request strategy and use of modifiers

This section is concerned with the relationship between request strategies and the use of modifiers.

8.3.2.1 Main request strategies and the use of modifiers

Table 8.6 shows the distribution of requests with and without modification in relation to the main strategies.

Table 8.6 Distribution of requests with and without modifiers in relation to main strategies

	Strategy			
	Direct	*Conventional*	*Non-conventional*	*Total*
Request	*n* *%*	*n* *%*	*n* *%*	*n* *%*
Without modifiers	596 64.9	327 71.4	29 78.4	952 67.4
With modifiers	322 35.1	131 28.6	8 21.6	461 32.6
Total no. of requests	918 100.0	458 100.0	37 100.0	1413 100.0

One third of the requests are modified and two thirds not. Of those modified, direct requests are more frequent than conventionally indirect or nonconventionally indirect requests. It seems reasonable that a greater proportion of direct requests than indirect requests are modified. If a request is direct, it is more likely to face confrontation and therefore has a greater need to mitigate the impositive force. On the other hand, conventionally indirect requests have a degree of built-in mitigation.

As pointed out above, there were in the data many more requests without than with modification. Two factors may have contributed to this. First, this may be the consequence of Yao's socialisation and experience. Even though these experiences were brief, they gave her a sense of the likelihood that requests were going to be successful, and if she guessed that one was not going to be, she would then add some form of modification to try to increase the chances of success. Secondly, in her play situations, the purposes were largely cooperative, and therefore, in general, she did not need to supply a large number of modifiers to make her requests acceptable. It is likely that certain situations within her play settings were more challenging, and in such situations she sensed the need to modify her requests.

Table 8.7 shows the relationships between the main request strategy types and their modifiers. In this table we will look only at those modifiers that represent greater than 8% of either direct strategies or conventionally indirect strategies out of the total number of requests of each strategy type. We have adopted this rather arbitrary criterion because it allows for the identification of those things that are sufficiently frequent to be noticed as substantial elements.

The relationship between the type of request strategy type and the occurrence of modifiers is not arbitrary. Although nearly everything appears to be potentially available as a modifier for both direct and conventionally indirect strategies, certain kinds of modifiers appear to cluster with certain type of strategies.

'Please' collocated substantially more frequently with the conventionally indirect strategy than with the direct strategy. However, a nonconventionally indirect strategy does not accept 'please' (House, 1989). This may be because the use of 'please' is a conventionalised behaviour. Gibbs (1981: 438) suggests that the addition of 'please' makes the conventionally indirect requests (i.e. *query preparatory*) more conventional. The addition of 'please' also makes the intention as a request explicit. Blum-Kulka's (1985) study offers reasons for this. She asked native speakers of English and native speakers of Hebrew to evaluate conventionally indirect requests (i.e. *query preparatory*) with and without 'please' to see how they perceive

Table 8.7 Distribution of modifiers in relation to requests using different main strategies

Modifier	Direct		Conventional		Non-conventional		Total	
	n	*%*	*n*	*%*	*n*	*%*	*n*	*%*
Nil	596	64.9	327	71.4	29	78.4	952	67.4
Please	31	3.4	45	9.8	0	0.0	76	5.4
Appealer	25	2.7	3	0.7	1	2.7	29	2.1
Toner	87	9.5	26	5.7	1	2.7	114	8.1
Attention getter	37	4.0	13	2.8	3	8.1	53	3.8
Subjectiviser	5	0.5	0	0.0	0	0.0	5	0.4
Repetition	81	8.8	6	1.3	0	0.0	87	6.2
Paraphrase	18	2.0	4	0.9	0	0.0	22	1.6
Elaboration	52	5.7	14	3.1	2	5.4	68	4.8
Preparator	3	0.3	3	0.7	0	0.0	6	0.4
Option giver	4	0.4	7	1.5	0	0.0	11	0.8
Reason	54	5.9	39	8.5	2	5.4	95	6.7
Other	0	0.0	1	0.2	0	0.0	1	0.1

(The table is based on multiple modifiers per request. Percentages are calculated in relation to the total number of requests for each strategy. Therefore, as requests can have more than one modifier, the total percentage for modifiers may be greater than 100%.)

them. Both groups of native speakers interpreted the utterances without 'please' as either questions and requests. The utterances with 'please', however, were perceived as requests only, thereby ruling out any literal meaning of the utterance. Therefore, '"please" used with conventional indirectness is a clear illocutionary force indicator, while simultaneously serving as a marker of politeness' (1985: 222). Because of the ambiguity inherent in conventionally indirect strategies, without 'please' the utterance in Example 59 could be interpreted as either a question and a request. Yao's use of 'please' with conventionally indirect strategies has probably to do the high conventionality of the strategy, as well as its possible interpretation as only a request.

59 *can you rub this out please mum?*
     (Yao and Hannah are making collages. Yao has written letters on some cardboard but does not like them. When she tries to erase them, she cannot because she has pressed too heavily.)

'Toners' were substantial modifiers with direct strategies but also collocated substantially with conventionally indirect strategies. 'Reasons' co-occurred both with direct and conventionally indirect strategies but appeared more frequently with the latter. 'Repetitions', on the other hand, were predominantly associated with direct strategies. Many of the utterances modified by 'repetitions' in the present data expressed a state of urgency (Example 60), Yao's desire to stop her addressee's action forcefully (Example 61), or even her criticism of her interlocutor's behaviour (Example 62). As Labov and Fanshel (1977: 214) have pointed out, 'if a request is repeated in exactly the same words, the action is normally heard as a sharp criticism'. It is very likely that modifiers with these attributes will cluster around direct strategies.

60   *tub quick!/ quick* [H48-53-2]
      (Hannah and Yao are decorating Easter eggs. One of the eggs is leaking. She wants Hannah to bring a tub.)

61   ***don't*** push it/ *don't push it* [PB-12-18]
      (Yao and her peer are working on jigsaw puzzles. The peer tries to put the wrong pieces together.)

62   *don't be silly/ don't be silly* [H38-34]
      (Hannah and Yao are playing with toy animals. Hannah does not show much interest and is acting silly.)

There are two patterns of employment that emerge from the above. One is that most modifiers appear to be used across two main strategy types, the direct and conventionally indirect strategies. 'Toners' and 'reasons' appear more frequently with these strategies than do other modifiers. The other is that a modifier is used with a particular strategy: 'Please' works with conventionally indirect strategies and 'repetition' works with direct strategies.

8.3.2.2 Substrategies and the use of modifiers

The three main strategies in the previous section are now broken down into seven strategies to see if there are further clustering effects with the modifiers: 'please', 'toners', 'repetitions' and 'reasons'.

Table 8.8 shows the distribution of requests with and without modification in relation to substrategies, where *mood derivable* was the most frequently modified, followed by *query preparatory*.

Table 8.9 shows the relationship between the substrategies and their modifiers. It shows further clustering. Again there is a continuation of the same pattern found in the previous section: Certain kinds of modifiers clustered with specific strategies.

Table 8.8 Distribution of requests with and without modifiers in relation to strategy

Request	Strategy							
	Direct			Conventionally indirect			Nonconventionally indirect	Total
	Mood derivable	Obligation statements	Want statements	Suggestory formulae	Stating preparatory	Query preparatory	Hints	
	n / %	n / %	n / %	n / %	n / %	n / %	n / %	n / %
Without modifiers	482 / 63.3	55 / 67.1	59 / 78.7	110 / 84.6	65 / 67.7	152 / 65.5	29 / 78.4	952 / 67.4
With modifiers	279 / 36.7	27 / 32.9	16 / 21.3	20 / 15.4	31 / 32.3	80 / 34.5	8 / 21.6	461 / 32.6
Total no. of requests	761 / 100.0	82 / 100.0	75 / 100.0	130 / 100.0	96 / 100.0	232 / 100.0	37 / 100.0	1413 / 100.0

Table 8.9 Distribution of modifiers in relation to requests using different strategies

Modifier	Strategy							
	Direct			Conventionally indirect			Nonconventionally indirect	Total
	Mood derivable	Obligation statements	Want statements	Suggestory formulae	Stating preparatory	Query preparatory	Hints	
	n / %	n / %	n / %	n / %	n / %	n / %	n / %	n / %
Nil	482 / 63.3	55 / 67.1	59 / 78.7	110 / 84.6	65 / 67.7	152 / 65.5	29 / 78.4	952 / 67.4
Please	29 / 3.8	0 / 0.0	2 / 2.7	0 / 0.0	0 / 0.0	45 / 19.4	0 / 0.0	76 / 5.4
Appealer	19 / 2.5	5 / 6.1	1 / 1.3	1 / 0.8	2 / 2.1	0 / 0.0	1 / 2.7	29 / 2.1
Toner	79 / 10.4	5 / 6.1	3 / 4.0	1 / 0.8	14 / 14.6	11 / 4.7	1 / 2.7	114 / 8.1
Attention getter	31 / 4.1	2 / 2.4	4 / 5.3	5 / 3.8	1 / 1.0	7 / 3.0	3 / 8.1	53 / 3.8
Subjectiviser	0 / 0.0	3 / 3.7	2 / 2.7	0 / 0.0	0 / 0.0	0 / 0.0	0 / 0.0	5 / 0.4
Repetition	80 / 10.5	0 / 0.0	1 / 1.3	1 / 0.8	1 / 1.0	4 / 1.7	0 / 0.0	87 / 6.2
Paraphrase	17 / 2.2	0 / 0.0	1 / 1.3	2 / 1.5	0 / 0.0	2 / 0.9	0 / 0.0	22 / 1.6
Elaboration	41 / 5.4	8 / 9.8	3 / 4.0	4 / 3.1	2 / 2.1	8 / 3.4	2 / 5.4	68 / 4.8
Preparator	3 / 0.4	0 / 0.0	0 / 0.0	0 / 0.0	3 / 3.1	0 / 0.0	0 / 0.0	6 / 0.4
Option giver	3 / 0.4	1 / 1.2	0 / 0.0	0 / 0.0	6 / 6.3	1 / 0.4	0 / 0.0	11 / 0.8
Reason	48 / 6.3	5 / 6.1	1 / 1.3	7 / 5.4	10 / 10.4	22 / 9.5	2 / 5.4	95 / 6.7
Other	0 / 0.0	0 / 0.0	0 / 0.0	0 / 0.0	0 / 0.0	1 / 0.4	0 / 0.0	1 / 0.1

(The table is based on multiple modifiers per request. Percentages are calculated in relation to the total number of requests for each strategy. Therefore, as requests can have more than one modifier, total percentages for modifiers may add up to greater than 100%.)

'Please' collocated with *query preparatory* (19.4%). The majority of Yao's requests made with 'could . . .?'[6] clustered with 'please': 84% with 'could you ...?' and 60% with 'could I (we) ...?' (see Appendix 8.2).

This suggests there may well be some kind of formulaic triggering that makes these already conventional forms more conventional when modified by 'please'. The form 'could you (I, we) ...?' appeared in Phases III and IV but not earlier (see Appendix 4.4) and provided a particularly important context for 'please'. As Yao became better able to use this highly conventionalised form, she seemed to have become more fully aware of high conventionality of forms with 'please'.

While 'toners' appeared with *mood derivable* substantially (10.4%) within direct strategies, a very clear clustering was seen within conventionally indirect strategies, where 'toners' were used with *stating preparatory* (14.6 % of both 'you (we) can ...' and 'you (we) could ...' together). It is worth noting that the 'toner' used for 'you (we) could ...' was exclusively 'maybe'. The form, 'you (we) could ...' first appeared in Phase IV (see Appendix 4.4) and this form attracted the modifier, 'maybe', the majority of which also occurred in Phase IV (see Table 8.4). The pattern, 'you could' + 'maybe' is thus a later development.

'Repetitions' occurred characteristically with the most direct strategy type, *mood derivable* (10.5%) and rarely appeared with other types. As reported in the previous section (8.3.2.1), many of the requests modified by 'repetitions' conveyed a state of urgency, an urge to stop an addressee's action, or even to criticise it. Hence, modifiers with these attributes tend to collocate with *mood derivable*, most frequently with imperatives and contextually elliptical imperatives (see Appendix 8.2).

'Reasons' appeared in conventionally indirect strategies as well as direct strategies, but they were the more viable option in conventionally indirect strategies: they clustered with *stating preparatory* (10.4%) and *query preparatory* (9.5%) and within these strategies they spread across different forms without being associated with any particular one (see Appendix 8.2).

8.3.3 Request goals and the use of modifiers

Table 8.10 shows the distribution of requests with and without modification in relation to request goals.

All the types of request goals except requests for joint activity had a modification rate of over 30% of the total number of the requests for each goal. Out of those, requests for cessation of action were most frequently modified (37.7%). This may suggest that stopping the action of the addressee is not an easy task and that it is therefore necessary to modify these requests more frequently than others. Requests for joint activity, on the other hand, were the least modified (15.5%). This may be the consequence of the types of forms used for this goal. Requests for joint activity are most frequently realised by the use of *suggestory formulae* such as, 'let's ...', 'shall we ...?' or a type of *query preparatory* such as 'do you want to ...?' (see Chapter 6). These forms are not usually associated with modifiers.

Table 8.10 Distribution of requests with and without modifiers in relation to goal

| | Goal | | | | | | | | | |
| | Goods | | Initiation of action | | Cessation of action | | Joint activity | | Total | |
Request	n	%	n	%	n	%	n	%	n	%
Without modifiers	80	65.0	571	66.9	192	62.3	109	84.5	952	67.4
With modifiers	43	35.0	282	33.1	116	37.7	20	15.5	461	32.6
Total no. of requests	123	100.0	853	100.0	308	100.0	129	100.0	1413	100.0

Table 8.11 Distribution of modifiers in relation to requests for different goals

| | Goal | | | | | | | | | |
| | Goods | | Initiation of action | | Cessation of action | | Joint activity | | Total | |
Modifier	n	%	n	%	n	%	n	%	n	%
Nil	80	65.0	571	66.9	192	62.3	109	84.5	952	67.4
Please	24	19.5	40	4.7	11	3.6	1	0.8	76	5.4
Appealer	2	1.6	17	2.0	8	2.6	2	1.6	29	2.1
Toner	12	9.8	90	10.6	9	2.9	3	2.3	114	8.1
Attention getter	6	4.9	38	4.5	4	1.3	5	3.9	53	3.8
Subjectiviser	0	0.0	5	0.6	0	0.0	0	0.0	5	0.4
Repetition	0	0.0	53	6.2	34	11.0	0	0.0	87	6.2
Paraphrase	0	0.0	11	1.3	11	3.6	0	0.0	22	1.6
Elaboration	5	4.1	41	4.8	18	5.8	4	3.1	68	4.8
Preparator	0	0.0	6	0.7	0	0.0	0	0.0	6	0.4
Option giver	0	0.0	10	1.2	0	0.0	1	0.8	11	0.8
Reason	11	8.9	39	4.6	40	13.0	5	3.9	95	6.7
Other	0	0.0	0	0.0	1	0.3	0	0.0	1	0.1

(The table is based on multiple modifiers per request. Percentages are calculated in relation to the total number of requests for each goal. Therefore, as requests can have more than one modifier, total percentages for modifiers may add up to greater than 100%.)

Table 8.11 shows the relationship between request goals and the use of modifiers. We will look only at modifiers that represent greater than 8% of any goal out of the total number of requests for each type of goal. We have again adopted this rather arbitrary criterion to be better able to identify those things which are sufficiently frequent to be considered as substantial elements.

'Please' occurred predominantly with requests for goods (19.5%). 'Toners' clustered with both requests for the initiation of action (10.6%), and requests for goods (9.8%). 'Repetitions' mainly modified requests for the cessation of action (11.0%). 'Reasons' collocated with requests for the cessation of action (13.0%) and also occurred fairly frequently with requests for goods (8.9%).

As we have seen, 'please' is a very conventional behaviour. 'Toners' are likely to be used to mitigate the impact of requests rather than to reinforce or aggravate them. Therefore, they were rarely used with requests for the cessation of action, but more frequently with requests for the initiation of action and requests for goods. On the other hand, with requests for the cessation of action, which require more persuasiveness and forcefulness to obtain compliance, 'reasons' and 'repetitions' were used.

The previous section indicated that there were some groupings between certain strategy types and certain modifiers. In this section we have demonstrated that certain request goals and modifiers are strongly inter-related. These results suggest that there are some combinatory patterns between the use of modifiers, strategy types and request goals. Those dominant patterns are summarised in Table 8.12, where the modifiers make up at least 8% of the modification in at least one strategy type and in one type of goal. 'Please' and 'repetition' each most frequently modify only one strategy and are predominantly used for only one goal. 'Toners' and 'reasons', on the other hand, are available for the modification of a wider range of strategies, including *stating preparatory*, as well as for a wider range of goals.

The frequency of *stating preparatory* is never high for any request goal (see Table 6.3, Chapter 6). Yet, in spite of the low frequency of those *stating preparatory* as a whole, 'toners' and 'reasons' are most commonly associated with *stating preparatory*. One reason for this may be that since *stating preparatory*, as well as *query preparatory*, is less impositive than other strategy types, it requires further modification to assert the requestive force. Another is that the inclusion of a modifier probably makes *stating preparatory* sound more like a request, as in Example 63.

Table 8.12 Summary of findings: dominant patterns

Modifiers	Strategies	Request goals
please	query preparatory	goods
toners	stating preparatory mood derivable	initiation of action goods
repetitions	mood derivable	cessation of action
reasons	stating preparatory query preparatory mood derivable	cessation of action goods

63   *you can just rub that out/ just over there/ so it gets colourful*
     (Hannah and Yao are drawing a donkey for 'Pin the Tail on the
     Donkey'. Yao wants a saddle on the donkey, and wants Hannah to
     colour it green and orange.)

Example 63 has three modifiers: The first 'just' is a toner, 'just over
there' is an elaboration, and 'so it gets colourful' is a reason. The second
'just' is not a toner but is used to emphasise the exact place to rub out. If
you say this example without modification ('you can rub that out'), it
may be perceived more like a statement of information. *Stating preparatory* and modifiers together perhaps reduce the informational character
of an utterance and give it a greater requestive force. In that sense, Yao
was beginning to grasp the way statements are overtly marked as requests.

8.3.4 Addressees and the use of modifiers

Table 8.13 shows the distribution of requests with and without modification in relation to addressee.

Yao's mother received a greater frequency of requests with modification than did any other addressee. This might be explained in terms of
context – of play situations vs. non-play situations. In a play world, the
power relationships of addressees are less clear. In a sense, the power
relationships, which normally exist elsewhere, may be temporarily
suspended or weakened. Peers, the teenager and the adult were actively
involved in the play. In contrast, Yao's mother was never fully involved
in the play, but in the usual relationship between mother and child. In
addition, as noted in Chapter 7 (on Addressees), Yao was aware of what
her mother was doing and seemed to show sensitivity to disrupting her
on-going activity.

Table 8.13 Distribution of requests with and without modifiers in relation to addressee

	Addressee									
	Peer		Teenager		Adult		Mother		Total	
Request	n	%	n	%	n	%	n	%	n	%
Without modifiers	222	64.0	225	69.7	149	71.6	56	56.0	652	66.7
With modifiers	125	36.0	98	30.3	59	28.4	44	44.0	326	33.3
Total no. of requests	347	100.0	323	100.0	208	100.0	100	100.0	978	100.0

Table 8.14 Distribution of modifiers in relation to requests with different addresses

	Addressee									
	Peer		Teenager		Adult		Mother		Total	
Modifier	n	%	n	%	n	%	n	%	n	%
Nil	222	64.0	225	69.7	149	71.6	56	56.0	652	66.7
Please	13	3.7	14	4.3	13	6.3	19	19.0	59	6.0
Appealer	12	3.5	5	1.5	2	1.0	3	3.0	22	2.2
Toner	42	12.1	34	10.5	15	7.2	9	9.0	100	10.2
Attention getter	10	2.9	4	1.2	1	0.5	9	9.0	24	2.5
Subjectiviser	1	0.3	1	0.3	3	1.4	0	0.0	5	0.5
Repetition	22	6.3	17	5.3	5	2.4	4	4.0	48	4.9
Paraphrase	8	2.3	5	1.5	1	0.5	2	2.0	16	1.6
Elaboration	16	4.6	16	5.0	10	4.8	7	7.0	49	5.0
Preparator	3	0.9	2	0.6	1	0.5	0	0.0	6	0.6
Option giver	6	1.7	1	0.3	1	0.5	0	0.0	8	0.8
Reason	27	7.8	22	6.8	13	6.3	17	17.0	79	8.1
Other	1	0.3	0	0.0	0	0.0	0	0.0	1	0.1

(The table is based on multiple modifiers per request. Percentages are calculated in relation to the total number of requests for each addressee. Therefore, as requests can have more than one modifier, total percentages for modifiers may add up to greater than 100%.)

One additional fact shown by Table 8.13 is that out of the three addressees except for her mother, peers received the most frequently modified requests, followed by the teenager, and then the adult. This may be because of the consequence of peers being far less likely to comply and therefore required more modifiers. Conversely, the adult clearly understands her role in play situations and also the dual capacity she has as a play partner and a sort of caretaker. Therefore, the adult is more likely to comply without many modifiers. The teenager to a degree understands those roles, but less so than the adult.

Table 8.14 shows the relationship between the addressees and the use of modifiers. The frequency of the use of different modifiers was not found to vary systematically across peers, the teenager, and the adult. However, it did vary substantially between those addressees and Yao's mother. Her mother received more specific kinds of modifiers than the other addressees did. The use of 'please' in requests to her mother stands out (19.0%). 'Please' occurred predominantly with requests for goods (see Table 8.11). Yao directed requests for goods more to her mother than to any other addressee. (see Appendix 8.3). This explains her more frequent use of 'please' with her mother than with the other addressees (Example 64).

64   *could you please pass me that bowl?* [H62-28]
      (To Yao's mother, while Yao and Hannah are making muffins.)

'Reasons' were widely employed across different addressees but were addressed most to her mother and next most frequently to peers. Of all the requests addressed to the mother, 17.0% had 'reasons', as did 7.8% of those addressed to peers (Example 65). These results are related to those for goals in the previous section, which showed 'reasons' were attached more to requests for the cessation of action and requests for goods than to other goals (see Table 8.11). Among the four categories of addressee, peers and the mother received the highest frequency of requests for the cessation of action and requests for goods respectively (see Appendix 8.3). Therefore, it would appear to follow that 'reasons' should be frequently directed to her mother and the peers.

65   *here/ don't eat too much because you might get tummy ache* [PJ63-16]
      (Yao and her peer are making muffins. Yao offers some dough for her to lick.)

'Elaborations' were used more frequently by Yao with her mother than with others. Again this is probably because her mother was usually outside the play situations and therefore Yao had to supply additional information in order to clarify what she wanted her mother to do. For instance, in Example 66, when Yao asked her mother for a lid the first time, her mother thought she wanted a saucepan lid. In the course of several turns with stimulus (i.e. a response) from the mother, Yao made clear exactly what she needed. Her mother had earlier let Linda, a peer, use the lid of a bottle for the thing she was making.

66   **Y:**   *mum have you got a lid?* [PL69-38]
      (Yao and her peer are making things out of various materials. Yao wants a lid.)

M: *yes but I'm going to use it at supper time*

Y: *no just a lid thing/ any lid*

M: *anything?*

Y: *oh you know the ones that you let Linda use/ maybe that please*

Yao used a higher frequency of 'attention getters' with her mother than with other addressees. This may be evidence that her mother was outside the play situation and so Yao felt the need to alert her mother to the ensuing request.

'Toners' occurred reasonably consistently with all the addressees but most frequently with peers. 'Toners' clustered with *mood derivables* as well as *stating preparatory* (see Table 8.9). *Mood derivables* and *stating preparatory* were more frequently directed to peers than to others (see Table 7.2 in Chapter 7 for details). 'Toners' were probably needed more with peers (Example 67) because they were far less likely to comply. Therefore, they received more *mood derivables* and *stating preparatory* with 'toners'.

67   **Y:**   *okay just pretend you didn't listen* [PE40-54]
           (Yao and her peer are playing a game in which Yao is
           supposed to play the piano perfectly. Yao plays the piano, but
           makes a mistake.)

     PE: *okay*

'Repetitions', in a sense, are a relatively blunt form of modification. They collocate with requests for the cessation of action (see Table 8.11). Peers show the highest frequency among the four addressees for requests for the cessation of action (see Appendix 8.3). As Example 68 shows, the direct impositive force of 'repetitions' does not conflict with the equal power relationship between Yao and her peers. This makes 'repetitions' a more viable modification for use with peers.

68   *wait a minute/ wait a minute/ not yet* [PE40-37-1]
     (A peer tries to start a game before Yao is ready.)

8.3.5 Mitigators, reinforcers and aggravators

So far we have looked at the types of modification available to Yao across phases, their occurrence in different strategies, with different forms, for different goals, and with different addressees. In this section, following the definition given earlier (see Section 8.0), we will examine whether or not those modifiers mitigate, reinforce, or aggravate the degree of the coerciveness the requests are likely to have on the addressee.

Modifiers are multifunctional in their sociopragmatic functions, in that they can serve to mitigate, reinforce, or aggravate a request. In spoken language, whether a certain modifier acts as a *mitigator*, a *reinforcer*, or an *aggravator* depends as much on how it is said, especially tone of voice, as on the grammatical or lexical choices made in constructing the utterance. Example 69 illustrates this point. The situation is that Hannah and Yao are making an animal zoo out of various materials. Hannah is using blu-tack for the zoo she is making. Yao wants some for the animal she is working on. But her request is ignored. So her tactic is now to add mitigation by the use of 'toners' (i.e. 'only' and 'this much'). She utters the request in a soft voice. Had she said it with angry voice, these modifiers would have served as *aggravators*.

69   *I need to put blu-tack on the bottom as well* [H73-35-1]
      (Yao asks Hannah for some blu-tack.)

      would you please hold this like this? [H73-35-2] / *thank you/ oopsy*
      (Yao asks her mother to hold the animal she is making, so she can use both hands to put something on the animal's head.)

      I only need this much/... thank you [H73-35-3]
      (Yao asks Hannah a second time for some blu-tack. Hannah gives it to her.)

Although modifiers are in principle multifunctional, it seems that with requests they serve predominantly as either *mitigators* or *reinforcers*, as seen in Table 8.15. In English, as a general rule, the use of *aggravators*, including 'threats', seems to be rare in combination with requests, while the use of softeners is frequent (Sifianou, 1992). This is also the case with the present data. About two thirds of the modifiers serve as *mitigators*, while nearly one third function as *reinforcers*. Only a few instances of *aggravators* are observed in the data, including only one instance of a threat (see Example 30).

Lexical/phrasal modifiers (of which 'toners' were the most frequent, as in Example 69) and *support moves* tend to decrease the impositive force, and since the former are shorter and more routinised than *support moves* (see Section 8.3.1.2 for detail), they appear to be easier devices to mitigate the impact of the request. Amongst *support moves*, 'reasons' were the preferred mitigating strategy (Example 29). 'Reasons and justifications that assume cooperation and lead the hearer to see the reasonableness of the act' (Blum-Kulka, 1990: 271) serve to reduce the threat to the addressee's face. Hence, as we have observed earlier, giving reasons is 'an efficient mitigating strategy' (Faerch & Kasper, 1989: 239).

Table 8.15 Distribution of *mitigators, reinforcers* and *aggravators* in the use of modifiers

Modifiers	Mitigators n	Reinforcers n	Aggravators n	Total n
Lexical/phrasal modifiers				
Please	72	4	0	76
Appealer	29	0	0	29
Toner	109	0	5	114
Attention getter	51	0	2	53
Subjectiviser	5	0	0	5
Reiterations				
Repetition	0	82	5	87
Paraphrase	0	20	2	22
Elaboration	0	65	3	68
Support moves				
Preparator	6	0	0	6
Option giver	11	0	0	11
Reason	94	0	1	95
Other	0	0	1	1
Total	377	171	19	567

Reiterations, on the other hand, do not mitigate the impact of a request but most frequently serve to reinforce a request without adding to the degree of intensification or aggravation. In *reiterations,* a feeling of urging in the speaker is expressed. Therefore, *reiterations* may have a stronger effect on the addressee than an unreiterated utterance. Out of the three types of *reiterations,* the feeling seems to be strongest in 'repetitions' (Example 18). Next comes 'paraphrase' (Example 20), and the feeling of urging is the least strong in 'elaboration' (Example 22).

While the above seems to suggest that an utterance, taken as a whole, is either mitigating, reinforcing, or aggravating, in fact, there are some examples where two conflicting elements (i.e. mitigation and aggravation) are contained in the same utterance, as in Example 70. Overall, the impositive force of an utterance depends on a balance between the different elements. However, in the present study what has been analysed is the mitigating, reinforcing, or aggravating nature of the modifiers in a context, but not as an utterance as a whole. The interest has not been the whole effect of the utterance but the different kinds of modifiers used. Example 70 has three different kinds of modifiers: a 'toner' (just); a 'repetition' (**don't don't**); and 'please'. The request started with mitigation, but the emphatic repetition added aggravation. Yao obviously thought she had made her request too aggravatedly and that it needed to be mitigated with the element 'please'.

70   *just don't **don't don't** do it any more please* [PC75-21]
     (Yao and her peer have finished making things out of plasticine
     and are now collecting half-used colours. The peer has mixed
     different colours though Yao had asked her not to. The peer,
     however, is going to mix the colours again.)

Let us now look more closely at 'please', since it seems to show how Yao came to expand her pragmatic awareness and competence

Yao used 'please' in several different ways: as a politeness marker, a request marker possessing an element of politeness, and a plea. The use of 'please' as a request marker was included in the category *mitigator*, since it softens the requestive force. On those few occasions when Yao produced 'please' as a way of pleading,[7] her initial request had been rejected and she was attempting to obtain compliance from her addressee. This type of 'please' reflects a greater engagement with the interlocutor, and shows that Yao was applying pressure on the interlocutor. Hence, 'please' as pleading is included in the category of *reinforcer* here. Yao uttered this type of 'please' in a whining tone, as in Example 71. In this example Yao and Hannah were playing school. Hannah was the teacher and Yao the student. Yao wanted to sing a song with Hannah, but Hannah did not want to. After several turns Hannah complied with Yao's request. Gleason *et al.* (1984: 498) call this a 'directive pleading routine'. According to them the use of 'please' as a form of pleading is a device that children resort to when they have to deal with reluctant adults.

71 **Y:** *Miss*
    H: *yes*
    Y: *I want to sing uh Red Nose Rudolf* [H32-64]
    H: *Rudolf Red Nose Reindeer/ have you got the music?/ do you know it?/*
            (Yao nods.)
            okay one two three four

Y: *Rudolf ... you have to sing too* [H32-65-1]
         (Yao does not look satisfied.)

H: *teachers don't sing/ the students sing*

Y: *please* [H32-65-2]
         (In a whining tone.)

H: *no no you can sing it*

Y: *please*
         (In a whining tone.)

H: *I'll put in the extra words*

Y: *um*
         (Yao still wants Hannah to sing with her.)

H: *okay*
         (Hannah gives in. Both sing.)

The use of 'please' as a *mitigator* is conventional behaviour. As Becker (1988) and Snow *et al.* (1990) have demonstrated, English speaking parents, in socialising their children, train them in politeness formulae such as 'please' and 'thank you'. They prompt their children to say the words, by using phases such as 'say please' or more indirectly by phrases such as 'what do you say?', when a child violates Manner, one of Grice's (1975) four maxims. By insisting on 'please', parents help children to gain pragmatic awareness (Gleason *et al.*, 1984). From the unstructured observation of the conversations between Yao's peers and their mothers, the children were often prompted by their parents to say 'please' in making requests. Yao did not receive this kind of sociolinguistic training in English from her mother. However, there was an instance in the data in which Yao was prompted to say 'please' by Hannah when she expressed her intention in a blunt statement (Example 72). The situation is one in which Yao and Hannah are making things.

72 **Y:**   *I need the blu-tack*
             (There is a blu-tack beside Hannah.)

    H: *please*
             (Hannah prompting Yao.)

    Y: *please* [H73-18]

    H: (giggles)
             (Hannah passes the blu-tack to Yao.)

Apart from the above instance there were few examples in which Yao was explicitly socialised to be polite, but she must have often observed her friends' parents or her teachers prompting the behaviour. In fact, Yao commented that at her friend Amy's birthday party, Amy's mother prompted another of Yao's friends, Ann, to say 'please' when she failed to do so. The comments suggest Yao's pragmatic awareness:

> Ann is sometimes rude to her friends and she is rude to adults, too. Amy's mother said, *'please?'*, when Ann just said *'Can I have that?'*, pointing to some food on the table. Then, Ann said, *'can I have that, please?'*. Finally, Amy's mother gave her what she wanted.
>
> [Diary, 16-10-93]
>
> (Utterances in italics were said in English as they were; the others in Japanese.)

Yao may have been given such coaching by her teachers at school or by her friends' mothers when she was at their houses playing. There is some evidence in the diary data that may support this (Examples 73 and 74). In both examples, Yao prompted her mother to utter politeness formulae (i.e. 'thank you', and 'please'), using the phrases 'what do you say?' and 'excuse me'. Although 'thank you' and 'yes please' are not under investigation in the present study, the fact that she knew the prompt–response sequence indicates that she had ample opportunity to observe the employment of the formulae, thus allowing her to gain pragmatic awareness and increase her pragmatic competence.

73 **M:** *Yao chan, booshi kaketeoite* (=can you hang up my hat for me, Yao)
(Yao's mother notices that her hat is on the floor and asks Yao in Japanese to hang it up.)

   Y: *what do you say?* [Diary, 24-12-92]
(Yao hangs it up, but realises that her mother has not thanked her.)

   M: *thank you*

   Y: *that's better*

74 **Y:** *would you like one?*
(Yao offers her mother a scone.)

   M: *yes*
(Her mother has not attached 'please' to 'yes'.)

   Y: *excuse me*↑ [Diary, 18-9-93]

   M: *please*

Although Yao's pragmatic competence increased in terms of modification, the developmental process was not complete, especially with respect to the appropriate use of modifications in context. The purpose of the analysis in this chapter is not to establish whether or not the overall utterance is ultimately perceived as mitigated, reinforced, or aggravated, but whether a certain modifier in an utterance serves as such an element. Nevertheless, we should examine briefly the extent to which Yao, in a given context, was able to use modification appropriately. Compare Example 75 with Example 76. Both examples appeared in the same transcript at the beginning of Phase IV and were uttered to her mother, though in different situations. In both examples, 'please' is used as a politeness maker. However, Example 75 is an appropriate utterance in context, while Examples 76 is not. The formulation, 'go to your room' is a disciplinary formula. Regardless of how much you modulate it, it carries that force. In fact, in this example, a conventionally indirect form is modified with a 'please', and even a 'reason' is attached. Yet, the overall utterance ends up being perceived as rude and very face-threatening. Certainly the roles of 'please' and 'reason' in this request are there to mitigate the request, but they are not sufficient to mitigate the utterance to an acceptable level. Appropriate utterances in the situation would be 'Mum would it be all right if we played here on our own?' or 'Mum do you think you could work in another room?' rather than Example 76. This may be a very difficult request to make even for children whose mother tongue is English.

75   *could you please help us mum?* [PJ63-3]
     (Yao and her peer are making Banana Muffins. It is not easy for
     them to mash the bananas. Yao wants her mother to help.)

76   *well we want to play here/ so could you please go to your room?*
     [PJ63-62-2]
     (Yao, her mother and her peer are in the living room. Yao wants to
     learn jazz dance from the peer who has been taking lessons. Yao
     does not want her mother to watch.)

8.4 Summary and Conclusion

In this chapter we have been concerned with a child's learning of request modification, focusing on *lexical/phrasal modifiers, reiterations,* and *support moves.*

First, the results show a steady developmental pattern, with Yao's use of 'toners', 'reasons' and 'please' increasing significantly, with a diminution of 'attention getters' and 'repetitions'. In addition, the use of 'please' increased consistently from phase to phase while changing its character.

Secondly, it was found that the relationship between the occurrence of modifiers and request strategy types was not arbitrary. Similarly, the relationship was systematic between the use of modifiers and request goals, suggesting that there are some combinatory patterns that relate the use of modifiers, strategy types, and request goals.

Thirdly, with respect to addressees, the frequency of requests with modification did not vary in any systematic way among peers, the teen-ager, and the adult. However, it was found to vary substantially between Yao's mother and the rest of the addressees. The greater frequency of requests with modification used with the mother may be the consequence of situational constraints, showing that request behaviour is bound to its temporal context.

Finally, although modifiers are in principle multifunctional, approximately two thirds of the modifiers served as *mitigators*, nearly one third as *reinforcers*, and only a few as *aggravators*. This supports the findings of Sifianou (1992), who points out that in English the use of mitigation is frequent and aggravation rare in requests. Yao may have been following the English norm.

The final chapter integrates what has been documented in the preceding chapters, summarises the findings, and presents the conclusions. It also discusses the questions arising from the conclusions and suggests some implications that can be drawn from the study.

Notes

1. In the general literature (e.g. Blum-Kulka *et al.*, 1989a; Blum-Kulka & Olshtain, 1984; Edmondson, 1981), this category is labelled as 'supportive moves' but for this classification the word 'support' has been chosen, instead, because it appears more neutral than the term 'supportive'.
2. Since this request is an information-seeking question, it is not dealt with in the present study. In another situation, Yao used 'excuse me' when she passed in front of someone. In this case this form was treated as a head act and a formulaic imperative, not as an attention getter.
3. There was no preparator of this type in the audio/video-recorded portion of the present data. But there were several in the diary data. The diary data is not used in the present study for quantification but only to provide clarification.
4. The subjects of all these studies are adults with different language backgrounds.
5. Liebling uses the terms 'explicit directives' and 'embedded directives' for direct and conventionally indirect requests respectively.
6. The majority of the requests made in 'could you …?' and 'could I (we) …?' had modifiers including 'please' (see Appendix 8.1). They were also the most frequently modified forms.
7. When 'please' was uttered repeatedly regardless of pleading, they were treated as a 'repetition' rather than a 'please'. As the results show both 'please' as pleading and as 'repetition' served as *reinforcers*.

Chapter 9
Summary and Conclusions

9.0 Introduction

In this study we have examined the acquisition of English requests by a Japanese girl over a period of 17 months, beginning at the age of seven years and two months. This period began with the onset of her second language learning experience during her residence in Australia. The principal purpose of the study was to determine what strategies and linguistic devices a second language learning child uses when making requests in English as a second language and what developmental path is followed. The data for this study were collected in Yao's home in Australia during her natural interaction with three types of interlocutor: a peer, a teenager, an adult neighbour; and with the mother, who conducted the research. Yao's interaction with each addressee was audio- and video- recorded. These recordings were supplemented by diary data. The coding scheme for the analysis of her request strategies used for this study was based on the CCSARP strategy types (Blum-Kulka *et al.*, 1989a) as modified to reflect more precisely the naturally occurring data gathered during the research.

The data was analysed not only to determine the strategies, the linguistic repertoire, and the modifications made, but also to see how these aspects varied in relation to goals and addressees. This examination of variation made it possible to discover certain developmental patterns in relation to goal and to unravel the complex process of acquisition of requests by a child learning a second language.

In this chapter, the findings from Chapters 4 through 8 are integrated and summarised and conclusions drawn. Then, the questions that arise from these conclusions are discussed. Finally, the implications and the major contribution of the study are presented.

9.1 A Child Second Language Learner's Request Realisation

As seen in Chapters 4 and 5, when we look at Yao's requests as a whole, the following picture emerges. Over the 17 months of data collection, her requests moved from initially formulaic and routinised forms to those progressively more differentiated. In the final phase, the expansion of her repertoire of indirect strategies is significant, especially in mitigated forms.

Consistent with the results for strategies or syntactic forms, modification also showed a steady developmental pattern, as seen in Chapter 8. In the initial phase, there was a high proportion of *reiterations*, which decreased by almost half in the final phase, while *lexical/phrasal modifiers* doubled and *support moves* more than tripled by the final phase. This means that Yao did not initially have many ways of modifying her requests other than by 'repetition' and some limited *lexical/phrasal modifiers*. Over the course of the observational period, she learned to use *support moves* much more frequently, a use which 'involves conscious planning decisions on the part of the speaker' (Faerch & Kasper, 1989: 244). The use of strategies that include a choice of syntactic form, and the use of modification indicate a growing ability to produce both cognitively and grammatically complex request forms. They also indicate an increased sophistication in Yao's capacity to adjust her requests in contexts where she might potentially impose upon an addressee or where there was a potential obstacle to her gaining compliance.

This, however, does not seem to present the full picture. As seen in Chapter 6, when we looked at the development of requests in relation to goal, we found that their patterns varied according to goal. Among requests for the cessation of action and for joint activity, there was little observable change in the main strategies used. In requests for the cessation of action, direct strategies were dominant from the beginning to the end of the data collection, while in requests for joint activity, conventionally indirect strategies were dominant throughout. However, requests for goods and for the initiation of action showed considerable change in the course of Yao's learning. With requests for goods, most of the requests in the initial phase were produced using direct strategies, whereas from Phase II onwards conventionally indirect strategies were dominant. For requests for the initiation of action, conventionally indirect strategies increased as direct strategies decreased and by the final phase there was little difference in the proportion of use of direct strategies and conventionally indirect strategies. Thus, there were quite different patterns of request realisation according to goal. Yao had developed different ways of handling requests with different goals.

In the following sections, we will consider more closely what has been outlined here. In Section 9.2, without taking into consideration any developmental sequence, we will look at strategies, perspectives, and modifications in relation to varying goals. In Section 9.3, the relationship between strategies and addressees are taken up. Some patterned relationships between addressees and modifications will then be summarised. Section 9.4 is concerned with the developmental sequence. In each phase, strategies, linguistic forms, and modifications are first looked at without considering the influence of goals. This is followed by the exploration of the development of strategies and linguistic forms in relation to goal.

9.2 Variation According to Goal

The following two sections summarise the findings for strategies, perspectives, and modification in relation to goal.

9.2.1 Strategies according to goal

As observed in Chapter 6, the analyses in the present study have revealed that goals strongly influence request strategies.

With regards to main strategies, for each goal, one level of directness dominated their use. For requests for the initiation of action and for the cessation of action, the direct strategy was the most frequent, while for requests for goods and for joint activity, conventionally indirect strategy dominated.

Yao's choice of substrategies also varied according to goal. The dominant substrategies for each goal were: with both requests for the initiation of action and for the cessation of action, *mood derivable*; with requests for goods, *query preparatory*; and with requests for joint activity, *suggestory formulae*. Thus, Yao varied her choice of request strategies in accordance with her goals. This suggests that requests for goods, for the initiation of action, for the cessation of action, and for joint activity emerge as distinct areas of learning behaviour.

Much of the literature conceives of requests as a single kind of act, especially the studies conducted in the framework of the CCSARP data, which show that the most frequently used main strategy type is a conventionally indirect strategy and substrategy type is *query preparatory*, such as 'can/could you (I) ...?' This is also in accord with the findings for role-playing data by House and Kasper (1981) and Trosborg (1995), which show a clear preference among adult native speakers of English for *preparatory strategies*.

However, as noted in Chapter 6, there are studies that report results consistent with the present study. For example, Blum-Kulka *et al.* (1985) and Blum-Kulka (1990) found that choice of request strategies varied according to goal. With requests for action, the direct mode was predominant, while with requests for goods, conventionally indirect forms were most frequently used. As we have seen, similar patterns of variation were found in the present data. There have been yet other studies that seem to support the findings of the present study, such as studies with children by Garvey (1975) and Trosborg (1985) (see Chapter 6). In neither study is there a direct mention of goals. However, a close look at their studies suggests that different request goals produce different results (i.e. direct strategies for requests for initiation of action and conventionally indirect strategies for requests for goods), and thus provide results parallel to those of the present study.

9.2.2 Perspectives and modification according to goal

In addition to the relationships between goals and strategies, it has been found that the perspectives (see Chapter 6) and the modifications of the requests (see Chapter 8) also vary according to goal.

The preferred choice of perspective for requests for goods was speaker oriented, which reflected the preponderance of *query preparatory* utterances such as 'can (could) I ...?'. On the other hand, the most frequent choice for requests for both the initiation and the cessation of action was hearer oriented, which reflected the predominance of *mood derivable* utterances such as imperatives. Requests for joint activity emphasised the inclusive 'we' perspective, which reflected the use of *suggestory formulae* such as 'let's ...'.

Concerning modification, requests for goods were predominantly modified by 'please', which in turn collocated with *query preparatory*. As Blum-Kulka (1985) points out, 'please' used with *query preparatory* has a clear illocutionary force indicator, while at the same time serving as a marker of politeness. Requests for the initiation of action were predominantly modified by 'toners', which are more likely to be used to mitigate the impact of the requests rather than to reinforce or aggravate them. Requests for the cessation of action, which require more persuasiveness and forcefulness to get compliance from the addressee, were collocated with 'reasons' and 'repetitions'. Requests for joint activity were rarely modified, and when they were, they were modified mainly by 'attention getters' and 'reasons'. Again, these differentiated patterns of perspectives and modifications in relation to goals suggest that Yao had come to develop different ways of handling requests with different goals.

9.3 Variation According to Addressee

As seen above, requests were differentiated by goal in terms of strategy, perspective, and modification. As observed in Chapter 7, requests also varied according to addressee. In the following two sections, the findings with respect to strategies, their linguistic exponents, and modification in relation to addressee will be summarised.

9.3.1 Strategies and their linguistic exponents according to addressee

There was some degree of patterned behaviour according to the addressee in terms of strategies and their linguistic exponents. The adult received *want statements* more frequently than did any other addressee. This reflects the caretaker characteristic associated with adults. Peers received requests in much more diverse forms than did other addressees, reflecting the perception that peers needed to be persuaded or approached in various ways because of their greater propensity not to conform. Yao's prominent use of an ambiguous request form, 'can you ...?' with the teenager shows the relative instability of their relationship. Her mother received a high frequency of an indirect strategy, *query preparatory*. This suggests Yao's sensitivity to being a possible disturbance. This interpretation coincides with the findings of Ervin-Tripp and Gordon (1986) as well as Gordon *et al.* (1980), who find this sensitivity in children around eight years of age (see Chapter 7). Yao had learned to mediate her intrusions by expressing herself indirectly in such contexts. However, at the same time, she used a direct strategy, *obligation statement*, with her mother almost as much as with her peers and the teenager. This may be attributable to the greater intimacy of the mother–child relationship. The finding that Yao's interaction with her mother could at times be direct again coincides with the findings of Hollos and Beeman (1978), Ervin-Tripp *et al.* (1984) and Andersen (1978; 1990a,b) as noted in Chapter 7. Thus, Yao's varied request behaviour reflects her consciousness of the different relationships she had with each addressee.

Another notable difference is a contrast between the adult and her mother on one hand and peers and the teenager on the other with respect to her use of the 'could you ...?' form. This form was produced predominantly with the former group.

The literature reviewed in Chapter 2 suggests that children by the age of 12 or even younger, when choosing request forms, show a sensitivity to the social meaning of the relative status of their addressee. This indicates that there is a differentiation to be made between adults and children who are younger than the speaker. However, for peers and adults, not all the research shows the same pattern of age-based distinctions. Some studies show that children are likely to produce direct requests with their peers and indirect requests with adults, while others find that speech addressed to peers is quite similar to that addressed to adults. In the present study, there is evidence that distinctions are made between addressees, including those between peers and the adult. Thus, the results suggest that there was some degree of patterned behaviour in terms of differences among addressees. Hence, Yao seemed to show an awareness of differences in addressee as a basis for differentiating request forms and this in turn suggests she was aware of some of the social meanings that help to determine appropriate request forms.

9.3.2 Modification according to addressee

The frequency of the use of modification in requests varied substantially between Yao's mother and the other addressees, especially in the use of 'please', 'reasons', and 'elaboration'; but did not vary greatly across peers, the teenager, and the adult. Her mother received requests with modification with greater frequency than did any other addressee. The use of requests with 'please' addressed to her mother stood out. One explanation for this is that nearly one third of all the requests made to her mother were requests for goods and 'please' was used predominantly with such requests. For interlocutors other than her mother, 'please' was directed to the adult, to the teenager and to peers in that order of decreasing frequency. This indicates, as Ervin-Tripp *et al.* (1990) suggest, that Yao used 'please' as a social index, rather than as a means of persuasion.

After her mother, peers received modified requests most frequently. This may be because her peers were far less likely to comply; and more than the teenager and the adult needed certain kinds of modifiers (i.e. 'toners', 'reasons', and 'repetitions'). Thus, in relation to the use of modification, Yao seemed to be aware of the social meanings associated with her addressees. This differentiation, however, was made most frequently between her mother and the other addressees, and to a lesser extent between peers and others.

In sum, Yao's choice of strategies, linguistic exponents, and modification showed some degree of patterned behaviour according to addressee. However, the major differentiation among addressees was between her mother (outside the play situation) and others (inside the play situation), and the differences within the play situation were more related to the goal of the request than to the addressee. In a supportive play setting, interlocutors are for the most part treated as one kind of addressee (i.e. play partners). Yao's mother was treated differently, we may presume, because she was outside the play situation. Addressees seem, therefore, to be less influential in shaping request behaviour than do goals in a support play setting.

9.4 A Developmental Profile

The previous sections have shown the effects of Yao's social awareness upon her production of requests, but to understand fully the significance of this social awareness we must relate her social perceptions to the growth of her linguistic repertoire. In this section, we will look more closely at what was outlined in 9.1 and presented in Chapters 4 through 8 in terms of the temporal development of request realisation. We will look at two aspects of this development. First, we will look phase by phase at Yao's repertoire (i.e. strategies, their linguistic exponents, and modification). In doing so we will see how it expanded over the course of the observational period. Second, we will look at how her repertoire was used for different goals in each phase (This second analysis does not include addressees and modification, because they were not formally analysed for this purpose). This profile shows both the social and linguistic expansion of Yao's second language acquisition. The descriptions of the phases will show how her growing social awareness and linguistic capacity were able to reinforce one another in different ways during different phases. Statements in relation to goal in each phase in the following sections refer to Figures 6.5–6.8 of Chapter 6 on pages 110–11.

9.4.1 Phase I

Repertoire of strategies and linguistic forms

Although Yao made use of all the strategy types (from *mood derivable* to *hints*) in Phase I, the linguistic forms were limited, and formulaic expressions, either routines or patterns predominated: for example, 'come on', 'just a minute', 'pass me …', 'it's your (my) turn', 'let's …', 'can you (I) …?', or 'do you want to …?'.

Modification

In Phase I, 'repetitions' were the predominant type of modification. There were some other resources available such as 'reasons' and 'elaboration'. However, the dominant, presumably the easiest, and the most readily available resource was 'repetitions', especially since Yao's linguistic resources were limited.

During this phase, the next most frequent use of modification after 'repetitions' was the use of 'attention getters', which was robust only in Phase I. They functioned in several ways, and their use, especially that of initial vocatives, was probably the shortest and quickest way to initiate a request. This was particularly true when Yao needed planning time or had only a few resources for the articulation of a request (see Chapter 8).

There was also a limited use of 'please'. However, in Phase I, when Yao's grammatical and lexical abilities were limited, 'please' appears to have functioned more as a marker to indicate that a request was being made (i.e. 'please' attached to a vocative only or to the name of an object) rather than as a politeness marker. In addition, in Phase I 'please' was added to the early-acquired basic request form (i.e. imperatives) but not to conventionally indirect forms.

Goal

In Phase I, because her linguistic forms were limited, Yao's expressions were characteristically formulaic. Within this limitation, the following was observed in relation to goal. For three goals (i.e. requests for goods, for the initiation of action, and for the cessation of action) *mood derivable* was dominant (e.g. 'pass me …', 'come on', or 'just a minute', respectively). In contrast, for requests for joint activity, *suggestory formulae* (e.g. 'let's …') were dominant, with *query preparatory* (e.g. 'do you want to …?') being relatively frequent.

9.4.2 Phase II

Repertoire of strategies and linguistic forms

In Phase II the formulaic use of English that characterised Phase I was dramatically reduced, and Yao began to make more extensive use of the forms that had emerged in Phase I, employing a wider range of lexical items and spontaneously produced longer requests. After Phase I there was a great increase in the use of the 'can you (I) …?' form. There was also the addition of a limited number of new request forms. However, requests with the past-tense modals such as 'could you (I) …?' had not yet emerged, and the use of *query preparatory* was limited to three different types: 'can you (I) …?', 'do you want to …?', and 'do you have …?'.

A further feature of this phase was the emergence of an awareness of the rules of English grammar. As shown in Chapter 4, Yao began to make a number of metalinguistic comments. During this phase, there were comments on the modals, the articles, and the sound system of English, as well as the difference in the word order between English and Japanese.

Modification

From Phase II through Phase IV, 'toners' were the most frequently employed means of modification. When all the toners were totalled from Phase I through Phase IV, the most frequently used were 'just' and 'maybe'. But in Phase II only 'just' was used. Both 'just' and 'maybe' are used 'to tone down the impositive force of the request' (Trosborg, 1995:

212). However, it seems that the use of 'maybe' requires a more conscious effort than 'just', apparently because 'just' is a more routinised part of the utterance and presumably used unconsciously. 'Reasons' and 'repetitions' were the second most frequently used modifiers during this phase.

Also in Phase II, the use of 'please' increased and seemed to change in character, now being used chiefly as a politeness marker, not as a request marker. This reverses the pattern characteristic of 'please' during Phase I. Another development seen in 'please' was in terms of its combination with strategy type. In Phase I, 'please' occurred only with the direct strategy but from Phase II onwards, it appeared more with a conventionally indirect strategy (i.e. *query preparatory*). This is in accordance with the results reported by other studies (see Chapter 8).

Goal

The great increase in the use of 'can you (I) ...?', as discussed above in relation to Yao's repertoire during Phase II, was observed in both requests for goods and for the initiation of action. This increase shows that Yao was learning to make such requests in an indirect way. For requests for goods, *mood derivable*, which was dominant in Phase I, was replaced by *query preparatory*. For this goal, *query preparatory* continued to be dominant from Phase II onwards, while *mood derivable* remained rare. For requests for the initiation of action, too, there was after Phase I a great increase in *query preparatory*. However, the frequency of *mood derivable* remained the most frequent. For requests for joint activity, *suggestory formulae* were dominant and the next most frequent substrategy was *query preparatory*, as in Phase I. For requests for the cessation of action, *mood derivable* was the single most frequent strategy, again, as it was in Phase I.

9.4.3 Phase III

Repertoire of strategies and linguistic forms

Phase III is marked by pragmatic expansion. Many new linguistic forms were added to Yao's repertoire of requests (i.e. 'you should ...', 'shall we ...?', 'may I ...?', 'will you ...?', and 'could you (I, we) ...?'), and many structurally differentiated requests appeared. All four types of *obligation statements* appeared in this phase (i.e. 'you have to', 'you should', 'you'd better', and 'you need to'). In addition, there was a substantial increase after Phase II in the use of 'you have to (you've got to) ....' The emergence of the 'could you (I, we) ...?' form, which is a syntactic modification of 'can you (I, we) ...?', was significant in terms of pragmatic development. Yao had become able to mitigate the impositive force of her requests syntactically by using a conditional. However, 'can you (I, we) …?' was still far more frequent than 'could you (I, we) …?'. Furthermore, the conditional, 'could' was used only in a question form (i.e. *query preparatory*) and not in a statement (i.e. *stating preparatory*). In addition, as the linguistic means to express her intentions expanded, the overall use of *hints* increased, especially after the middle of Phase III. The frequency of her use of *hints*, however, was low throughout the study.

A further feature of this phase was the extension of metalinguistic awareness, which was shown in Yao's playful manipulation of English (i.e. a pun on the meaning of a word), as illustrated in Chapter 4.

In spite of all these developments, further refinement of Yao's pragmatic system was yet to come.

Modification

'Toners' continued to be the most frequently selected means of modification. 'Reasons' increased in each phase and from Phase II onwards they were the second most frequently used modifiers. 'Reasons' were also the most frequent *support move*.

The findings of the present study agree with studies of adults (e.g. Faerch & Kasper, 1989; House & Kasper, 1987; Trosborg, 1995), which find 'reasons' to be the most frequently selected *support move*; however, as we have seen in Chapter 8, in studies with children concerning this ability the results are not consistent.

As also noted in Chapter 8, *support moves* are clausal and require a separate structure. Therefore, they are more difficult to produce than other modifiers. The most likely reason for the high frequency of 'reasons' in the present study, in spite of their difficulty, is that psychologically it is plausible, as noted by House & Kasper (1987: 1281), to make an addressee understand the reason behind a request. Thus, giving 'reasons' was very likely a useful device for Yao in her attempt to mitigate the impact of her requests. In the present study, Yao used 'reasons' to some extent even during Phase I, and as her grammatical competence increased, her use of them also increased. Furthermore, the fact that 'reasons' outnumbered the use of 'please' may also show that she was gaining insight into how to be persuasive. This suggests Yao's increasing awareness of social context and her growing ability to draw on her linguistic repertoire.

Goal

The pragmatic expansion in Yao's repertoire in Phase III is reflected most clearly in her requests for the cessation of action and for joint activity. The number of strategy types for these request goals here was the largest of any phase: *query preparatory* (i.e. 'could you please …?') was added to Yao's repertoire for the cessation of action, and *stating preparatory* (i.e. 'you (we) can ...') was added to requests for joint activity. With respect to requests for goods, the pattern did not change from Phase II; *query preparatory* being dominant. With respect to requests for the initiation of action, *mood derivable* continued to decrease but remained the most frequently used strategy type, with *query preparatory* remaining second, as it had been in Phase II. The substantial increase in the use of 'you have to (you've got to) ...' after Phase II is reflected in the increase in *obligation statements* in requests for the initiation of action. Thus, during Phase III, there was a significant expansion in Yao's capacity to differentiate her request behaviour depending on the goal.

9.4.4 Phase IV

Repertoire of strategies and linguistic forms

In Phase IV, Yao's pragmatic ability to express her intentions in indirect ways advanced rapidly, especially in *stating preparatory* and *query preparatory*. New forms in these strategies were added to her repertoire, including mitigated forms. All the new forms occurring in this phase were indirect strategies: the 'is there ...?' form, and syntactically mitigated forms ('would you ...?', 'would you like to ...?' and 'you (we) could ...'). Furthermore, 'do you have ...?', which first appeared in Phase II, was used more often in Phase IV. The 'could you (I) ...?', which became available in the Phase III, was constantly used in this phase.

According to Gordon *et al.* (1980), native speaking children of English under eight years of age rarely use 'is there ...?' or 'do you have ...?'. In the present data, in Phase IV, when Yao was eight years old, the 'is there ...?' form emerged, and the 'do you have ...?' form increased. Yao's use of 'is there ...?', which is a distancing device (Sifianou, 1992), shows her recognition of the social nuances of situations and her potential imposition on her addressees. This suggests that she was framing her requests so that they were only indirectly demanding. What Gordon et al. suggested for the first language development began happening in Yao's second language pragmatic development in Phase IV.

In regard to the 'do you have ...?' form, another development that was observed in Phase IV, was Yao's ability to add qualifying clauses, such as 'I could use', to 'do you have ...?' (e.g. *I need a blu tack/ do you have a blu tack I could use?* [PL69-58]). This is again very similar to what has been found in the child native speakers of English in the study by Gordon *et al.* (1980), where children less than eight years old never add this qualification. This suggests that within 17 months, Yao had begun to acquire the ability to make use of English that was, in many respects, equivalent to her native speaking peers.

Qualitative changes in the use of *hints* also occurred by Phase IV on both the propositional and the grammatical levels. On the former, it was during Phase IV that Yao was able to produce *hints* that masked both the requested objects and the action required of the addressee. Before Phase IV, the *hints* she produced made specific reference to desired objects or actions, although there was no reference to the addressee's responsibility. On the grammatical level, by the end of Phase IV, she was able to use a good number of syntactic forms in producing her *hints*. Some of them appeared as early as Phase I. But as *hints*, tag questions (e.g. 'oh yeah you've got blu-tack haven't you?' [PL-69-22]) and interrogatives without modal verbs (e.g. 'do you need two eyes?' [J74-28]) did not appear until Phase IV and their use as *hints* was rare.

A further feature of this phase is Yao's increased pragmalinguistic awareness. This can be seen in her question about the difference between 'could you ...?' and 'would you ...?', as illustrated in Chapter 4.

Yao's pragmatic development in the final phase is therefore a consequence of both social and linguistic achievements. Once she had acquired the grammar necessary to realise her requests, she was able to produce different forms in appropriate contexts, and in addition, she had developed a sense of social context that, as Gordon *et al.* (1980) suggest, a native speaker her age would have.

Modification

'Toners' were the most frequently selected means of modification from Phase II onwards. They increased quite dramatically from 1.3% in Phase I to 15.9% in Phase IV. Although 'just' and 'maybe' were the most frequently used 'toners' in total, 'just' appeared in every phase, while 'maybe' rarely occurred before Phase IV. The tendency to tone down the impact of a request through the use of 'maybe' in Phase IV is evidence that Yao had found a new dimension of modification and begun to recognise social nuances, all of which indicate a significant increase in her English language sophistication. The frequency of 'repetitions', which were the predominant type of modification in Phase I, decreased and in Phase IV only a few instances were observed.

Goal

The increase in Yao's pragmatic repertoire in Phase IV suggests that further refinements were taking place in this final phase. This is reflected in the growing differentiation observed for all the goals, especially with requests for the initiation of action and for joint activity, for which *stating preparatory* (e.g. 'you (we) could ...') became an increasingly important part of her repertoire.

In conclusion, Yao's developmental profile shows a steady developmental pattern for strategies, linguistic exponents, and modification. And by the end of Phase IV, there is a great deal of expansion, elaboration, and refinement in the repertoire. In addition to this increase in linguistic capacity, we observe a growing awareness of the social dimensions of requests. These include the recognition of the social nuances in situations, of the potential imposition on her addressees, and the understanding of how to operate within as well as outside the play situation. Yao's linguistic capacity and increased social understanding had come to reinforce each other to make her pragmatic development possible. However, regardless of the extent of the expansion of the repertoire, realisation of requests for one goal differed from that for others.

In the following three sections, the questions that arose in the summary and conclusions presented above are addressed.

9.5 Constraints on Variation in Request Forms According to Addressee

The variation in Yao's requests in relation to goal and addressee illustrate that the patterns of request realisation differ significantly according to goal, with the differences in addressees being less influential.

The bulk of the literature finds variation according to addressee. Although the present study shows a similar variation, the variation was much less than might have been expected. There were differences according to addressee, but they were small. This is in all likelihood the result of the dominant influence of the play situation. The setting for this study was one of supportive play. Within such a setting, interlocutors were treated largely as a single kind of addressee. Therefore, supportive play did not create the need for much face-work. The results suggest that the setting is so significant an influence that even the large differences in age and status between the peers and the adult were substantially reduced. However, her mother was not part of Yao's play, and to make requests Yao had to interrupt her, making the difference between her mother and the other addressees significant. By not distinguishing between her peers, the teenager, and the adult to any significant degree, but by distinguishing between her play partners and her mother, Yao showed a sensitivity to the role of social context and revealed an increased sophistication in her use of English.

Consistent with this, Yao showed sensitivity to the addressee in improvised role-play, where she was deliberately, consciously, and appropriately communicating with addressees, as in Chapter 4. One example of this is when Yao addressed 'Mr Doggy', she changed her request form from 'can I ...?' to 'may I ...?', since 'Mr Doggy' was the father of her friend. This example shows Yao's knowledge of polite request forms to be appropriate to specific contexts and addressees. Another example in improvised role-play is the use of the 'could I ...?' form where Yao was a customer and Janice was a sales clerk in a pretend store, suggesting that Yao had observed the protocol appropriate to a customer and a sales clerk in Australia. These instances, which occurred in Phase III, reveal that Yao was not just learning linguistic forms but that she had come to recognise certain essential, social features that shape English usage. Yao's request behaviour had become constrained by the temporal situation or setting.

There are also instances about the use of one modification type, 'preparators' to illustrate this. As described in Chapter 8, before uttering an actual request, a speaker can prepare the addressee for the subsequent request without making the actual request. There are several ways to do this. However, in the recorded data, there was only one type of 'preparators': announcing an addressee that he or she is to anticipate the assignment of a task. They were produced to the addressees except to her mother. On the other hand, in the diary data, where there were more opportunities for considered appeals to goals, there were additional types: getting some kind of pre-commitment from an addressee; or by making disarming statements. These were addressed to her mother. The situations where 'preparators' occurred in the diary data were usually when Yao came to her mother's room while she was studying. And Yao had to interrupt her mother to make her request. On the other hand, in the recorded play situations requests were far less premeditated. The context of a play situation is immediate, with the speaker and interlocutor engaged in quick conversational exchanges. The reason why 'preparators' were rare in the recorded data is not that Yao was unable to produce them, but that the context discouraged them. This also suggests that request behaviour is constrained by the temporal context. The present study is concerned with a specific type of temporal context, the play situation, where participants so frequently seek immediate need gratification. Consequently, Yao's use of 'preparators' was limited to only one type in the recorded data. Bohn (1986) suggests that learners (and probably also competent speakers) utilise their morphosyntactic knowledge only to a limited degree because the situational variable game may largely determine the use of specific structural types and specific lexical elements. (Bohn, 1986: 194)

This can be applied to the interpretation of the play situations in the recorded data, where the difference between interlocutors in the situation is substantially reduced.

9.6 Is One Kind of Data Enough?

Examples from the diary raise a very important question about how the type of data constrains the findings. The present study was based on recorded data, supported whenever necessary by the diary of Yao's language development, a diary kept by the researcher from the second day of Yao's residence in Australia until the end of the data collection period. Without this diary data, the findings would have identified only one type of 'preparator'. Another example, which was rare in the recorded data but occurred more frequently in the diary data, was the use of 'may I ...?'. In fact, this form with the verb, 'have', in requesting goods did not appear in the recorded data. However, it was reported several times in the diary, specifically in requests that Yao addressed to her mother when asking for sweets. These examples from the diary demonstrate that an analysis from only one kind of data would have resulted in an underestimation of Yao's command of the pragmatics in English. Also without the diary data, the metalinguistic comments, which Yao often made and which were so important in understanding how Yao was actually perceiving second language learning, would not have been captured. Her metalinguistic comments were not only on the differences between the two languages but were also directly related to request realisation as well as language socialisation. These were important for supplementing and validating what occurred in the recorded data. Of similar significance was improvised role-play. Her behaviour here was different from her more natural interactions. From these we can conclude that multiple data sources are an extremely important element in any longitudinal study of pragmatic development.

9.7 How Far Did Yao Get?

Pragmatic competence is the combination of a learner's ability to draw on a given linguistic repertoire and his or her understanding of socio-cultural contexts. As Bialystok (1993: 51) points out, 'selecting the appropriate form requires an assessment of contextual and social factors'. Thus, the expansion of linguistic resources is what enables pragmatic sophistication to be realised. Learners cannot become pragmatically more sophisticated until they have a greater variety of linguistic resources, since the expression of pragmatic concepts conforms to the level of grammatical complexity acquired (Koike, 1989b).

Unlike early first language acquisition, Yao as a second language learner, was already equipped with one set of pragmatic concepts. Like child native speakers of English, as Ervin-Tripp and Gordon (1986) and Gordon *et al.* (1980) suggest, Yao's sense of social context and relevant pragmatic concepts for her second language presumably developed rapidly around age eight in Australia. In addition, Yao seems to have gained her pragmatic awareness by 'noticing' (Schmidt 1993) how native speakers of English use a particular form or modification in situations with which she was already in part familiar. As was seen in Chapter 8, for example, there is evidence in the diary data that Yao noticed that her friends were explicitly told to use politeness formulae such as 'please' by their mothers, and she came to understand that failure to do so in a particular situation was inappropriate. Through such observation, Yao seems to have gained a greater pragmatic awareness and increased her overall pragmatic competence.

With respect to her linguistic resources, again, unlike her early first language acquisition, Yao as a second language learner, was 'already familiar with the syntactic principle of natural language' (Felix, 1978: 477) and, as Ellis (1982) has pointed out with respect to second language learners, Yao, too, used her awareness of contributory features such as word order and modals.

A small number of deviations from target-like request forms were observed even in Phase I of the data. Yao did not have to resort extensively to idiosyncratic forms, since during the early stages of her second language acquisition she was able to use her mother as a resource person, as well as an interpreter. Yao was free to use English or Japanese at home. This made her environment at home bilingual and thus conducive to her application of learned pragmatics across cultures.

Yao's pragmatic sophistication in the final phase is a reflection of her expanded linguistic resources and her better understanding of the sociocultural context. This understanding was achieved by her drawing on her general pragmatic knowledge and pragmatic rules particular to English. Consequently, her expanded linguistic repertoire enabled her pragmatic behaviour to become significantly more sophisticated by the end of the 17-month of observation period.

This study is not supported by baseline data from children who are native speakers of English, and consequently it is not possible to determine the exact extent to which Yao achieved what comparable native speakers would have in similar contexts. Nevertheless, we have seen that similar patterns have been reported in the literature for native speaking children. Since the data in this study did not seem to conflict with other research, it would seem reasonable to assume that within the space of 17 months Yao was able to achieve a level of pragmatic competence in making requests that was remarkably similar in many important respects to that of native speakers of English approximately the same age.

Although Yao's pragmatic competence increased significantly during the period of observation and consequently her requests became noticeably more sophisticated, we cannot conclude that the developmental process was complete. The example below, as discussed in detail in Chapter 8, produced at the beginning of Phase IV, illustrates that fine-tuning of the appropriate use of English in certain situations has yet to come.

> *well we want to play here/ so could you please go to your room?*
> [PJ63-62-2]

Although the intimacy of the mother and child relationship can lead to rudeness on the part of the child, as observed in this and other research, in this particular instance, Yao's rudeness was in all likelihood unintentional. As Kasper (1990: 208) points out, the unmotivated rudeness in children provides evidence that 'they have not yet mastered the socio-pragmatic and pragmalinguistic norms of their (adult) speech community'. The development of pragmatic competence requires a complex mapping 'between form and social context' (Bialystok, 1993: 51) that goes beyond just learning a linguistic repertoire. Although, the example above is the only instance of this sort found in the final phase, it suggests that Yao was still on the developmental path.

This study of one individual learner suggests strongly that more studies of this kind are needed. Its conclusions, therefore, are presented as points of departure for future discussion.

9.8 Implications of this Study

(1) This study has shown that Yao's requests differed in the choice of main strategies, substrategies, perspectives, and modification depending on their goal. The developmental patterns of requests for each goal were also shown to vary. This suggests that there is distinct

language behaviour for different goals, and that we must therefore understand requests as a differentiated system. Any single dimensional understanding would be unable to capture the incredible complexity of the task interlanguage users have to confront. What we have seen in this study is precisely how complicated the acquisition process is and how sophisticated the learner has to be when drawing different elements of the process together.

However, we do not know whether the patterns that were found for requests in this study are mirrored in other speech acts. They may or may not be more homogeneous. This study, therefore, points to the need to investigate other speech acts in order to determine if they are as differentiated as requests.

(2) This longitudinal case study has demonstrated that for an individual learner there is synchronic variation in the features of request realisation for different goals. It has further shown the details of diachronic variation. This kind of data cannot be obtained from any methodology other than the longitudinal study of an individual learner, and thus suggests a direction for future research, particularly in relation to data gathering. In order to determine the variation in the linguistic behaviour of an individual learner at different times, what we need are studies based on longitudinal data for an individual as he or she is observed interacting in a set of contexts, over an extended period of time.

(3) The findings of this study further suggest that although situations do not fully determine the choice of language they contribute significantly to it. That is to say, even though the individual makes choices about how to interact, the choice of strategy, linguistic form, and modification are significantly constrained by the situation. The data used in the quantitative part of the analysis was recorded in play situations with familiar people. A comparison with the diary data shows that play situations tend to reduce the status difference between addressees. A play situation is a specific temporal context, characterised by immediate need satisfaction. This points to the need for studies to be done in various situations to determine how other situational variables affect requests made to addressees. These might be classroom, playground, home-caregiver, or extended family situations.

(4) The difference between what was found by the analysis of the recorded data as opposed to the diary data strongly suggests that any extensive study using just one kind of data will be inadequate for a full description of the process by which a child acquires a second language. The diary data in this study supplied invaluable additional

information, as demonstrated in Sections 9.5 and 9.6, as did the improvised role-play recorded during the play sessions. Different kinds of data are needed to complement and verify the primary data set.

(5) There were four phases identified in the data. However, we do not know whether these phases intrinsically individual or whether they are generalisable. This points to the direction for future study.

9.9 Concluding Remarks

The task that a second language learning child confronts in acquiring the pragmatic knowledge needed to make requests is incredibly complex. The learner has to be able to map linguistic forms into social contexts in order to make appropriate requests in a second language. The learner's ever expanding linguistic knowledge and socio-cultural perceptions constantly influence the choice of strategies and linguistic devices.

As has been pointed out in Chapter 1, much of the research into interlanguage pragmatics has focused on second language use, frequently comparing native speakers' pragmatic knowledge with that of non-native speakers. Unlike most mainstream research into second language acquisition, which focuses on the acquisitional patterns or processes of the learners' language, research into interlanguage pragmatics has paid little attention to pragmatic development. While a rich literature exists on the acquisition of the formal linguistic properties of a learner's language, we know very little about the processes by which pragmatic knowledge is acquired.

This study has attempted to fill this gap in our current knowledge by exploring the learning process for a single aspect of pragmatics – requests. Further, in doing so, it has shown how request goals significantly affect the linguistic behaviour of a child learning a second language.

In-depth developmental studies of interlanguage pragmatics, such as this, can move the study of interlanguage pragmatics closer to the mainstream of second language acquisition research and shed further light upon the intricate relationship that exists between the development of a learner's linguistic and pragmatic competence.

References

Andersen, E. (1978) Will you don't snore please?: Directives in young children's role-play speech. *Papers and Reports on Child Language Development* 15, 140–50.

Andersen, E. (1990a) *Speaking with Style: The Sociolinguistic Skills of Children*. London: Routledge.

Andersen, E. (1990b) Acquiring communicative competence: Knowledge of register variation. In R. C. Scarcella, E. S. Andersen and S. D. Krashen (eds) *Developing Communicative Competence in a Second Language* (pp. 5–25). New York: Newbury House.

Austin, J. (1962) *How To Do Things With Words*. Oxford: Oxford University Press.

Bahns, J., Burmeister, H. and Vogel, T. (1986) The pragmatics of formulas in L2 learner speech: Use and development. *Journal of Pragmatics* 10, 693–723.

Bardovi-Harlig, K. and Hartford, B. (1993) Learning the rules of academic talk: A longitudinal study of pragmatic change. *Studies in Second Language Acquisition* 15, 279–304.

Bates, E. (1976a) *Language and Context: The Acquisition of Pragmatics*. New York: Academic Press.

Bates, E. (1976b) Pragmatics and sociolinguistics in child language. In D. Morehead and A. Morehead (eds) *Normal and Deficient Child Language* (pp. 411–63). Baltimore: University Park Press.

Becker, J. (1982) Children's strategic use of requests to mark and manipulate social status. In S. Kuczaj II (ed.) *Language Development: Language, Thought and Culture* (pp. 1–35). Hillsdale, NJ: Lawrence Erlbaum.

Becker, J. (1988) The success of parents' indirect techniques for teaching their preschoolers pragmatic skills. *First Language* 8, 173–82.

Beebe, L. and Takahashi, T. (1989) Variation in interlanguage speech act realization. In S. Gass, C. Madden, D. Preston and L. Selinker (eds) *Variation in Second Language Acquisition: Discourse and Pragmatics* (pp. 103–25). Clevedon: Multilingual Matters.

Bialystok, E. (1993) Symbolic representation and attentional control in pragmatic competence. In G. Kasper and S. Blum-Kulka (eds) *Interlanguage Pragmatics* (pp. 43–57). New York: Oxford University Press.

Blum-Kulka, S. (1982) Learning to say what you mean in a second language: A study of the speech act performance of learners of Hebrew as a second language. *Applied Linguistics* 3, 29–59.

Blum-Kulka, S. (1985) Modifiers as indicating devices: The case of requests. Paper presented at the Conference on Cognitive Aspects of the Utterance, Tel Aviv.

Blum-Kulka, S. (1987) Indirectness and politeness in requests: Same or different? *Journal of Pragmatics* 11, 131–46.

Blum-Kulka, S. (1989) Playing it safe: The role of conventionality in indirectness. In S. Blum-Kulka, J. House and G. Kasper (eds) *Cross-cultural Pragmatics: Requests and Apologies* (pp. 37–70). Norwood, NJ: Ablex.

Blum-Kulka, S. (1990) You don't touch lettuce with your fingers: Parental politeness in family discourse. *Journal of Pragmatics* 14, 259–88.

Blum-Kulka, S. and House, J. (1989) Cross-cultural and situational variation in requesting behavior. In S. Blum-Kulka, J. House and G. Kasper (eds) *Cross-cultural Pragmatics: Requests and Apologies* (pp. 123–54). Norwood, NJ: Ablex.

Blum-Kulka, S. and Olshtain, E. (1984) Requests and apologies: A cross-cultural study of speech act realization patterns (CCSARP). *Applied Linguistics* 5, 196–213.

Blum-Kulka, S. and Olshtain, E. (1986) Too many words: Length of utterance and pragmatic failure. *Studies in Second Language Acquisition* 8, 47–61.

Blum-Kulka, S., Danet, B. and Gherson, R. (1985) The language of requesting in Israeli society. In J. Forgas (ed.) *Language and Social Situations* (pp. 113–39). New York: Springer-Verlag.

Blum-Kulka, S., House, J. and Kasper, G. (eds) (1989a) *Cross-cultural Pragmatics: Requests and Apologies.* Norwood, NJ: Ablex.

Blum-Kulka, S., House, J. and Kasper, G. (1989b) Investigating cross-cultural pragmatics: An introductory overview. In S. Blum-Kulka, J. House and G. Kasper (eds) *Cross-cultural Pragmatics: Requests and Apologies* (pp. 1–34). Norwood, NJ: Ablex.

Bohn, O. (1986) Formulas, frame structures, and stereotypes in early syntactic development: Some new evidence from L2 acquisition. *Linguistics* 24, 185–202.

Brown, P. and Levinson, S. (1978, 1987) *Politeness: Some Universals in Language Usage.* Cambridge: Cambridge University Press.

Bruner, J., Roy, C. and Ratner, N. (1982) The beginnings of request. In K. E. Nelson (ed.) *Children's Language* (pp. 91–138). Hillsdale, NJ: Lawrence Erlbaum.

Camras, L., Pristo, T. and Brown, M. (1985) Directive choice by children and adults: Affect, situation, and linguistic politeness. *Merrill-Palmer Quarterly* 31, 19–31.

Cathcart, R. (1986) Situational differences and the sampling of young children's school language. In R. Day (ed.) *Talking to Learn: Conversation in Second Language Acquisition* (pp. 118–40). Cambridge, MA: Newbury House.

Cazden, C., Cancino, E., Rosansky, E. and Schumann, J. (1975) *Second Language Acquisition Sequences in Children, Adolescents and Adults.* Final report submitted to the National Institute of Education, Washington, DC.

Celce-Murcia, M. and Larsen-Freeman, D. (1983) *The Grammar Book: An ESL/EFL Teacher's Course.* Rowley: Newbury House.

Clancy, P. (1985) The acquisition of Japanese. In D. Slobin (ed.) *The Crosslinguistic Study of Language Acquisition: The Data* (pp. 373–524). Hillsdale: Lawrence Erlbaum.

Clancy, P. (1986) The acquisition of communicative style in Japanese. In B. Schieffelin and E. Ochs (eds) *Language Socialization Across Cultures* (pp. 213–50). Cambridge: Cambridge University Press.

Clark, H. (1979) Responding to indirect speech acts. *Cognitive Psychology* 11, 430–77.

Clark, H. and Schunk, D. (1980) Polite responses to polite requests. *Cognition* 8, 111–43.

Clark, P. (1996) Investigating second language acquisition in preschools: A longitudinal study of four Vietnamese speaking children's acquisition of English in a bilingual preschool. Unpublished doctoral thesis, La Trobe University, Australia.

Cook, G. (1989) *Discourse*. Oxford: Oxford University Press.

Cook, H. (2001) Why can't learners of JFL distinguish polite from impolite speech styles? In K. Rose and G. Kasper (eds) *Pragmatics in Language Teaching* (pp. 80–102). Cambridge: Cambridge University Press.

Cook-Gumperz, J. (1977) Situated Instructions: Language socialization of school age children. In S. Ervin-Tripp and C. Mitchell-Kernan (eds) *Child Discourse* (pp. 103–21). New York: Academic Press.

Dore, J. (1977a) Children's illocutionary acts. In R. O. Freedle (ed.) *Discourse Production and Comprehension* (pp. 227–44). Norwood, N.J: Ablex.

Dore, J. (1977b) 'Oh them sheriff': A pragmatic analysis of children's responses to questions. In S. Ervin-Tripp and C. Mitchell-Kernan (eds) *Child Discourse* (pp. 139–63). New York: Academic Press.

Dore, J., Gearhart, M. and Newman, D. (1978) The structure of nursery school conversation. In K. Nelson (ed.) *Children's Language* (pp. 337–95). New York: Gardner Press.

Edmondson, W. (1981) *Spoken Discourse*. London: Longman.

Ellis, R. (1982) The origins of interlanguage. *Applied Linguistics* 3, 207–23.

Ellis, R. (1984) Formulaic speech in early classroom second language development. In J. Handscombe, R. Orem and B. Taylor (eds) *On TESOL '83: The Question of Control* (pp. 53–65). Washington, DC: TESOL.

Ellis, R. (1988) *Classroom Second Language Development*. New York: Prentice Hall.

Ellis, R. (1992) Learning to communicate in the classroom: A study of two language learners' requests. *Studies in Second Language Acquisition* 14, 1–23.

Ellis, R. (1994) *The Study of Second Language Acquisition*. Oxford: Oxford University Press.

Ervin-Tripp, S. (1976) Is Sybil there? The structure of some American English directives. *Language in Society* 5, 25–66.

Ervin-Tripp, S. (1977) Wait for me, roller skate! In S. Ervin-Tripp and C. Mitchell-Kernan (eds) *Child Discourse* (pp. 165–88). New York: Academic Press.

Ervin-Tripp, S. and Gordon, D. (1986) The development of requests. In R. L. Schiefelbusch (ed.) *Language Competence: Assessment and Intervention* (pp. 61–95). London: Taylor & Francis.

Ervin-Tripp, S., Guo, J. and Lampert, M. (1990) Politeness and persuasion in children's control acts. *Journal of Pragmatics* 14, 307–31.

Ervin-Tripp, S., O'Connor, M. and Rosenberg, J. (1984) Language and power in the family. In C. Kramarae, M. Schulz and W. O'Barr (eds) *Language and Power* (pp. 116–35). Beverly Hills, CA: Sage.

Ervin-Tripp, S., Strage, A., Lampert, M. and Bell, N. (1987) Understanding requests. *Linguistics* 25, 107–43.

Faerch, C. and Kasper, G. (1989) Internal and external modification in interlanguage request realization. In S. Blum-Kulka, J. House and G. Kasper (eds) *Cross-cultural Pragmatics: Requests and Apologies* (pp. 221–47). Norwood, NJ: Ablex.

Felix, S. (1978) Some differences between first and second language acquisition. In N. Waterson and C. Snow (eds) *The Development of Communication* (pp. 469–78). Toronto: John Wiley & Sons.

Fraser, B. (1975) Hedged performatives. In P. Cole and J. Morgan (eds) *Syntax and Semantics 3: Speech Acts* (pp. 187–210). New York: Academic Press.

Fraser, B. and Nolen, W. (1981) The association of deference with linguistic form. *International Journal of the Sociology of Language* 27, 93–109.

Fraser, B., Rintell, E. and Walters, J. (1980) An approach to conducting research on the acquisition of pragmatic competence in a second language. In D. Larsen-Freeman (ed.) *Discourse Analysis in Second Language Research*. Rowley, MA: Newbury House.

Fukushima, S. (1990) Offers and requests: Performance by Japanese learners of English. *World Englishes* 9, 317–25.

Garvey, C. (1975) Requests and responses in children's speech. *Journal of Child Language* 2, 41–63.

Gerhardt, J. (1991) The meaning and use of the modals HAFTA, NEEDA and WANNA in children's speech. *Journal of Pragmatics* 16, 531–90.

Gibbs, R. (1979) Contextual effects in understanding indirect requests. *Discourse Processes* 2, 1–10.

Gibbs, R. (1981) Your wish is my command: Convention and context in interpreting indirect requests. *Journal of Verbal Learning and Verbal Behavior* 20, 431–44.

Gibbs, R. (1983) Do people always process the literal meanings of indirect requests? *Journal of Experimental Psychology: Learning, Memory and Cognition* 9, 524–33.

Gillis, M. and Weber, R. (1976) The emergence of sentence modalities in the English of Japanese-speaking children. *Language Learning* 26, 77–94.

Gleason, J., Perlmann, R. and Greif, E. (1984) What's the magic word: Learning language through politeness routines. *Discourse Process* 7, 493–502.

Gordon, D. and Ervin-Tripp, S. (1984) The structure of children's requests. In R. L. Schiefelbusch and J. Pickar (eds) *The Acquisition of Communicative Competence* (pp. 295–321). Baltimore, MD: University Park Press.

Gordon, D. and Lakoff, G. (1975) Conversational postulates. In P. Cole and J. Morgan (eds) *Syntax and Semantics 3: Speech Acts* (pp. 83–106). New York: Academic Press.

Gordon, D., Budwig, N., Strage, A. and Carrell, P. (1980) *Children's Requests to Unfamiliar Adults: Form, Social Function, Age Variation*. Fifth Annual Boston University Conference on Language Development, Boston. (ERIC Document Reproduction Service No. ED 205-053.)

Grice, H. (1975) Logic and conversation. In P. Cole and J. Morgan (eds) *Syntax and Semantics 3: Speech Acts* (pp. 41–58). New York: Academic Press.

Hakuta, K. (1974) Prefabricated patterns and the emergence of structure in second language acquisition. *Language Learning* 24 (2), 287–97.

Hakuta, K. (1976) A case study of a Japanese child learning English as a second language. *Language Learning* 26, 321–51.

Hatch, E., Peck, S. and Wagner-Gough, J. (1979) A look at process in child second-language acquisition. In E. Ochs and B. Schieffelin (eds) *Developmental Pragmatics* (pp. 269–78). New York: Academic Press.

Hill, T. (1997) The development of pragmatic competence in an EFL context. Unpublished doctoral dissertation, Temple University, Tokyo, Japan.

Hollos, M. and Beeman, W. (1978) The development of directives among Norwegian and Hungarian children: An example of communicative style in culture. *Language in Society* 7 (3), 345-55.

Holtgraves, T. (1986) Language structure in social interaction: Perceptions of direct and indirect speech acts and interactions who use them. *Journal of Personality and Social Psychology* 305–14.

House, J. (1989) Politeness in English and German: The functions of please and bitte. In S. Blum-Kulka, J. House and G. Kasper (eds) *Cross-cultural Pragmatics: Requests and Apologies* (pp. 96–119). Norwood, NJ: Ablex.

House, J and Kasper, G. (1981) Politeness markers in English and German. In F. Coulmas (ed.) *Conversational Routine* (pp. 157–85). The Hague: Mouton.

House, J. and Kasper, G. (1987) Interlanguage pragmatics: Requesting in a foreign language. In W. Lörscher and R. Schulze (eds) *Perspectives on Language in Performance*, vol. 2 (pp. 1250–88). Tübingen: Narr.

Huang, J. and Hatch, E. (1978) A Chinese child's acquisition of English. In E. Hatch (ed.) *Second Language Acquisition: A Book of Readings* (pp. 118–31). Rowley, MA: Newbury House.

Itoh, H. and Hatch, E. (1978) Second language acquisition: A case study. In E. Hatch (ed.) *Second Language Acquisition* (pp. 76–88). Rowley: Newbury House.

James, S. (1978) Effect of listener age and situation on the politeness of children's directives. *Journal of Psycholinguistic Research* 7, 307–17.

Kasper, G. (1989) Variation in interlanguage speech act realization. In S. Gass, C. Madden, D. Preston and L. Selinker (eds) *Variation in Second Language Acquisition: Discourse and Pragmatics* (pp. 37–58). Clevedon: Multilingual Matters.

Kasper, G. (1990) Linguistic politeness. *Journal of Pragmatics* 14, 193–218.

Kasper, G. (1995) Routine and indirection in interlanguage pragmatics. *Pragmatics and Language Learning* 6, 59–78.

Kasper, G. (1996) Introduction: Interlanguage pragmatics in SLA. *Studies in Second Language Acquisition* 18, 145–8.

Kasper, G. (1997) *Can Pragmatic Competence be Taught?* (NFLRC Net Work No. 6.) Honolulu: University of Hawaii at Manoa, Second Language Teaching & Curriculum Center.

Kasper, G. and Blum-Kulka, S. (eds) (1993) *Interlanguage Pragmatics*. New York: Oxford.

Kasper, G. and Dahl, M. (1991) Research methods in interlanguage pragmatics. *Studies in Second Language Acquisition* 13, 215-47.

Kasper, G. and Rose, K. (1999) Pragmatics and SLA. *Annual Review of Applied Linguistics* 19, 81–104.

Kasper, G. and Rose, K. (2001) Pragmatics in language teaching. In K. Rose and G. Kasper (eds) *Pragmatics in Language Teaching* (pp. 1–12). Cambridge: Cambridge University Press.

Kasper, G. and Schmidt, R. (1996) Developmental issues in interlanguage pragmatics. *Studies in Second Language Acquisition* 18, 149–69.

Koike, D. (1989a) Requests and the role of deixis in politeness. *Journal of Pragmatics* 13, 187–202.

Koike, D. (1989b) Pragmatic competence and adult L2 acquisition: Speech acts in interlanguage. *The Modern Language Journal* 73, 279–89.

Krashen, S. and Scarcella, R. (1978) On routines and patterns in language acquisition and performance. *Language Learning* 28, 283–300.

Lakoff, R. (1973) The logic of politeness: Or minding your p's and q's. In C. Corum, T. Smith-Stark and A. Weiser (eds) *Papers from the Ninth Regional Meeting of the Chicago Linguistic Society* (pp. 292–305). Chicago: Chicago Linguistic Society.

Lee-Wong, S. (1993) Requesting in Putonghua: Politeness, culture and forms. Unpublished doctoral thesis, Monash University, Australia.

Leech, G. (1983) *Principles of Pragmatics.* London: Longman.

Levin, E. and Rubin, K. (1983) Getting others to do what you want them to do: The development of children's requestive strategies. In K. Nelson (ed.) *Children's Language* (pp. 157–86). Hillsdale, NJ: Lawrence Erlbaum.

Liebling, C. (1988) Means to an end: Children's knowledge of directives during the elementary school years. *Discourse Processes* 11, 77–99.

Liu, G. (1991) Interaction and second language acquisition: A case study of a Chinese child's acquisition of English as a second language. Unpublished doctoral thesis, La Trobe University, Australia.

Matsumori, A. (1981) Hahaoya no kodomo e no gengo ni yoru koodoo kisei - yookyuu hyoogen no nichibei hikaku. [A comparative study of American and Japanese mothers' directives]. In M. Hori and F. Peng (eds) *Gengo Shuutoku no Shosoo* [*Aspects of Language Acquisition*] (pp. 320–39). Hiroshima: Bunka Hyoron.

McTear, M. (1979) 'Hey! I've got something to tell you': A study of the initiation of conversational exchanges by preschool children. *Journal of Pragmatics* 3, 321–36.

McTear, M. (1980) Getting it done: The development of children's abilities to negotiate request sequences in peer interaction. *Belfast Working Papers in Language and Linguistics* 4 (1), 1–29.

McTear, M. (1985) *Children's Conversation.* New York: Basil Blackwell.

Mitchell-Kernan, C. and Kernan, K. (1977) Pragmatics of directive choice among children. In S. Ervin-Tripp and C. Mitchell-Kernan (eds) *Child Discourse* (pp. 189–208). New York: Academic Press.

Morgan, J. (1978) Two types of convention in indirect speech acts. In P. Cole (ed.) *Syntax and Semantics* (pp. 261–80). New York: Academic Press.

Nicholas, H. (1987) A comparative study of the acquisition of German as a first and as a second language. Unpublished doctoral thesis, Monash University, Australia.

Ninio, A. and Snow, C. (1996) *Pragmatic Development.* Oxford: Westview.

Nippold, M., Leonard, L. and Anastopoulos, A. (1982) Development in the use and understanding of polite forms in children. *Journal of Speech and Hearing Research* 25, 193–202.

Owens, R. (1992) *Language Development* (3rd edn). New York: Macmillan.

Peters, A. and Boggs, S. (1986) Interactional routines as cultural influences upon language acquisition. In B. Schieffelin and E. Ochs (eds) *Language Socialization Across Cultures* (pp. 80–96). Cambridge: Cambridge University Press.

Piaget, J. (1959) *The Language and Thought of the Child* (M. Gabain and R. Gabain, Trans.) (3rd edn). London: Routledge & Kegan Paul.

Pienemann, M. (1980) The second language acquisition of immigrant children. In S. Felix (ed.) *Second Language Development.* Tübingen: Narr.

Quirk, R., Greenbaum, S., Leech, G. and Svartvik, J. (1985) *A Comprehensive Grammar of the English Language.* Longman: New York.

Read, B. and Cherry, L. (1978) Preschool children's production of directive forms. *Discourse Processes* 1, 233–45.

Rescorla, L. and Okuda, S. (1987) Modular patterns in second language. *Applied Psycholinguistics* 8, 281–308.

Rose, K. (1994) On the validity of DCTs in non-western contexts. *Applied Linguistics* 15, 1–14.

Rose, K. (2000) An exploratory cross-sectional study of interlanguage pragmatic development. *Studies in Second Language Acquisition* 22, 27–59.

Rose, K. and Ono, R. (1995) Eliciting speech act data in Japanese: The effect of questionnaire type. *Language Learning* 45, 191–223.

Sawyer, M. (1992) The development of pragmatics in Japanese as a second language: The sentence-final particle *ne*. In G. Kasper (ed.) *Pragmatics of Japanese as a Native and Foreign Language* (Tech. Rep. no. 3, pp. 83–125). Honolulu: University of Hawaii at Manoa, Second Language Teaching & Curriculum Center.

Scarcella, R. and Brunak, J. (1981) On speaking politely in a second language. *International Journal of the Sociology of Language* 27, 59–75.

Schmidt, R. (1983) Interaction, acculturation, and the acquisition of communicative competence: A case study of an adult. In N. Wolfson and E. Judd (eds) *Sociolinguistics and Second Language Acquisition* (pp. 137–74). Rowley, MA: Newbury House.

Schmidt, R. (1993) Consciousness, learning and interlanguage pragmatics. In G. Kasper and S. Blum-Kulka (eds) *Interlanguage Pragmatics* (pp. 21–42). New York: Oxford University Press.

Scollon, R. and Scollon, S. (1983) Face in interethnic communication. In J. Richards and R. Schmidt (eds) *Language and Communication* (pp. 156–90). London: Longman.

Searle, J. (1969) *Speech Acts: An Essay in the Philosophy of Language.* Cambridge: Cambridge University Press.

Searle, J. (1975) Indirect speech acts. In P. Cole and J. Morgan (eds) *Syntax and Semantics 3: Speech Acts* (pp. 59–82). New York: Academic Press.

Searle, J. (1976) A classification of illocutionary acts. *Language in Society* 5, 1–23.

Sifianou, M. (1992) *Politeness Phenomena in England and Greece: A Cross-cultural Perspective*. Oxford: Clarendon Press.

Sifianou, M. (1993) Off-record indirectness and the notion of imposition. *Multilingua* 12, 69–79.

Snow, C., Perlmann, R., Gleason, J. and Hooshyar, N. (1990) Developmental perspectives on politeness. *Journal of Pragmatics* 14, 289–305.

Takahashi, S. and DuFon, P. (1989) *Cross-linguistic Influence in Indirectness: The Case of English Directives Performed by Native Japanese Speakers*. University of Hawaii at Manoa, Honolulu. (ERIC Document Reproduction Service no. ED 370-439).

Takahashi, T. and Beebe, L. (1987) The development of pragmatic competence by Japanese learners of English. *JALT Journal* 8, 131–55.

Tanaka, N. (1988) Politeness: Some problems for Japanese speakers of English. *JALT Journal* 9, 81–102.

Tarone, E. and Liu, G. (1995) Situational context, variation and second language acquisition theory. In H. Widdowson (ed.) *Principle and Practice* (pp. 107–24). Oxford: Oxford University Press.

Thomas, J. (1983) Cross-cultural pragmatic failure. *Applied Linguistics* 4, 91–112.

Thomas, J. (1995) *Meaning in Interaction*. London: Longman.

Thomas, J. (manuscript). Methods in cross-cultural politeness phenomena research.

Trosborg A. (1985) May I/ can I/ I would like to: A study of requests in 3 to 5 year-old children. In O. Togeby (ed.) *Papers from the Eighth Scandinavian Conference of Linguistics* (pp. 51–73). Copenhagen.

Trosborg, A. (1995) *Interlanguage Pragmatics*. Berlin: Mouton.

Vihman, M. (1982) Formulas in first and second language acquisition. In L. K. Obler and L. Menn (eds) *Exceptional Language and Linguistics* (pp. 261–84). New York: Academic Press.

Walters, J. (1979a) The perception of politeness in English and Spanish. In C. Yorio, K. Peters and J. Schachter (eds) *On TESOL '79: The Learner in Focus* (pp. 288–96). Washington, DC: TESOL.

Walters, J. (1979b) Strategies for requesting in Spanish and English. *Language Learning* 29 (2), 277–93.

Walters, J. (1980) Grammar, meaning, and sociocultural appropriateness in second language acquisition. *Canadian Journal of Psychology* 34, 337–45.

Walters, J. (1981) Variation in the requesting behavior of bilingual children. *International Journal of Sociology of Language* 27, 77–92.

Weizman, E. (1989) Requestive hints. In S. Blum-Kulka, J. House and G. Kasper (eds) *Cross-cultural Pragmatics: Requests and Apologies* (pp. 71–95). Norwood, NJ: Ablex.

Weizman, E. (1993) Interlanguage requestive hints. In G. Kasper and S. Blum-Kulka (eds) *Interlanguage Pragmatics* (pp. 123–37). New York: Oxford.

Wolfson, N. (1986) Research methodology and the question of validity. *TESOL Quarterly* 20, 689–99.

Wolfson, N. (1988) The bulge: A theory of speech behavior and social distance. In J. Fine (ed.) *A Textbook of Current Research* (pp. 21–38). Norwood, NJ: Ablex.

Wolfson, N. (1989) *Perspectives: Sociolinguistics and TESOL*. New York: Newbury House.

Wong-Fillmore, L. (1976) The second time around: Cognitive and social strategies in second language acquisition. Unpublished doctoral dissertation, Stanford University, USA.

Wood, B. and Gardner, R. (1980) How children 'Get their way': Directives in communication. *Communication Education* 29, 264–71.

Yorio, C. (1980) Conventionalized language forms and the development of communicative competence. *Tesol Quarterly* 14, 433–42.

Appendices

Appendix 3.1

Recording schedule

Play contexts	1	2	3	4	5	6	7	8	9	10	11	12	13	14	15	16	17	18	19	20
with peer						*						*	*				*			
with teenager				*		*					*			*			*			
with adult								*		*					*					*

Play contexts	21	22	23	24	25	26	27	28	29	30	31	32	33	34	35	36	37	38	39	40	41	42
with peer					*			*				*								*		
with teenager	*					*					*		*			*						
with adult				*					*				*					*				

Play contexts	43	44	45	46	47	48	49	50	51	52	53	54	55	56	57	58	59	60	61	62	63	64	65	66
with peer					*					*					*						*			
with teenager	*					*						*							*					
with adult	*							*					*							*				

Play contexts	67	68	69	70	71	72	73	74	75
with peer			*					*	
with teenager						*			*
with adult	*						*		

Numbers from 1 to 75 indicate week. Asterisks (*) indicate a recording session. The recording sessions were approximately one hour long, but the two sessions in the 6th week were 30 minutes long and were therefore analysed as one recording.

Appendix 3.2

Transcription conventions for the data

(1) All the speech is written in standard letters with standard spelling, except for noticeably non-standard pronunciations in which case the word is written as it sounds, but using normal spellings.

(2) Capital letters are only used for proper nouns; not to indicate the beginnings of sentences.

(3) Bold type indicates marked emphasis.

(4) / marks slight final fall indicating temporary closure and that more is to be said on the topic.

(5) ? indicates question forms regardless of whether they are fully formed or marked only by rising intonation.

(6) ! indicates an exclamation.

(7) – is a self-editing marker when a speaker interrupts her own utterance to change or correct it.

(8) = indicates where one speaker is interrupted by another. The interruption begins with = directly under the = in the preceding speaker's turn. The beginning of another speaker's turn is also marked with = to indicate interruption of the utterance to the preceding one.

   e.g. **Y:**   how come there's not =

   PL: = I had one here a moment ago

(9) < > indicates overlap. The overlapped portions of the utterances of both speakers are enclosed separately in < >.

(10) ( ) indicates an approximation to an unclear word.

(11) (xxx) indicates an unintelligible word or sound or segment.

(12) ↑ indicates rising intonation but not question.

(13) . (A single period) indicates a short pause, approximately two seconds.

(14) ... (Three periods) indicate pauses greater than two seconds.

(15) .... (Four periods) indicate that an utterance is trailing off.

(16) (=) is for translation or for paraphrase.

Appendix 4.1   Recording schedule and time

Play contexts	Time 1					Time 2					Time 3					Time 4				
	1	2	3	4	5	6	7	8	9	10	11	12	13	14	15	16	17	18	19	20
with peer						*							*				*			
with teenager				*			*							*				*		
with adult										*						*				*

Play contexts	Time 5					Time 6						Time 7						Time 8				
	21	22	23	24	25	26	27	28	29	30	31	32	33	34	35	36	37	38	39	40	41	42
with peer					*							*			*					*		
with teenager	*						*							*					*			
with adult				*						*								*				

Play contexts	Time 9					Time 10						Time 11								Time 12				
	43	44	45	46	47	48	49	50	51	52	53	54	55	56	57	58	59	60	61	62	63	64	65	66
with peer					*					*					*						*			
with teenager	*						*						*							*				
with adult		*							*			*							*					

Play contexts	Time 13						Time 14		
	67	68	69	70	71	72	73	74	75
with peer			*						*
with teenager	*						*		
with adult		*						*	

Numbers from 1 to 75 indicate week. Asterisks (*) indicate a recording session. The recording sessions were approximately one hour long, but the two sessions in the 6th week were 30 minutes only and were therefore analysed as one recording.

Appendix 4.2

Distribution of main request strategy types over time

Strategy type								Time									
		1	2	3	4	5	6	7	8	9	10	11	12	13	14	Total
Direct	n	111	123	33	31	73	50	119	97	87	37	26	40	49	42	918
	%	81.6	72.4	70.2	63.3	62.9	51.0	68.0	67.8	77.7	52.9	53.1	58.0	55.1	44.7	65.0
Conventionally indirect	n	20	42	15	16	41	48	51	39	25	32	19	27	38	45	458
	%	14.7	24.7	31.9	32.7	35.3	49.0	29.1	28.1	22.3	45.7	38.8	39.1	42.7	47.9	32.4
Nonconventionally indirect	n	5	5	0	1	1	1	2	0	2	4	5	2	4	5	37
	%	3.7	2.9	0.0	2.0	0.9	1.0	1.1	0.0	1.8	5.7	10.2	2.9	4.5	5.3	2.6
Total	n	136	170	47	49	116	98	175	139	112	70	49	69	89	94	1413
	%	100.0	100.0	100.0	100.0	100.0	100.0	100.0	100.0	100.0	100.0	100.0	100.0	100.0	100.0	100.0

Total percentages with decimals were rounded off to 100%.

Appendix 4.3
Distribution of request strategy types over time

Strategy type		1	2	3	4	5	6	7	8	9	10	11	12	13	14	Total
Mood derivable	n	106	116	26	25	65	47	89	77	54	25	22	35	41	33	761
	%	77.9	68.2	55.3	51.0	56.0	48.0	50.9	55.4	48.2	35.7	44.9	50.7	46.1	35.1	53.9
Obligation statements	n	0	2	0	6	2	3	25	17	6	4	2	3	7	5	82
	%	0.0	1.2	0.0	12.2	1.7	3.1	14.3	12.2	5.4	5.7	4.1	4.3	7.9	5.3	5.8
Want statements	n	5	5	7	0	6	0	5	3	27	8	2	2	1	4	75
	%	3.7	2.9	14.9	0.0	5.2	0.0	2.9	2.2	24.1	11.4	4.1	2.9	1.1	4.3	5.3
Suggestory formulae	n	17	26	3	4	14	20	18	8	1	6	4	2	1	6	130
	%	12.5	15.3	6.4	8.2	12.1	20.4	10.3	5.8	0.9	8.6	8.2	2.9	1.1	6.4	9.2
Stating preparatory	n	1	1	3	5	3	4	9	11	9	6	0	4	17	23	96
	%	0.7	0.6	6.4	10.2	2.6	4.1	5.1	7.9	8.0	8.6	0.0	5.8	19.1	24.5	6.8
Query preparatory	n	2	15	9	7	24	24	24	20	15	20	15	21	20	16	232
	%	1.5	8.8	19.1	14.3	20.7	24.5	13.7	14.4	13.4	28.6	30.6	30.4	22.5	17.0	16.4
Hints	n	5	5	0	1	1	1	2	0	2	4	5	2	4	5	37
	%	3.7	2.9	0.0	2.0	0.9	1.0	1.1	0.0	1.8	5.7	10.2	2.9	4.5	5.3	2.6
Total	n	136	170	47	49	116	98	175	139	112	70	49	69	89	94	1413
	%	100.0	100.0	100.0	100.0	100.0	100.0	100.0	100.0	100.0	100.0	100.0	100.0	100.0	100.0	100.0

Total percentages with decimals were rounded off to 100%.

Appendix 4.4
Distribution of linguistic forms by phase

Strategy type and form	Phase									
	I		II		III		IV		Total	
	n	%	n	%	n	%	n	%	n	%
Mood derivable										
ordinary imperatives	128	41.8	136	43.9	199	36.5	74	29.4	537	38.0
you + imperatives	5	1.6	8	2.6	20	3.7	16	6.3	49	3.5
contextually elliptical										
imperatives	85	27.8	18	5.8	43	7.9	18	7.1	164	11.6
formulaic imperatives	1	0.3	1	0.3	5	0.9	1	0.4	8	0.6
others	3	1.0	0	0.0	0	0.0	0	0.0	3	0.2
Obligation statements										
you (we) have to	0	0.0	8	2.6	49	9.0	8	3.2	65	4.6
you (we) should	0	0.0	0	0.0	1	0.2	5	2.0	6	0.4
you'd better/										
you better	0	0.0	1	0.3	1	0.2	1	0.4	3	0.2
you need to/you need	2	0.7	2	0.6	3	0.6	1	0.4	8	0.6
Want statements										
I want to (I wanna)/										
I want	1	0.3	10	3.2	35	6.4	1	0.4	47	3.3
I need to/I need	5	1.6	3	1.0	10	1.8	6	2.4	24	1.7
others	4	1.3	0	0.0	0	0.0	0	0.0	4	0.3
Suggested formulae										
let's	12	3.9	20	6.5	20	3.7	6	2.4	58	4.1
how about/										
what about	1	0.3	10	3.2	2	0.4	2	0.8	15	1.1
why don't you (we)	0	0.0	1	0.3	5	0.9	1	0.4	7	0.5
shall we	0	0.0	0	0.0	3	0.6	0	0.0	3	0.2
it's your (my) turn/										
your (my) turn	16	5.2	10	3.2	5	0.9	0	0.0	31	2.2
it goes here/										
it's here (there)	6	2.0	0	0.0	0	0.0	0	0.0	6	0.4
that's enough	4	1.3	0	0.0	2	0.4	0	0.0	6	0.4
others	4	1.3	0	0.0	0	0.0	0	0.0	4	0.3
Stating preparatory										
you (we) can	1	0.3	14	4.5	32	5.9	21	8.3	68	4.8
you (we) could	0	0.0	0	0.0	0	0.0	23	9.1	23	1.6
you're not allowed to/										
that's not allowed	1	0.3	1	0.3	3	0.6	0	0.0	5	0.4
Query preparatory										
can you (I, we)	9	2.9	51	16.5	69	12.7	22	8.7	151	10.7
could you (I, we)	0	0.0	0	0.0	14	2.6	21	8.3	35	2.5
will you	0	0.0	0	0.0	2	0.4	0	0.0	2	0.1
would you	0	0.0	0	0.0	0	0.0	4	1.6	4	0.3
do you want to										
(do you wanna)	8	2.6	12	3.9	7	1.3	1	0.4	28	2.0
would you like to	0	0.0	0	0.0	0	0.0	2	0.8	2	0.1
may I	0	0.0	0	0.0	1	0.2	0	0.0	1	0.1
do you have/										
have you (we) got	0	0.0	1	0.3	1	0.2	5	2.0	7	0.5
is there	0	0.0	0	0.0	0	0.0	2	0.8	2	0.1
Hints	10	3.3	3	1.0	13	2.4	11	4.4	37	2.6
Total	306	100.0	310	100.0	545	100.0	252	100.0	1413	100.0

Appendix 6.1
Distribution of main request strategies by request goals in phase

Request for goods

| | Phase | | | | | | | |
| Strategy | I | | II | | III | | IV | |
	n	%	n	%	n	%	n	%
Direct	16	66.7	7	29.2	13	32.5	8	22.9
Conventionally indirect	5	20.8	15	62.5	24	60.0	21	60.0
Nonconventially indirect	3	12.5	2	8.3	3	7.5	6	17.1
Total	24	100.0	24	100.0	40	100.0	35	100.0

Request for the initiation of action

| | Phase | | | | | | | |
| Strategy | I | | II | | III | | IV | |
	n	%	n	%	n	%	n	%
Direct	147	81.7	110	61.8	228	69.3	88	53.0
Conventionally indirect	28	15.6	67	37.6	93	28.3	75	45.2
Nonconventially indirect	5	2.8	1	0.6	8	2.4	3	1.8
Total	180	100.0	178	100.0	329	100.0	166	100.0

Request for the cessation of action

| | Phase | | | | | | | |
| Strategy | I | | II | | III | | IV | |
	n	%	n	%	n	%	n	%
Direct	67	88.2	62	93.9	120	89.6	30	93.8
Conventionally indirect	7	9.2	4	6.1	12	9.0	0	0.0
Nonconventially indirect	2	2.6	0	0.0	2	1.5	2	6.3
Total	76	100.0	66	100.0	134	100.0	32	100.0

Request for joint activity

| | Phase | | | | | | | |
| Strategy | I | | II | | III | | IV | |
	n	%	n	%	n	%	n	%
Direct	4	15.4	8	19.0	5	11.9	5	26.3
Conventionally indirect	22	84.6	34	81.0	37	88.1	14	73.7
Nonconventially indirect	0	0.0	0	0.0	0	0.0	0	0.0
Total	26	100.0	42	100.0	42	100.0	19	100.0

Appendix 6.2
Distribution of request strategies by request goals in phase

Request for goods

Strategy	Phase I		Phase II		Phase III		Phase IV	
	n	%	n	%	n	%	n	%
Mood derivable	13	54.2	2	8.3	4	10.0	3	8.6
Want statements	3	12.5	5	20.8	9	22.5	5	14.3
Query preparatory	5	20.8	15	62.5	24	60.0	21	60.0
Hints	3	12.5	2	8.3	3	7.5	6	17.1
Total	24	100.0	24	100.0	40	100.0	35	100.0

Request for the initiation of action

Strategy	Phase I		Phase II		Phase III		Phase IV	
	n	%	n	%	n	%	n	%
Mood derivable	139	77.2	105	59.0	151	45.9	79	47.6
Obligation statements	1	0.6	4	2.2	44	13.4	7	4.2
Want statements	7	3.9	1	0.6	33	10.0	2	1.2
Suggestory formulae	24	13.3	17	9.6	12	3.6	6	3.6
Stating preparatory	0	0.0	13	7.3	24	7.3	38	22.9
Query preparatory	4	2.2	37	20.8	57	17.3	31	18.7
Hints	5	2.8	1	0.6	8	2.4	3	1.8
Total	180	100.0	178	100.0	329	100.0	166	100.0

Request for the cessation of action

Strategy	Phase I		Phase II		Phase III		Phase IV	
	n	%	n	%	n	%	n	%
Mood derivable	66	86.8	55	83.3	112	83.6	27	84.4
Obligation statements	1	1.3	7	10.6	8	6.0	3	9.4
Suggestory formulae	5	6.6	2	3.0	3	2.2	0	0.0
Stating preparatory	2	2.6	2	3.0	5	3.7	0	0.0
Query preparatory	0	0.0	0	0.0	4	3.0	0	0.0
Hints	2	2.6	0	0.0	2	1.5	2	6.3
Total	76	100.0	66	100.0	134	100.0	32	100.0

Request for joint activity

Strategy	Phase I		Phase II		Phase III		Phase IV	
	n	%	n	%	n	%	n	%
Mood derivable	4	15.4	1	2.4	0	0.0	0	0.0
Obligation statements	0	0.0	0	0.0	2	4.8	5	26.3
Want statements	0	0.0	7	16.7	3	7.1	0	0.0
Suggestory formulae	14	53.8	22	52.4	22	52.4	3	15.8
Stating preparatory	0	0.0	0	0.0	6	14.3	6	31.6
Query preparatory	8	30.8	12	28.6	9	21.4	5	26.3
Total	26	100.0	42	100.0	42	100.0	19	100.0

Appendix 6.3

Query preparatory and its linguistic exponents according to goal and phase

Requests for goods					
	Phase				
	I	*II*	*III*	*IV*	*Total*
Exponent	*n*	*n*	*n*	*n*	*n*
can I	5	12	12	7	36
could I			3	5	8
can we			3	1	4
could we				1	1
can you		2	1		3
could you			4		4
have we got				1	1
do you have/have you got		1	1	4	6
is there				2	2
Total number of query preparatory	5	15	24	21	65
Total number of requests for goods	24	24	40	35	123

Requests for the initiation of action					
	Phase				
	I	*II*	*III*	*IV*	*Total*
Exponent	*n*	*n*	*n*	*n*	*n*
can I	1	6	12	6	25
can you	3	31	37	7	78
could you			5	14	19
will you			2		2
would you				4	4
may I			1		1
Total number of query preparatory	4	37	57	31	129
Total number of requests for the initiation of action	180	178	329	166	853

Requests for the cessation of action					
	Phase				
	I	II	III	IV	Total
Exponent	n	n	n	n	n
can you			2		2
could you			2		2
Total number of query preparatory			4		4
Total number of requests for the cessation of action	76	66	134	32	308

Requests for joint activity					
	Phase				
	I	II	III	IV	Total
Exponent	n	n	n	n	n
can we			2	1	3
could we				1	1
do you want to (do you wanna)	8	12	7	1	28
would you like to				2	2
Total number of query preparatory	8	12	9	5	34
Total number of requests for joint activity	26	42	42	19	129

Appendix 8.1
Distribution of requests with and without modifiers in relation to form

Mood derivables

Request	Ordinary imperative		you + imperative		Contextually elliptical imperative		Formulaic imperative		Others		Total	
	n	%	n	%	n	%	n	%	n	%	n	%
Without modifiers	337	62.8	31	63.3	105	64.0	7	87.5	2	66.7	482	63.3
With modifiers	202	37.6	18	36.7	59	36.0	1	12.5	1	33.3	279	36.7
Total	537	100.0	49	100.0	164	100.0	8	100.0	3	100.0	761	100.0

Obligation statements

Request	you (we) have to		you (we) should		you'd better/ you better		you need to/ you need		Total	
	n	%	n	%	n	%	n	%	n	%
Without modifiers	47	72.3	2	33.3	2	66.7	4	50.0	55	67.1
With modifiers	18	27.7	4	66.7	1	33.3	4	50.0	27	32.9
Total	65	100.0	6	100.0	3	100.0	8	100.0	82	100.0

Want statements

Request	I want to (I wanna)/ I want		I need to/ I need		Others		Total	
	n	%	n	%	n	%	n	%
Without modifiers	43	91.5	14	58.3	2	50.0	59	78.7
With modifiers	4	8.5	10	41.7	2	50.0	16	21.3
Total	47	100.0	24	100.0	4	100.0	75	100.0

Suggestory formulae

Request	let's		how about/what about		why don't you (we)		shall we		Total	
	n	%	n	%	n	%	n	%	n	%
Without modifiers	50	86.2	13	86.7	5	71.4	3	100.0	110	84.6
With modifiers	8	13.8	2	13.3	2	28.6	0	0.0	20	15.4
Total	58	100.0	15	100.0	7	100.0	3	100.0	130	100.0

Request	it's your (my) turn/your (my) turn		it goes here/it's here (there)		that's enough		Others	
	n	%	n	%	n	%	n	%
Without modifiers	21	87.5	4	100.0	5	83.3	9	69.2
With modifiers	3	12.5	0	0.0	1	16.7	4	30.8
Total	24	100.0	4	100.0	6	100.0	13	100.0

Stating prepatory

Request	you (we) can		you're not/you (we) could		you're not allowed to/that's not allowed		Total	
	n	%	n	%	n	%	n	%
Without modifiers	50	73.5	13	56.5	2	40.0	65	67.7
With modifiers	18	26.5	10	43.5	3	60.0	31	32.3
Total	68	100.0	23	100.0	5	100.0	96	100.0

Query preparatory

Request	can you		can I (we)		could you		could I (we)		will you		would you	
	n	*%*	*n*	*%*	*n*	*%*	*n*	*%*	*n*	*%*	*n*	*%*
Without modifiers	55	66.3	54	79.4	4	16.0	2	20.0	1	50.0	2	50.0
With modifiers	28	33.7	14	20.6	21	84.0	8	80.0	1	50.0	2	50.0
Total	83	100.0	68	100.0	25	100.0	10	100.0	2	100.0	4	100.0

Request	do you want to (do you wanna)		would you like to		may I		do you have/ have you (we) got		is there		Total	
	n	*%*	*n*	*%*	*n*	*%*	*n*	*%*	*n*	*%*	*n*	*%*
Without modifiers	26	92.9	2	100.0	1	100.0	3	42.9	2	100.0	152	65.5
With modifiers	2	7.1	0	0.0	0	0.0	4	57.1	0	0.0	80	34.5
Total	28	100.0	2	100.0	1	100.0	7	100.0	2	100.0	232	100.0

Hints

Request	Hint		Total	
	n	*%*	*n*	*%*
Without modifiers	29	78.4	29	78.4
With modifiers	8	21.6	8	21.6
Total	37	100.0	37	100.0

Appendix 8.2

Distribution of modifiers in relation to requests in different forms

Tables are based on multiple modifiers per request. Percentages are calculated in relation to the total number of requests for each form (see Appendix 8.1 for the total number). Therefore, as requests can have more than one modifier, total percentages for modifiers may add up to greater than 100%.

Mood derivable

Modifier	Ordinary imperative		you + imperative		Contextually elliptical imperative		Formulaic imperative		Others		Total	
	n	%	n	%	n	%	n	%	n	%	n	%
Nil	337	62.8	31	63.3	105	64.0	7	87.5	2	66.7	482	63.3
Please	13	2.4	0	0.0	16	9.8	0	0.0	0	0.0	29	3.8
Appealer	14	2.6	2	4.1	2	1.2	0	0.0	1	33.3	19	2.5
Toner	68	12.7	7	14.3	4	2.4	0	0.0	0	0.0	79	10.4
Attention getter	23	4.3	3	6.1	4	2.4	1	12.5	0	0.0	31	4.1
Subjectiviser	0	0.0	0	0.0	0	0.0	0	0.0	0	0.0	0	0.0
Repetition	55	10.2	3	6.1	22	13.4	0	0.0	0	0.0	80	10.5
Paraphrase	10	1.9	0	0.0	7	4.3	0	0.0	0	0.0	17	2.2
Elaboration	24	4.5	2	4.1	14	8.5	0	0.0	1	33.3	41	5.4
Preparator	2	0.4	1	2.0	0	0.0	0	0.0	0	0.0	3	0.4
Option giver	3	0.6	0	0.0	0	0.0	0	0.0	0	0.0	3	0.4
Reason	38	7.1	2	4.1	8	4.9	0	0.0	0	0.0	48	6.3
Other	0	0.0	0	0.0	0	0.0	0	0.0	0	0.0	0	0.0

Obligation statements

Modifier	you (we) have to n	you (we) have to %	you (we) should n	you (we) should %	you'd better/ you better n	you'd better/ you better %	you need to/ you need n	you need to/ you need %	Total n	Total %
Nil	47	72.3	2	33.3	2	66.7	4	50.0	55	67.1
Please	0	0.0	0	0.0	0	0.0	0	0.0	0	0.0
Appealer	5	7.7	0	0.0	0	0.0	0	0.0	5	6.1
Toner	2	3.1	2	33.3	0	0.0	1	12.5	5	6.1
Attention getter	1	1.5	0	0.0	0	0.0	1	12.5	2	2.4
Subjectiviser	0	0.0	2	33.3	1	33.3	0	0.0	3	3.7
Repetition	0	0.0	0	0.0	0	0.0	0	0.0	0	0.0
Paraphrase	0	0.0	0	0.0	0	0.0	0	0.0	0	0.0
Elaboration	6	9.2	0	0.0	0	0.0	2	25.0	8	9.8
Preparator	0	0.0	0	0.0	0	0.0	0	0.0	0	0.0
Option giver	1	1.5	0	0.0	0	0.0	0	0.0	1	1.2
Reason	3	4.6	1	16.7	0	0.0	1	12.5	5	6.1
Other	0	0.0	0	0.0	0	0.0	0	0.0	0	0.0

Want statements

Modifier	I want to (I wanna)/ I want n	I want to (I wanna)/ I want %	I need to/ I need n	I need to/ I need %	Others n	Others %	Total n	Total %
Nil	43	91.5	14	58.3	2	50.0	59	78.7
Please	0	0.0	2	8.3	0	0.0	2	2.7
Appealer	0	0.0	0	0.0	1	25.0	1	1.3
Toner	0	0.0	3	12.5	0	0.0	3	4.0
Attention getter	2	4.3	1	4.2	1	25.0	4	5.3
Subjectiviser	0	0.0	2	8.3	0	0.0	2	2.7
Repetition	0	0.0	1	4.2	0	0.0	1	1.3
Paraphrase	1	2.1	0	0.0	0	0.0	1	1.3
Elaboration	3	6.4	0	0.0	0	0.0	3	4.0
Preparator	0	0.0	0	0.0	0	0.0	0	0.0
Option giver	0	0.0	0	0.0	0	0.0	0	0.0
Reason	0	0.0	1	4.2	0	0.0	1	1.3
Other	0	0.0	0	0.0	0	0.0	0	0.0

Suggestory formulae								
	let's		how about/ what about		why don't you (we)		shall we	
Modifier	n	%	n	%	n	%	n	%
Nil	50	86.2	13	86.7	5	71.4	3	100.0
Please	0	0.0	0	0.0	0	0.0	0	0.0
Appealer	1	1.7	0	0.0	0	0.0	0	0.0
Toner	1	1.7	0	0.0	0	0.0	0	0.0
Attention getter	2	3.4	0	0.0	0	0.0	0	0.0
Subjectiviser	0	0.0	0	0.0	0	0.0	0	0.0
Repetition	0	0.0	0	0.0	0	0.0	0	0.0
Paraphrase	0	0.0	1	6.7	0	0.0	0	0.0
Elaboration	1	1.7	0	0.0	1	14.3	0	0.0
Preparator	0	0.0	0	0.0	0	0.0	0	0.0
Option giver	0	0.0	0	0.0	0	0.0	0	0.0
Reason	4	6.9	1	6.7	1	14.3	0	0.0
Other	0	0.0	0	0.0	0	0.0	0	0.0

	it's your (my) turn/ your (my) turn		it's your here/it's here (there)		it goes that's enough		Others		Total	
Modifier	n	%	n	%	n	%	n	%	n	%
Nil	21	87.5	4	100.0	5	83.3	9	69.2	110	84.6
Please	0	0.0	0	0.0	0	0.0	0	0.0	0	0.0
Appealer	0	0.0	0	0.0	0	0.0	0	0.0	1	0.8
Toner	0	0.0	0	0.0	0	0.0	0	0.0	1	0.8
Attention getter	2	8.3	0	0.0	0	0.0	1	7.7	5	3.8
Subjectiviser	0	0.0	0	0.0	0	0.0	0	0.0	0	0.00
Repetition	0	0.0	0	0.0	1	16.7	0	0.0	1	0.8
Paraphrase	1	4.2	0	0.0	0	0.0	0	0.0	2	1.5
Elaboration	0	0.0	0	0.0	0	0.0	2	15.4	4	3.1
Preparator	0	0.0	0	0.0	0	0.0	0	0.0	0	0.0
Option giver	0	0.0	0	0.0	0	0.0	0	0.0	1	0.8
Reason	0	0.0	0	0.0	0	0.0	1	7.7	7	5.4
Other	0	0.0	0	0.0	0	0.0	0	0.0	0	0.0

Stating prepatory								
	you (we) can		*you (we) could*		*you're not allowed to/ that's not allowed*		*Total*	
Modifier	*n*	*%*	*n*	*%*	*n*	*%*	*n*	*%*
Nil	50	73.5	13	56.5	2	40.0	65	67.7
Please	0	0.0	0	0.0	0	0.0	0	0.0
Appealer	2	2.9	0	0.0	0	0.0	2	2.1
Toner	6	8.8	8	34.8	0	0.0	14	14.6
Attention getter	1	1.5	0	0.0	0	0.0	1	1.0
Subjectiviser	0	0.0	0	0.0	0	0.0	0	0.0
Repetition	1	1.5	0	0.0	0	0.0	1	1.0
Paraphrase	0	0.0	0	0.0	0	0.0	0	0.0
Elaboration	2	2.9	0	0.0	0	0.0	2	2.1
Preparator	2	2.9	1	4.3	0	0.0	3	3.1
Option giver	3	4.4	3	13.0	0	0.0	6	6.3
Reason	5	7.4	2	8.7	3	60.0	10	10.4
Other	0	0.0	0	0.0	0	0.0	0	0.0

Query preparatory

Modifier	can you		can I (we)		could you		could I (we)		will you		would you	
	n	%	n	%	n	%	n	%	n	%	n	%
Nil	55	66.3	54	79.4	4	16.0	2	20.0	1	50.0	2	50.0
Please	9	10.8	7	10.3	21	84.0	6	60.0	0	0.0	2	50.0
Appealer	0	0.0	0	0.0	0	0.0	0	0.0	0	0.0	0	0.0
Toner	6	7.2	2	2.9	0	0.0	0	0.0	1	50.0	0	0.0
Attention getter	3	3.6	1	1.5	0	0.0	0	0.0	0	0.0	0	0.0
Subjectiviser	0	0.0	0	0.0	0	0.0	0	0.0	0	0.0	0	0.0
Repetition	2	2.4	1	1.5	1	4.0	0	0.0	0	0.0	0	0.0
Paraphrase	1	1.2	0	0.0	1	4.0	0	0.0	0	0.0	0	0.0
Elaboration	2	2.4	0	0.0	2	8.0	1	10.0	0	0.0	0	0.0
Preparator	0	0.0	0	0.0	0	0.0	0	0.0	0	0.0	0	0.0
Option giver	0	0.0	0	0.0	0	0.0	0	0.0	0	0.0	0	0.0
Reason	11	13.3	5	7.4	2	8.0	2	20.0	0	0.0	0	0.0
Other	0	0.0	0	0.0	1	4.0	0	0.0	0	0.0	0	0.0

Query preparatory continued

Modifier	do you want to (do you wanna) n	%	would you like to n	%	may I n	%	do you have/ have you (we) got n	%	is there n	%	Total n	%
Nil	26	92.9	2	100.0	1	100.0	3	42.9	2	100.0	152	65.5
Please	0	0.0	0	0.0	0	0.0	0	0.0	0	0.0	45	19.4
Appealer	0	0.0	0	0.0	0	0.0	0	0.0	0	0.0	0	0.0
Toner	2	7.1	0	0.0	0	0.0	0	0.0	0	0.0	11	4.7
Attention getter	1	3.6	0	0.0	0	0.0	3	42.9	0	0.0	7	3.0
Subjectiviser	0	0.0	0	0.0	0	0.0	0	0.0	0	0.0	0	0.0
Repetition	0	0.0	0	0.0	0	0.0	0	0.0	0	0.0	4	1.7
Paraphrase	0	0.0	0	0.0	0	0.0	0	0.0	0	0.0	2	0.9
Elaboration	0	0.0	0	0.0	0	0.0	3	42.9	0	0.0	8	3.4
Preparator	0	0.0	0	0.0	0	0.0	0	0.0	0	0.0	0	0.0
Option giver	0	0.0	1	50.0	0	0.0	0	0.0	0	0.0	1	0.4
Reason	0	0.0	0	0.0	0	0.0	2	28.6	0	0.0	22	9.5
Other	0	0.0	0	0.0	0	0.0	0	0.0	0	0.0	1	0.4

Hints				
	Hint		Total	
Modifier	n	%	n	%
Nil	29	78.4	29	78.4
Please	0	0.0	0	0.0
Appealer	1	2.7	1	2.7
Toner	1	2.7	1	2.7
Attention getter	3	8.1	3	8.1
Subjectiviser	0	0.0	0	0.0
Repetition	0	0.0	0	0.0
Paraphrase	0	0.0	0	0.0
Elaboration	2	5.4	2	5.4
Preparator	0	0.0	0	0.0
Option giver	0	0.0	0	0.0
Reason	2	5.4	2	5.4
Other	0	0.0	0	0.0

Appendix 8.3
Distribution of request goals by addressee

	Addressee									
	Peer		Teenager		Adult		Mother		Total	
Goal	n	%	n	%	n	%	n	%	n	%
Goods	21	6.1	24	7.4	14	6.7	27	27.0	86	8.8
Initiation of the action	199	57.3	203	62.8	157	75.5	52	52.0	611	62.5
Cessation of the action	96	27.7	71	22.0	25	12.0	20	20.0	212	21.7
Joint activity	31	8.9	25	7.7	12	5.8	1	1.0	69	7.1
Total	347	100.0	323	100.0	208	100.0	100	100.0	978	100.0

Index

Authors

220

Subjects